LANGUAGE, TRUTH AND POLITICS

Towards A Radical Theory for Communication

LANGUAGE, TRUTH AND POLITICS

Second Edition, revised and enlarged

by

TREVOR PATEMAN

JEAN STROUD *Publisher*
PO BOX 12 LEWES EAST SUSSEX BN7 1AZ

First edition published in 1975
by Jean Stroud and Trevor Pateman
Second edition published in 1980
by Jean Stroud
All Rights Reserved

ISBN 0 9504400 2 7

PRINTED IN GREAT BRITAIN BY
LATIMER TREND & COMPANY LTD PLYMOUTH

Contents

Preface to the Second Edition   *page* 7

Acknowledgements   11

Chapter I
A Conception of Philosophy   13

Chapter II
Rational Error   45

Chapter III
Not so Inquiring Man   65

Chapter IV
Repressive Discourse   83

Chapter V
Impossible Discourse   122

Chapter VI
Tolerance   151

Chapter VII
Concluding Remarks   177

APPENDICES

1. The Experience of Politics   181
2. Review of Claus Mueller, *The Politics of Communication*   198
3. Liberals, Fanatics and Moral Philosophers   203
4. Remarks on *L'Empire des Signes* of Roland Barthes   211
5. How to do things with Images   215
6. Is there Power in Words?   238

Bibliography   250

In Memory of My Mother
HILDA MAY PATEMAN
1907–1978

Preface to the Second Edition

Jean Stroud and I published *Language, Truth and Politics* in July 1975 in an edition of 2,000 copies. That edition is now sold out, despite our efforts to make the book impossible to obtain: we moved house three times in two years, and apologise to those whose orders went astray *en route* between Church Green, Castle Crescent, Alexandra Road, and Lambarde Road. This time around my publisher has opted for a box number.

This second edition does differ from the first. I decided against a simple reprint of a book written in 1973 and worked out over the preceding four or five years. But also I decided against a rewriting, for that way I would have written the next book I hope to write, on the social reproduction of language. This would have deprived the reader of a very different text, apparently still of interest, judging by the continuing trickle of orders, reviews, and commentary. So what does the reader get in this second edition? The text of the first edition largely intact, with one new section added in (on Barthes' *Mythologies*); a much expanded apparatus of footnotes and references (the new notes and references identifiable by their letter subscripts) which make the book less readable but, hopefully, more usable for those interested in furthering the study of 'language worked by power' (14d Barthes, p. 33); and, finally, half a dozen appendices—the last two of which provide samples of recent work. Three of the remaining four were written after the completion of the first edition of this book.

Language, Truth and Politics is centrally concerned with what might be called the seamier side of social and cultural reproduction, and specifically with the part played in the reproduction of class- and status-divided societies by cultural domination: Marx's *ideology*, Lukacs' *false consciousness*, Gramsci's *hegemony*, and so on. The focal chapters develop accounts of linguistic and cognitive exclusion (Chapter V); of linguistic repression and cognitive mystification (Chapter IV); and of linguistic alienation as the consequence of real exclusion from power (Chapter III; see also Appendix 1, 'The Experience of Politics').

Chapter II assorts badly with these central concerns, partly because it dates from the earliest phase of the work out of which the book grew, and in a proper rewrite the whole chapter would need to be rethought in the communicational framework adopted for subsequent chapters. One possible approach to this would be through the concern with the relation between argumentation and knowledge in a book like Stephen Toulmin's *Uses of Argument* (119a).

Chapter VI might also seem disconnected from the central chapters, but can be connected up more straightforwardly. The 'tolerance' which is discussed in Chapter VI is tolerance by the State or its citizens of an arena in which debate can be carried on and opinion formed on public matters. Jürgen Habermas uses the term *'Öffentlichkeit'* ('the public sphere') to conceptualise the space which classical liberal theorists like Mill sought to establish between civil society and the State, protected from both the tyranny of the former and the despotism of the latter (see 48b, 48j Habermas). Now for Mill, what goes on or should go on in the public sphere is a specialised variety of conversation, namely, dialectical debate, the model for which is provided (quite explicitly in Mill) by the dialectics of the Ancients, and above all by Plato's Socrates. And this is to open the question of language use in a pretty direct way. I have given a fair number of footnote references to the relevant literature on this topic, and therefore don't repeat them here.

The Ancients were perfectly aware of the non-identity of language and reason, and of the fact that the former is not necessarily transparent to the latter (the goal of all logical formalisms from Leibniz onwards). Though the relationship between them changes, the co-existence from the time of the Greeks onwards of an art of rhetoric and an art of logic is the most obvious sign of the recognition of the difference and the way it was conceptualised. Now Chapter IV should really be connected up to rhetorical theories, but I have found myself instead getting interested in psycholinguistic questions about the effectivity of forms of utterance: Appendix 6 ('Is There Power in Words?') offers what is almost certainly a false start, but illustrates one direction in which I think the ideas of Chapter IV can be pursued fruitfully.

In contrast, Chapter VI should be connected up to theories

of what one might call 'practical logic': not only with the dialectics of the Ancients, but also with important contemporary formulations of the relation between discourse processes and practical reasoning. I have in mind Habermas' concept of the ideal speech situation; Rawls' account of a hypothetical Original Position (which Habermas mentions as similar to his own idea of representatively simulated discourse: 48c Habermas, p. 265; see also 48i Habermas, pp. 113-117); Grice's theory of conversation (47a Grice); and, more technically, Hamblin's formal theory of dialogue (51a Hamblin ch. 8; see also his 51b). Further relevant literature will be found in footnotes to Chapter VI and elsewhere.

Finally, Chapter I is concerned to theorise one of the many possible activities which exist and can be developed to unmask and disrupt the practices described in the rest of the book. But the trouble here, and throughout, is the absence of a properly articulated social theory (theory of society or social formations): a theory of the articulations of the structures in which reproduction occurs, or fails to occur, and their articulation with the structures which sustain and are sustained by the reproductive apparatuses. There is no real theory of social institutions and the practices which constitute them, of the sort one might find in recent 'sociology of education' (22b Bowles and Gintis; 22a Bourdieu and Passeron, etc.). The book is all-too face-to-face, and though this has been its attraction for many readers, the absences to which I refer have been singled out by several reviewers for criticism (25a Callinicos and 89c Mey from a Marxist position; 66d Kochman from within the ethnography of speaking). I do not feel able to fill here and now the absences of the first edition; for being structural absences they cannot just be filled in, leaving everything else unchanged. Not least, to write a theory of structures, institutions, society, would involve me in a rewriting of my political position (criticised at length by one reviewer, 45a Graham; and more briefly, but just as forcefully, in 104g Quinton). For the present, I can usefully do no more than say that I now regard most of the politics of this book (in the sense of 'big P' Politics) as misguided, and I do not recommend it to anyone. To say more would be to record my own confusions about what to put in place of what I have said here. Fortunately, some of the ideas about language and knowledge advanced in this book, which proved to be of greatest interest to its readers, do not depend entirely for their validity on my grasp of major political questions.

TREVOR PATEMAN

Acknowledgements

The first edition of *Language, Truth and Politics* (*LTP*) grew out of a number of papers and talks. For criticisms of those, of drafts of the book, and for bibliographical help, I am grateful to Chris Allen, Chris Arthur, Jairus Banaji, Anne Bellis, Andy Bennett, Basil Bernstein, Maggie Boden, G. A. Cohen, Selwyn Hughes, David Ingleby, John Jervis, John Kaler, John Krige, Steven Lukes, John Mepham, Ralph Miliband, Carole Pateman Denise Riley, Chris Sinha, Aaron Sloman, Rod Snell, Tim Sprigge, and, especially, to Roy Edgley, who read and criticised in detail most versions of the parts and whole of the book. Gay Best gave extensive secretarial help, Denise Riley did the cover for the first edition, and Jean Stroud worked with me to publish it.

For 1968–70, when work used in *LTP* was begun, I had a Major State Studentship to pursue graduate work under the supervision of Richard Wollheim at University College, London. For 1971–72 the award of a Leverhulme Research Trust European Studentship allowed me to study semiology at the sixth section of the École Pratique des Hautes Etudes, Paris, under the direction of Roland Barthes.

It is to the readers and reviewers of the first edition of *LTP* that I am indebted for the encouragement I needed to get together a revised second edition. At various points I have referred to their ideas and criticisms, without doing anything like justice to them. Most of the reviews I have seen and letters I have received are not even mentioned. By way of excuse, I can only say that the file of reviews and letters would fill a small book, even without any reply from me. I attribute the volume of response to *LTP* to the fact that it was seen to be self-published. Though Jean Stroud and I could not distribute the book as extensively as a real publisher (which tempted us to look for a capitalist publishing house to do this second edition), we were compensated by an immediacy of response that I doubt we would have got otherwise: from an author's point of view, commercial publications easily fall dead-born from the press, if and when they fall (these words are being written in September 1979; they will be published on 1st January 1980.)

I am grateful to Maria Amaral for doing the cover for this edition, and to Betty Beytagh, Ruth Davis, Gill Lowe, and Margaret Ralph for typing a long and untidy manuscript.

CHAPTER I

A Conception of Philosophy

The materialist doctrine concerning the changing of circumstances and education forgets that circumstances are changed by men and that the educator must himself be educated. This doctrine has therefore to divide society into two parts, one of which is superior to society.

The coincidence of the changing of circumstances and of human activity, or self-changing, can only be grasped and rationally understood as revolutionary practice

Marx *Third Thesis on Feuerbach*

1. The Significance of Insignificant Acts

In this book I shall criticise a variety of everyday communicational acts and omissions, including both those which occur in face-to-face situations and those which are produced in the mass media. I do so in the context of an attempt to theorise a practice or practices of *intervention*[0a] already carried on in opposition to such phenomena but which I think might well be developed further. It is therefore not the object of this book to contribute to any one, or even several, academic disciplines (though I do draw on a range of academic work), but rather to produce a sort of manual which might be used in the conduct of daily life.

In the course of the book I change perspective several times: in this chapter I write from a philosophical perspective, and the focus is narrowed in Chapter II to the theory of knowledge. But then Chapters III to V draw on psychological and linguistic ideas to produce what I hope is a recognisably communicational approach. Chapter VI can be read either as political philosophy or as sociology. Such shifts should be illuminating, and have a cumulative effect, if the reader keeps in mind the practical aspirations of this book.

But why is everyday life important? Why should making it different make any difference? I answer these questions by stating and illustrating a central assumption of the book, namely, that nothing one may say or do is non-significant; every action has meaning, even if that meaning is unconscious to oneself or others.[0b] In contrast to this position, when an action is taken for granted,[1] it is treated as non-significant, that is, without meaning. Such taking for granted is habitual, unavoidable if we are to get on with a job in hand, but often disastrous in its consequences when it is never challenged. To take for granted an action is equivalent to *naturalising* it, that is, consigning it to the realm of nature external to people and lacking meaning in itself. Thus, the action hardens into an alien thing, over and against people, unamenable to control or change—despite the fact that it is nothing but human action which is being thus reified. When generalised, such reification gives rise to a metaphysics of meaninglessness, and its practical consequences are variously theorised as alienation, privatisation and apathy. The causes of such a development do not lie in the mind of the individual, but in the specific forms of social organisation which generate such a consciousness. And the irony is that the very consciousness which is generated by these social forms is incapable of understanding the processes which have given rise to it and, thus, unable to criticise those processes in theory, it reproduces and strengthens them in practice.

Developments in Western society—bureaucratisation, technologisation—intensify the process of reification in everyday thought and behaviour: the use of phrases such as 'I only work here' or 'I'm only doing my job' reveal a state of mind and a state of affairs in which my work or my job is something other than I, as if I did not *do* my work or my job. Of course, such phrases can have a non-reified and positive use, as when a worker uses them to reject demands, from those who exploit him, for greater 'involvement' in his work—that is, demands for higher productivity, and, hence, higher profits. But much of the time such phrases are not used like this.[2]

Some political developments are working against the taken for grantedness and hence the naturalisation or reification of meaningful acts, and it is by reference to them that I can answer the questions with which this short discussion began and illustrate the central assumption which I stated above.

Consider then, that one of the small effects of the rise of the Women's Liberation movement has been to make it more difficult for quite a few men unselfconsciously to use such expressions as 'chick' or 'bits of stuff' in referring to women. Previously, the use of these terms was taken for granted, and

their use could be seen simply in terms of drawing on the resources of the vocabulary, where 'the vocabulary' is seen as an
objective store of words to be drawn on as and when needed.
Whilst the general reification of vocabulary into an entity outside our control may be maintained, the use of 'chicks' and 'bits
of stuff' can no longer be seen in the neutral way just characterised. Many men have been made aware of the fact that the use
of such expressions is actively depersonalising, and that this is
something for which they are responsible.

But what are the effects of giving up the use of such offensive
expressions? Certainly, it does not follow that in giving up the
use of such terms a man ceases to depersonalise women; he may
continue doing it in other ways. So do the effects of giving up
such words exhaust themselves just in the giving up itself? Or
do such small acts have wider consequences? I think they do,
and I shall try to show how.

Suppose, then, that the man who gives up using 'chick' or
'bits of stuff' has undergone no conversion, no fundamental
change of heart. He still has a fundamentally depersonalising
attitude to women. (Equally, a man with a fundamentally
human relation to women might use depersonalising terms
simply through failure to reflect on their meaning.) Such an
unreconstructed chauvinist as I am supposing may still have
an effect on his *hearers*, if they notice the absence from his
speech of the common terms for women, and they may be
affected by their understanding of the reason for this absence,
even if the speaker is not. Further, the speaker may be inwardly
transformed as a result of giving up outward depersonalising practices. This is an old idea: Pascal recommends a procedure of
adherence to outward ritual as a *means* toward inner faith for
the person who wants to believe in God but can't.[3]

But how could an outer change affect an inner attitude, that
is, a general orientation to the world? It seems to me that it can
because the change in outward practice *constitutes* a restructur-
ing of at least one aspect of one social relationship, and that
experience in the new social relationship thereby created
(artificially, one could say) can effect the 'inner' change.
Crudely, if you haven't tried it, you can't know whether you
like it or not, but having tried it and liked it, you can try it
again, wanting to.

Finally, the simple vocabulary change can not only affect others and oneself in the new social relationships in which people have put themselves, but can have a spill-over effect on to (for example) general awareness of the nature and functions of language. For to cut words out of one's vocabulary must be one of the better ways of generating a generalised awareness of the human character of language. For in my act I have asserted that I can control language; I have stopped acting as if language necessarily controls me.

In summary, then, it is not unimportant that a man uses 'chick' nor unimportant that he stops using it.[4] The generalisation which permits the above analysis and the conclusion just arrived at can be stated as follows: that every act reproduces or subverts a social institution (in the above case, relations between men and women). If every social institution is an organisation of power (I think it is), then every act is political for it either sustains or subverts a given organisation of power. Certainly, enough social institutions are organisations of power for it to be possible to speak significantly of a politics of everyday life, though where reification has petrified consciousness, such an assertion will not be intelligible (see below, Chapter V). It is, I think, the idea of a politics of everyday life which generates much of the discourse of this book.

But isn't the idea of a politics of everyday life oppressive in its practical implications? For to take seriously the critique of naturalisation as it applies (for example) to the use of language surely implies the need for self-conscious reflection on the meaning of all one's everyday linguistic acts, including the most intimate and those in the spontaneity and naturalness of which one may take, and surely should take, great delight. The position does, indeed, imply this sort of self-awareness, but I think that there are a number of lines of defence which can be taken against the objection.

First, there is the argument that what is taken to be natural or spontaneous is generally something which is just well learnt, like going to the lavatory.[5] Second, that the delight derived from such 'spontaneous' practices as wolf-whistling women, thumping kids, or—for that matter—writing allusively, has to be offset against the oppression, suffering and mystification they cause. Third, that many things which have been learnt can be unlearnt or forgotten and new things learnt, which then in turn become 'spontaneous'. Fourth, and polemically, isn't there something to be said for knowing what one is doing in life—that is, to one-self, others and for the future? Where has 'spontaneous' patriotism got soldiers but to an early grave? What has the 'spontaneity' of the maternal 'instinct' produced, except frustrated women and unhappy children?

If, in spite of these summary arguments, my across-the-board defence of self consciousness is rejected, it remains open to the reader to pick and choose between those areas in which she thinks self awareness is important, and those in which she thinks it is not. There is a lot to be said for half measures.

But to conclude this section, I want to indicate one area in which I think reflection is important, that of *reading*, and I want to do it here because you are just beginning to read my book.

Does a reader generally have any clear idea of what she is doing in the act of reading a book? Does she know how to read it, when her task is not to extract a number of key points in order to write an essay? Does she enjoy reading? If such questions can now be asked and make some sense, it must in part be due to the efforts of modern writers, such as the creators of the *Nouveau Roman* in France (on which see 54, Heath), to frustrate the expectations which the average reader has when she picks up a book. If the reader of the *Nouveau Roman* takes it seriously, she will end up posing questions about her expectations, their legitimacy, possible alternatives to her own practice of reading. Otherwise, she will write off the writer. Barthes summarises the mechanism: 'I don't understand you; therefore you're an idiot' (10, Barthes, p. 35).

Rhetoric, or the Art of Speaking
Logic, or the Art of Thinking
———, or the Art of Reading[6]

2. What's your Subject?

For me, it was a *discovery* that I could reflect on the significance of my everyday acts; that they could form the starting point for theoretical exploration; and that they might be changed in an informed way. This discovery was slowly made, and I am sure

B

that its application is far from complete. But however in-
complete, the possible unity of knowledge (as theory) and
everyday life (as practice) had to be *discovered* because formal
(i.e. school) education forecloses the awareness of this possibility. Certainly, it doesn't *realise* the possibility. Formal education
equates knowledge with a range of subjects, thrown up hap-
hazardly in history—and parochial history at that. A first effect
of this equation is to inhibit people from realising that they
know a great deal which school has never taught them: Everyman is a geographer and Everyman detests Geography, and in
doing so fails to recognise that already he is a geographer.
Geography is then a directionless, disorienting knowledge. A
second effect is to obscure the usefulness of knowledge. Whilst
Everyman recognises that reading, writing and arithmetic have
a Utilitarian value, he does not see that this could be true of
other 'subjects', because the present structure of their teaching
bears no clear relation to human needs.[6a] Ivory towers may never
have existed, but the alienation of which the term is a symptom
certainly does. Third, because subjects are made and taught as
theories of an object, not of a practice (cf. 53, Harvey), they
further obscure the possible usefulness of knowledge. This does,
of course, fulfil an ideological function, and the uses to which
the subject is put may contradict its own theory. Thus, whilst
economics is presented as the neutral theory of an object—the
economy—outside of and not including the researcher, it can
be and is given a non-neutral application as the theory of a
practice such as 'managing the economy', i.e. managing other
people. And the theory may be useless for certain economic
practices, certain ways of operating on the 'object', in which
case its claim to neutrality falls (cf. 33, Dugdale).[6b]

The effects of the equation of knowledge with subjects is
evident in the stereotyped critical oppositions of everyday
philosophy: *experience* counterposed to *theory, practical knowledge*
to *book learning* and so on. The academic researcher is as
affected by the equation as anyone. There may be and often is
a vast disparity between his professional and his 'personal'
knowledge. Social scientists often don't 'see' how their discipline's concepts apply to their own behaviour and how they
might be used in understanding or changing it. Freudian
psychoanalysts seem to provide a notable exception (the de-

velopment of a theory of the analyst's counter-transference is evidence for the claim) and it is partly from Althusser's sketch of the structure of Freudianism that I have derived my own theory of the relation of theory and practice (3, Althusser, pp. 181–202). In the following two sections I contrast one area of knowledge, P/philosophy, conceived on the one hand as a subject and on the other as theory and everyday practice. (I use 'Philosophy' to refer to the subject; and 'philosophy' to the alternative.)

3. Philosophy as a Subject

I studied Philosophy as an undergraduate and graduate student. In Philosophy as a subject, one of the things you do is read Great Books, or—more frequently—bits of Great Books. You read a bit of Locke's *Essay Concerning Human Understanding* dealing with 'the Problem of Universals'. In doing so, you fail to discover at least the following: why Locke wrote the *Essay*; what *his* Problems were; how he thought his book might be useful (see his own Preface; 75, Locke); how his treatment of universals fits into his overall approach or paradigm—for it is possible to 'do Locke' yet never discover what that approach is. Again, you can read (I read), within the context of writing an Essay on some Problem, the whole of Descartes' *Discourse on Method* without noticing that it is, among other things, an autobiography (my eyes were opened here by 66, Kenner), an appeal for funds (?),[6c] a Preface to three other essays (the Dioptrics, Meteors and Geometry, themselves described as applications (*essais*) of the Method), and a practical manual. You can even fail to notice the full title of the work which emphasises the last item on the list: the *Discourse on Method* is really a *Discourse on the Method of rightly directing one's reason and of seeking Truth in the Sciences* (in the original: Discours de la Méthode Pour bien conduire sa raison, chercher la verité dans les sciences).[7]

In general, historical and structural appropriation of a philosopher's work is obstructed by the way you are made to read the Great Works, as grist for the weekly essay mill. More precisely, Locke, Descartes or whoever are seen as having an a-historical existence, as occupying a *place* (Greek *topoi* English *topic*) in the eternal architecture of Philosophy. The result is that the young essayist can only come to the conclusion that Locke or Descartes or whoever was a muddle-headed old fool. For he didn't 'solve' 'the problem' to the satisfaction of the latest local contributor to *Mind*.

As a Philosophy student you don't only read the Great Works like a schoolboy reading *Lady Chatterley's Lover*. You also read the contemporary journal articles on the Problems of Philosophy. Usually, you are sent off to read them without having any idea of any wider perspective in which the Problem might exist, or why it is important. The journal article itself will almost certainly have nothing to say on such matters. In consequence, the Problems and problem-solving exist for the student in an intellectual and practical vacuum. He can only interpret what he is doing in the most wretchedly formalistic manner and, given the context in which he is working, most likely on the model of a competitive game, in which you make moves, counter-moves, annihilate an opponent (this is rare) or imitate the style of some Grandmaster (this is common).

The socialisation into a competitive game, whether theorised as such or not, is probably a more important ideological function of instruction in Philosophy than any substantive content or method which is transmitted, many of which have been well criticised elsewhere (see 42, Gellner; 83, Marcuse, especially ch. 7; 1, Adelstein and the journal *Radical Philosophy*). Most people give up Philosophy when given their B.A.s; what they do not give up is their formalism and competitiveness.

4. Philosophy as Theory and Practice

In contrast to doing Philosophy as a subject, I want to indicate a number of everyday activities which seem to me paradigmatically philosophical and with which a conception of philosophy as a theory *and* a practice can be generated. These paradigmatic activities are already engaged in by almost everybody; they might well be done more frequently, systematically and self-consciously for reasons which the remainder of this book will try to display.

Consider the following minimal list, comprising four everyday activities:

—pausing to think;
—querying the truth or reasonableness of an assertion;
—answering 'I don't know' when you don't know;
—asking 'What do you mean by the word "x"?'

It will be said that this list is trivial. I shall try to counter this charge by bringing out the significance of these trivial acts in the rest of this section. The points made below will be returned to throughout the book.

—Pausing to think

To speak 'without thinking' is usually, though not necessarily, to utter a conventional, predictable response. The exact form of words may differ from person to person in the same context, but the meaning remains invariant. To speak without thinking implies unselfconsciousness of what one is saying, its status and even of the very fact of speaking. In Orwell's theory of Newspeak (93, Orwell), *duckspeak* is the ideal type of speaking without thinking. Basil Bernstein has a paper in *Class, Codes and Control* (21, Bernstein, Ch. 5) in which he speaks of hesitation as being a condition for lexical and structural selection in verbal planning and thus for greater appropriateness between the speech sequences and their referents. Yet dominant in the culture in which I live is the demand to be able to think and act quickly, a demand most clearly revealed (and success rewarded) in the exam-system. Compare the furious rush to 'get it all down' in an exam with the hesitation involved in trying to mean exactly what one writes when outside an exam room. I think that the social premium on quickness is destructive of accurate and original thought, and it is for this reason that I think the little act of pausing to think is *socially* significant. Its philosophical character I try to show later in this section.

Academics suffer from a variant of the premium on quickness, namely, the premium on quantity. Academic success is measured by the volume of articles produced. No matter how thoughtless they may be, so long as no one chooses to hold them up for ridicule, all such articles *count*.[7a]

—Querying the truth or reasonableness of an assertion
In many situations, to let an assertion pass without challenge is tacitly to endorse the truth or reasonableness of the belief it expresses.[7aa] Though it may not imply that you share or agree with the assertion, to fail to challenge where you do disagree may suggest to the speaker that you do not know *how* to challenge the assertion, and this may be enough to convince him that his position is irrefutable.

Of course, there are often conventional reasons for not challenging an assertion with which you disagree and sometimes they are good reasons. There are unwritten, context-specific rules of conversational etiquette which, for example, keep families from becoming scientific battlegrounds. There are also therapeutic situations in which listening to the patient without challenging him is a condition of successful therapy, though the therapy may, however, involve getting the patient to challenge his own assertions. But there are important considerations about the appropriateness of all these rules, the circumstances in which they should be overriden and the definitions of (for example) therapeutic situations. Further, as indicated above, it is not the case that people always challenge assertions with which they disagree even when the conventions give them the right to do so.

Things turn into their opposites, and whilst failure to challenge an assertion may sometimes be taken to confirm it and strengthen the conviction with which it is held, a general policy of not challenging assertions serves to invalidate them and their utterers, especially when a mechanism operates of tacitly converting claims to knowledge (which must be true or false) into expressions of personal opinion (which are neither and, therefore, cannot demand assent). There is a sort of conversational liberalism or positivism which devalues what people are saying and the status which they might give to it (see 5, Arendt and Chapter VI of this book).[7b]

In the light of such considerations as the above, I think that the activity of 'querying the truth or reasonableness of an assertion' should not *go without saying*.

—Answering 'I don't know' when you don't know
In *Teaching as a Subversive Activity*, Neil Postman and Charles
Weingartner (103) go so far as to recommend that teachers
reply 'I don't know' even where they do know the answer to a
student's question. Their object is to get teachers to change
from being people who convey discrete bits of information into
people who teach the skills needed to carry out information
search and retrieval. They want to encourage cognitive self-
sufficiency (even if collective rather than traditionally individual) and discourage reliance on Authority.[7c]
 Outside of school, most people seldom have nothing substantive to say in answer to a question,[8] not because they know
but because they would rather guess at an answer than say 'I
don't know' or more helpfully 'I don't know, try ...'. In
different circumstances, I'm sure there are different reasons for
the premium put on being able to give an answer: in quiz programmes, it's money! In general, I would say we are too quick
to give an answer because that is what is socially demanded. It
is not some psychological weakness which is to be held responsible. It is significant when people give an answer when
really they don't know, because they create an illusion of knowledge, which at the collective level may function as a real
obstacle to understanding. An impression of certainty is created
which disguises a pervading doubt.

—Asking 'What do you mean by the word "x"?'
In a society in which knowledge competes with wealth as the
supreme conventional value, ignorance becomes more and more
difficult to admit and puzzlement is no longer an admirable
state of mind. The illiterate go to vast lengths to cover up
their illiteracy and more and more people claim fictitious 'O'-
and 'A'-level successes; some actually buy Ph.D.s from box
numbers. To an assertion containing a problematic word it is
unusual to respond with a request for clarification; you assume
that you ought to understand and thus conversations can go on
in which key words are bandied about in different senses of
which no one seems aware. Worse, the introduction of words
not in the vocabulary of undergraduate textbooks makes supposedly educated people feel threatened. Rather than ask for

clarification, they resent the speaker and uncritically treat any such word as unnecessary jargon.[8a] In consequence, they are unable to learn anything new or think anything dangerous, let alone allow other individuals their self-expression. If the reader of this book comes across a word he doesn't know, will he fume at the author or get down from the shelf his dictionary? (I think that for an educated person, the non-possession of a good dictionary is as sure a sign as any of *hubris*.)

Philosophy students *are* specially instructed in asking questions about the meaning of words, but this does not always produce a good result. For the question can cease to be asked as a genuine one, as an expression of a desire to understand. It comes to assert plenitude rather than want, fixed in the mythic function[9] of connoting to the hearer that the speaker knows how to do Philosophy.

Yet the original emphasis on asking questions about the meaning of words remains, in my view, valid and important, though I do not accept the notion which generally accompanies such an emphasis, namely, that the meaning of a word should remain the same throughout a given discourse. But that is by the way.

What do the above four activities have in common that makes me want to call them 'philosophical'?[10] It is that they are all in their paradigmatic uses, means of promoting the reasonableness and truth of assertion, belief and argument, of which understanding what is said is a presupposition. They provide a model of the kind of everyday philosophical intervention which I have briefly characterised. Indeed, I should like to propose a philosophical practice whose scope might be defined in a formula as that of *reflecting on one's own thought and discourse and intervening in discourse and thereby in social relationships from the point of view of promoting the truth of what is thought and said; the rationality of thought, discourse and action; and the conditions of possibility of these things.*[10a] As well as those four activities listed above, philosophical activity could include such political and practical things as leafleting a meeting or operating a Trades Description Act.[10b]

The conception of a philosophical practice can itself be subsumed under a more general conception of communicational practice as concerned with promoting, (1) the conditions for and actuality of 'appropriate' reciprocal emission and reception of messages and, (2) the adequacy of the codes used in such messages. (In this book, I shan't confine myself just to the development of the theory of a philosophical practice, which is why I use 'communication' rather than 'philosophy' in the sub-title.) Thus, for example, one could have—and does have—practices concerned with the expression of feelings. The psychotherapy of neurosis is a good example of helping someone find and use a code appropriate for what it is that they wish to express but have been stopped from doing. If a wish gets expressed in an unintelligible hysterical symptom, it must be translated into a code intelligible to the patient (see, for example, 23, Breuer and Freud). Only in this way does it become operable—e.g., can catharsis take place. Such practices need not be carried on by professionals or in separate and watertight compartments, psychotherapists can also be philosophers. Perhaps they should be (see 96, Pateman).

Of course, both the existing and my proposed everyday philosophical practice inevitably perform functions other than the promotion of reason and truth. A major difficulty with the practice I have suggested is precisely whether one could engage in it without inevitably doing other things which contradict the philosophical impulse toward reason and truth. Especially, can the enterprise avoid becoming one in which those who know or think they know dominate those who don't know, don't think they know or can't successfully assert that they do? I shall be arguing that a whole range of existing communicational activities make people ignorant, mystified, repressed and unfree. Can the philosophical or more generally communicational practices which I want to promote be part of collective and democratic, that is, non-dominating endeavours? In the next section of this chapter, I try to show how I see the ideas of this book in the context of my own political beliefs. But before I do that there is one major question which perhaps should be confronted now.

Paul Feyerabend asks the question 'Can the abstract aim to come closer to the truth be reached in an entirely rational manner, or is it perhaps inaccessible to those who decide to rely on argument only?' (36, Feyerabend, p. 80.) I am convinced by Feyerabend's own work that this question has to be answered in the negative, if by 'in an entirely rational manner' is meant the sticking to any logic as the sole heuristic device. There are many more patterns of discovery than are dreamt of in logic. But what can remain, even in the maverick remark or action, is the impulse toward truth, and this Feyerabend has not yet (to my knowledge) challenged. When Feyerabend uses a maverick device it is with an educational intent; he uses it to get his audience or reader to see things in a radically different perspective, and this is something attempted in all revolutionary science.[11] If I provide no canon of rules for the conduct of the practice I have proposed it is because I share Feyerabend's position. But this doesn't entail that one abandons the pursuit of useful knowledge; only that one will pursue it in many different ways, the development of which would only be stunted by the laying down of rules (see also Chapter VII).

5. The Politics of this Philosophy

By 1969, I thought I was a revolutionary socialist and was a graduate student in search of a thesis topic. I was engaged in student politics (where the key issue was the University's complicity in imperialism), living for a while in a North London commune, trying to do some community work, and doing some adult education teaching. I believed that the material conditions were ripe for a socialist revolution and that the system was held together by little else but bourgeois ideology. But since I was trying to engage in day-to-day contact with people who were not, for the most part, self-conscious revolutionaries, my intellectual interest focussed not so much on structural features of ideological thought, or on the means of its transmission, but more on the hold which ideology had on individuals or, equally, on the way in which they held to ideology. In this context, it was unsurprising that my research supervisor, Professor Richard Wollheim, should suggest that work on my thesis-to-be-written should proceed under the title 'False Consciousness'. Of course, since I was a Ph.D. student in Philosophy, I was meant to get on with a conceptual rather than a substantive analysis, and the impossibility or emptiness of doing such a thing is one reason why this book exists and not a thesis shelved in the Library of the University of London. In any case, this book refocuses the problem of consciousness in a communicational perspective.

The most important point I should like to make is that my work has proceeded under the pressure of political impulses. I do not now know what it would be like to write a 'disinterested' work.[11a]

In 1968–9, like many radicalised students, I read most of the available work of Herbert Marcuse and many of the ideas worked out in the chapters which follow derive from those of *One Dimensional Man* (83) and the essay on *Repressive Tolerance* (84). In particular, there are the Orwellian themes of the 'closure of the universe of discourse', the themes of lexical, syntactic, semantic and pragmatic pathology in the uses of language (themes which Marcuse seems to develop from the work of Karl Kraus[12]); and the reformulation of a theory of repressive tolerance (in Chapter VI below). Most generally, what I think I take from or share with Marcuse is the concern to establish the non-economic context within which radical or revolutionary discourse can be effective. I see the philosophical practice proposed in section 4 above as one of the means of realising such a context.

Similar themes to those of Marcuse appear in the work of George Steiner (116, 117, 118), though the political perspective is different[13] and his concern is with high culture, whereas Marcuse's (as also my own) is mainly with face-to-face interaction and the relation of the mass media to their audiences.

I no longer believe that all the obstacles to revolutionary change are ideological, even when 'ideological' has the very broad sense it has been given in recent Marxist work, for example, in Althusser's essay on the ideological state apparatuses (3, Althusser, pp. 121–73). And I think my project can escape the charge of idealism (in the Marxist sense). For I am not going to say that the world can be changed by converting the majority of (abstract) 'people' to general ideas upon which they then proceed to act. What I say is that *unless* certain channels of communication are open, and used in certain ways, within those groups capable of bringing about social change, and *unless* certain forms of communication between rulers and ruled are stopped, disrupted or combatted, *then* radical and revolutionary groups will not be able to expand and mobilise their base among the relevant people, nor will organised large-scale action be possible. This has nothing to do with improving

the 'dialogue' between rulers and ruled. That particular
'dialogue' can only be broken off as of no use to the ruled.[14]
What it does have to do with are differences between revolutionaries and 'ordinary' people in cognitive and linguistic behaviour
(as also other behaviours) some of which differences make the
former ineffectual and serve to maintain the latter in exploited
and oppressed positions, and all of which are obstacles to
revolutionary social change.

6. Rationalism, conservative and radical

Perhaps I can make my position clearer on a number of issues
raised so far by outlining what I take to be features of an implicit theory of Establishment rationalism and by stating criticisms and alternatives, in particular, criticisms to show how the
theory can't or doesn't work in practice for radicals and
revolutionaries, though it tells them that they can use the procedures it specifies to achieve their ends.[15]

Here is a list of the assumptions of what I take to be an
Establishment rationalism:

—that everyone is interested to discover the T/truth;
—that T/truth will out in the dialectic of argument;
—that everyone can contribute to this argument;
—that where the T/truth is practical, people will act upon it
to bring about the situation which accords with their needs,
interests, etc., and that if only they are a majority there are
no institutional obstacles to their bringing about this accord.

I shall examine each of these features in turn but first I must
indicate what are the different meanings I attribute to 'Truth'
with a capital T and 'truth' with a small t.

A diversion: Truth and truth

I reject the position that there is a single Truth in favour of the
idea that there is no Truth, that is to say, I adopt a relativist
position. I use 'Truth' to refer to absolute Truth, and 'truth' to
refer to truth established relative to a given set of conventional
rules—rules which may always be, and sometimes are, incommensurable and ultimately unjustifiable by reference to any
higher order set of rules.[15a]

A few pages back (p. 24) I defined a practice of philosophy in terms of the promotion of reason and truth, and this is consistent with my relativism because the injunction 'pursue truth' and my assertion 'There is no Truth' are made at different levels. Whilst I do not believe that there is an absolute Truth, it is clear that—of necessity—all societies have conventional rules for assigning truth to propositions, and when I urge 'pursue truth' I use 'truth' (without a capital) in this conventional sense. But it may then be further objected that this position is a rather conservative one for a supposed radical alternative. If there is no Truth, why not throw away conventional logical rules and language, as do surrealists, dadaists and schizophrenics? Would not this be more revolutionary?

My responses to this objection are *ad hominem*. First, that surrealists, dadaists and schizophrenics have never been able to build up a political movement, or even convert people to their way of life. Second, that the possibilities of 'working within the system' should not in this area be underestimated. Consider the following two instances of changes which might be effected through restricting oneself to the rules which conventionally define rationality and truth:

At the level of isolated truths, consider that a person may at one moment express a belief in the sovereignty of British political institutions and at another speak of the determination of policy by the US government or international financial institutions. By conventional logical standards and given the conventional meaning of terms, not both of the propositions can be simultaneously true. In an argument, one could demonstrate their inconsistency and seek to get a person to choose the more justifiable of them. Note that one of the propositions embodies a conventional principle or definition which one might learn at school, and the other an empirical (or quasi-empirical) counter-instance which one might pick up from reading the right newspapers or the wrong newspapers in the right kind of way. I think this structure of a principle contradicted by evidence is fairly common in people's political consciousness and also important: if the principles dominate consciousness, they may prevent a person from *noticing* counter instances; and if the counter instances are spotted but no alternative principles are available, the person may become cynical, confused or apathetic, for a

crisis in a political belief system need not be resolved in the way
scientific crises typically get resolved. In science, a paradigm
shift[16] will sooner or later occur, whereas in a political belief
system the paradigm may simply disintegrate. A person can
more easily give up on politics than a scientist can on science,
for the latter risks losing his job, his reputation or both if he
does give up. A person who gives up on politics seems to risk
nothing.[16a]

The above example concerns beliefs inconsistent in terms of
the logical 'processing mechanism' which is accepted for use in
evaluating consistency, etc. But what of the processing mechanism itself? Can this, or parts of it, be challenged internally?
Consider the following example:

The reason for admitting memory as a ground for a claim to
knowledge is that it is reliable. You have a right to say 'I know
she was wearing a green jacket' if you can truly say 'I remember
she was wearing a green jacket'. Invoking memory allows one
to pass through one of the gates which are placed on the path
to justified knowledge claims. But memory is not a fixed, in-
variable capacity, the same for all individuals in all times and
places. Suppose one had empirical evidence to show that, as a
result of developments in the media of communication, or
geographical or social mobility, that people's memories were
getting poorer. Though this claim may itself be entered using
the existing memory-criterion, it could be used as a ground for
arguing the need for a change in the memory criterion itself.
The philosopher could say: for a large class of cases, we now
need not merely a memory claim, but a Diary entry to vindicate
the knowledge claim, if knowledge claims are to serve the
purpose for which they are intended by us. (The State might
have different ideas about the purpose of knowledge claims:
Winston Smith, the hero of *1984*, commits a crime in keeping a
Diary. For Harold Wilson, part of his power rested on the fact
that, as he put it, a week in politics is a long time—i.e. that
people forget). In summary, I think this memory example does
illustrate how part of the knowledge processing mechanism can
be challenged internally, and Chapter II will illustrate further
possibilities of challenge. However, the critique which follows
seems to me to be independent of a decision between absolute and
relative T/truth. Readers who reject my personal relativism are

not in consequence obliged to reject the critique which follows.

—The interest in T/truth assumption
Texts like J. S. Mill's *On Liberty* tend to assume that people in general want to know the T/truth. Mill argues that if some people are silenced, this is not because they are believed to have found out the T/truth but because they are believed to be wrong. But is this assumption plausible? That is, is it a guide to reality? As evidence against the plausibility of the assumption, consider how there are not only situations in which those in power suppress information about themselves, but more wide-spread phenomena of disregard of one's own logical standards (irrationalism properly speaking), large-scale self-deception, and even simple lack of curiosity: people do not want to know and in extreme cases shut themselves off to an extraordinary degree: they switch off the TV when the news comes on, they don't read newspapers, they taboo (like the Army) political and religious discussion. In short, they try not to think about things.

If people do not want to know, there is little point in trying to conduct with them rational argument leading to positive conclusions, at least until the necessary preliminary task of explaining and overcoming the 'negative orientation' towards knowledge has been accomplished. My own feeling is that not wanting to know is closely connected to feelings of powerless-ness, themselves to be explained by the real powerlessness most people experience. The desire to know may, symmetrically with this situation, only become established as people discover the possibility of changing the world in changing it, in the dis-covery of their own strength and the recognition of repressed desires. It is not knowledge which makes people feel free; it is more likely that struggling for freedom makes people want and need knowledge. This is part of the meaning of the third thesis on Feuerbach, which forms the epigraph of this chapter.[17]

It is not always necessary to eliminate the cause in order to eliminate the effect; not all situations are symmetrical in this way. Thus, for example, to come by a belief irrationally—i.e. by ignoring one's own cognitive standards—does not entail that one is not now amenable to rational argument with respect to it.[18] After all, to come by a belief irrationally (as opposed to non-rationally) is to ignore rules which one possesses and the

authority of which one in some sense acknowledges: this is perhaps why people make great efforts to rationalise after the event
beliefs they have come by irrationally. Similarly, self-deception
can only occur in people who have a commitment to being
reasonable but where reasonableness is over-ridden by a conflicting force, usually the prospect of pain; knowledge is avoided
because it threatens suffering. In cases where the suffering cannot be mitigated or removed, I don't see why knowledge should
be defended at all costs. It seems to me a defensible position not
to tell people that they are suffering from incurable diseases.
But, in practice, I think we avoid knowledge in cases where the
suffering is eliminable. For example, if we reify the social order—
that is, regard it as unchangeable—then we may avoid knowing
about its defects. And even if we don't reify society, we may still
avoid knowledge—and is this justifiable? One could pose a
general question in these or similar terms: does Bad Faith have
any rights? That is to say, in what circumstances if any is the
avoidance of knowledge to be treated as legitimate, that is, free
from sanction? My own position is that where another person's
refusal to know affects the prospects of my happiness and freedom, I have a right to try to make him know. That is to say, I
can legitimately impose sanctions upon him for his refusal to
know, though only—of course—if those sanctions are effective
as a means of getting him to know.

—The 'T/truth will out' and free access assumptions
If people don't want to know, truth will out in argument purely
by chance. Even if they do want to know, it only seems plausible
to think that the truth will out if everyone who has something
to say can say it. Here I share the classical liberal position. But
in that position it tends to be assumed that because everyone
has the *legal* right to speak the condition of access is fulfilled.
But quite aside from the existing multitude of legal, quasi-legal,
and conventional impediments to free speech, the assumption
based on legal freedom is clearly unrealistic, especially in the
age of the mass media. What is required is that everyone with
something to say can actually say it, effectively as well as without fear, and this means that the media of communication must
be open and available, and not only that a vast number of
sanctions must be got rid of.

In Mill's *On Liberty* what strikes me forcibly is the relative insensitivity to the vast problem of the social distribution of the possibilities of contributing to debate and discussion. This cannot be put down simply to his having written before the age of the mass media, which have forced an awareness of this problem upon us. In my opinion, the omission results from the peculiar ideological nature of Mill's project: Mill's interests were particularistic; he wished to defend the freedom of thought and expression specifically of intellectuals in opposition to the masses (by which he means the middle classes),[19] in order that the intellectuals could have a directing role in public affairs (see 24, Burns). But Mill couched his particularistic interests in universal terms; yet a properly universalistic treatment would require much closer attention to the problems I have indicated.

To achieve some sort of equality of access to means of communication requires political action of a sort which may mean that the desired situation cannot be brought about independently of much broader social change; for example, the question of access to the means of communication cannot be separated from questions about media ownership and legal constraints on the freedom to broadcast and receive. Prior to radical changes of ownership and control being achieved, one has to ask what can be done, in a situation of inequality of access, to maximise the possibility of truth emerging. Many radical students came to the conclusion in 1968–70 that the *denial* of freedom of expression to individuals and groups and disrupting the workings of certain media might be the most effective means of maximising the possibilities of reason and truth prevailing. This position is only paradoxical if it is assumed that the necessary background conditions for free and equal debate are fulfilled. The radical argument is meant to cope with the situation in which they are not. (For further discussion, see Chapter VI below.)

Finally, let me note that there are situations in which because of cognitive or linguistic deprivation some people can't have anything to say on some subjects, just as skill deprivation means that some people can't say effectively what they want to say, and are thus even more clearly excluded from the Great Debate out of which Truth is supposed to emerge. (See Chapter V below.)

C

—The unity of theory and practice assumption

It is difficult to prove that, where someone knows how to satisfy a need in a situation where there appears to be no conflicting, overriding need, failure to act to satisfy the need is to be explained in terms of weakness of will or apathy. Isn't it usually the case that the person estimates the probability of success relatively low and the risks of things going unpleasantly wrong relatively high and thus, quite rationally, does not act? This is the idea which lies behind the claim that the workers have much more to lose than their chains.

But what would you say of a person who prefers a situation of present misery to action he knows would probably bring about a better situation with very little risk involved? I can think, for example, that though he knows what is required, he does not know how to go about it. Again, might it be that the desire for security is so great that he has what economists call 'high risk-aversion'? But might not such an aversion eventually become pathological—that is, dysfunctional for his survival? You have to take risks to avoid risks.[20] Even where some 'men' do act to transform social reality, other 'men' may oppose them and even though a minority, may be more powerful. If on no other ground, the establishment theory of rationalism founders on the fact of class society.

In summary, what I have tried to indicate in this section are some of the ways in which philosophical, educational or political work which based itself on the four assumptions listed at the beginning of the preceding discussion would founder, simply because reality does not correspond to the assumptions. On the other hand, what I have not done is to counterpose reliance on History to reliance on Argument. Rather, I have—if indirectly —tried to indicate the sort of space in which a philosophical, educational or political practice could operate effectively. In Marxist terms, I have been trying to find a path between the opposites of voluntarism (the Establishment and activist positions are voluntarist ones) and mechanism (historical inevitability). The third thesis on Feuerbach, which forms the epigraph for this chapter, remains a sign-post to such a path.

7. Concluding Remarks

These opening sections should indicate some of the main areas and themes of this book and some of the reasons why I think them important enough to write about. The reader will already have noticed that my style of argument and writing leaves many imprecisions, gaps and unanswered questions. Some of these are deliberately there. I believe in trying to create an 'open' discourse which the reader must criticise, contribute to, engage with and interpret *as* she is reading—and not just afterwards. I don't want her to be confronted with a Final Solution to a given Problem which she can then forget, confident that somewhere it exists.

It is also true that in trying to work outside a *subject*, I assemble my discourse from concepts and techniques out of different disciplines. In this process of *bricolage* (doing a job as an amateur, using whatever happens to be around) I hope it is something useful I am creating and not a myth, for Lévi-Strauss tells us that myths are created in the same way as I am working (74, Lévi-Strauss).

There are, of course, non-theoretical reasons for the structure of this book. There are my own intellectual limitations, and laziness. There are the facts of daily life, too, such as that this chapter was drafted in between knocks at the front door from members of a village Youth Club, bringing in what they have scavenged for their jumble sale. I think it is important to avoid doing without such eruptions of daily life—at least, most of the time.

NOTES TO CHAPTER I

0_a. The idea of 'intervention' was actually taken from R. D. Laing's *Interventions in Social Situations* (72a, Laing). [References are to the numbered bibliography at the back of the book.]

0_b. This statement is either tautologous, if 'action' is used to contrast with 'behaviour', or else it represents a failure to recognise the difference between informative and communicative action (on which see 47c, Grice; 78c, Lyons; 78g, McKay).

1. The concept of 'taken-for-grantedness' plays an important part in phenomenological sociology (see, notably, 19, Berger and

Luckmann). 'Reification' is a central concept of the early work of George Lukacs (77, Lukacs; an important critical article dealing with Marx's use of the concept is 43, Geras).

2. Still the best discussion of the worker and his work is 86, Marx. An important recent sociological study is 45, Goldthorpe, Lockwood, *et al.*

3. 'You want to find faith and you do not know the road . . . learn from those who were once bound like you and who now wager all they have . . . follow the way by which they began. They behaved just as if they did believe, taking holy water, having masses said, and so on. That will make you believe quite naturally, and will make you more docile.' (94, Pascal, p. 152.)

4. But note the following from Denise Riley's comments on a draft of this chapter: 'About the effects of the women's movement. You say that "fewer men can now unselfconsciously refer to", etc. But I don't think that's true. Precisely the people who talk about "chicks" and "bits of stuff" go on doing so. You say "he may lose more of his chauvinism in giving up 'outward' chauvinist practices than is entailed by that giving up alone" and you quote Pascal. But what do you base that supposition on, apart from optimism? The forms of chauvinism or any other social nastiness are endlessly changeable and can endlessly recuperate any inroads.

   'So it happens that because of where I am socially/politically, I don't end up in the "chick" box; but being called a "feminist" or even "an unsupported mother" can function in ways that are more sinisterly reductive. And arguments against that sort of role-reduction aren't easily acceptable in the way that arguments against "chick" are. So I don't accept your microanalysis. Which isn't to say I don't accept your generalisation, "every act reproduces or subverts a given social institution, which means that every act is political", but then that's a wide and familiar generalisation which you could have reached from many other places.'

5. Going to the lavatory can be full of meaning. See 35, Esterson, especially Ch. 8. Denise Riley wrote 'I think you've missed the main point, which isn't the aetiology of what's "natural", or whether or not some learning has been involved in it. It's more important that the "spontaneous" and the "natural" are both extremely and transparently *bourgeois* categories. Look at who uses them and who has used them (e.g., which manufacturers of Hitlerjugend ideologies or shampoos . . .).'

6. Denise Riley corrects me: 'Rhetoric is, classically, the art of organisation of verbal material, and so could include reading—and would have, in its original scholastic sense.'

6ₐ. I find it impossible to dispense with the concept of 'human needs' as a standard of value. My Appendix 1 makes some attempt to ground the concept, and I have another go in 99d.

6_b. This seems to be a *non sequitur*. A good explanation of any phenonemon is precisely one which shows 'certain ways of operating on the "object" ' to be impossible or counter-productive. But this is only to say that a good explanation is not "neutral" with respect to truth: a tautologous claim out of which I attempt to get a political trade-off.

6_c. Compare Jonathan Ree's *Descartes* (105c, Ree, p. 43).

7. The themes of this and the following paragraphs recur more fully in my article 97. [For a historical approach to doing Philosophy, see now 48k, 48m, Hacking, influenced by 39a, Foucault.]

7ₐ. The preceding two paragraphs are far from being theorised in terms antagonistic to contemporary analytical philosophy; in fact, they are derivative from it. For in the philosophy of language, in the tradition of Frege, Wittgenstein and Austin, there is a considerable body of discussion of such questions as, What is it to *say* something in *speaking*? Frege distinguishes the *force* of an utterance from its *sense* (39b, Frege); Wittgenstein writes about 'language idling' as opposed to 'doing work' (126, Wittgenstein, para. 132); and Austin devoted a lifetime to the analysis of the force of utterances (5b, Austin; see the appreciation in 45b, Graham, and the critique there of the reactionary aspects of 'ordinary language' philosophy).

When Orwell writes about 'Duckspeak' it seems to me that he is concerned with the same kinds of question as have preoccupied philosophers of language: what is it that distinguishes an utterance from a string of sounds or from a well-formed sentence uttered without force?

Anyone interested in theorising the practice of 'pausing to think' would learn a great deal from Frege, Wittgenstein, Austin and their successors: Michael Dummett writes in his *Frege* that 'a theory of meaning is . . . a theory of the practice of using a language' (33a, p. 682), and P. F. Strawson, in 'Grammar and Philosophy', writes in similar vein of stating the theory of our practice of using a language (118a, p. 455). On the relation between theory and practice in analytic philosophy, see also App. 3 on R. M. Hare's work (pp. 203–10 below). And see n. 10

7$_{aa}$. This is at least partly a simple consequence of what a *conversation* is: see, for example, 74aa Lewis.

7$_b$. Anything can be said, but it won't be taken very seriously. Arendt's ideas have been taken up, commented on and criticised by, among others, Richard Bernstein (21a) and Jürgen Habermas (48h). The opposite of 'conversational liberalism or positivism' might be called *dialectics*. J. S. Mill, on whom I rely heavily in Chapter VI, was himself almost wholly indebted to Plato for his justification of liberty of discussion as permitting dialectical refutation, and also to him for a dialectical theory of the pursuit of truth. See, for instance, Mill's review of 'Grote's *Plato* (91c). Sparshott's Introduction to the same volume is also valuable. Parts of Grote's *Plato* are themselves well worth reading. See especially the *Preface* and Ch. VIII (47e, Grote). There is some discussion of Mill as a Platonist in my 99c, and an overview of the classical influence on the Utilitarians in 93a, Pappé.

7$_c$. Very little of what we believe to be true has or can have any other support than the testimony of others. It is accepted, and much will always have to be accepted, 'on authority'. What follows from the realisation of the impossibility of generally following the maxims of Cartesian or Lockean individualism is explored in some nineteenth-century writings. See, for instance, George Cornewall Lewis' *An Essay on the Influence of Authority in Matters of Opinion* (74c, Lewis; discussed in my 99c). It would be more useful to think about changing the social organisation of the (necessary) social division of intellectual labour than suggesting that such a division will go away if only we pretend it doesn't exist (as Rousseau in *Emile* proposes to make social constraints vanish by acting *as if* they were laws of nature. See 110b, Rousseau, pp. 100–1).

8. Both Carole Pateman and Denise Riley have queried the truth of this assertion. Perhaps, then, what follows is merely self-criticism.

8$_a$. Adorno gives a helpful functional definition and many examples of 'jargon'. Jargon 'sees to it that what it wants is on the whole felt and accepted through its mere delivery, without regard to the content of the words used. It takes under its own control the preconceptual, mimetic element in language . . . [For example, in existentialism] "Statement" thus wants to make believe that the existence of the speaker has communicated itself simultaneously with his subject matter and has given the latter its dignity.' (1a, Adorno, pp. 8–9; compare the journalistic use of

such phrases as 'Solzhenitsyn speaks', drawn to my attention by John Mepham.)
There are also interesting and possibly incompatible remarks in Benjamin's essay on Kraus (18d, Benjamin, especially p. 248).

9. I use 'mythic' here in the sense it has in Roland Barthes' theory of myth, as roughly equivalent to connotation. (See 11, Barthes, second part 'Myth today'.) The opposition denotation/connotation is criticised by 16, Baudrillard. (For an attempt to rethink 'connotation' in terms of Gricean 'implicature', see App. 5.)

10. Roy Edgley comments on the preceding section:
   The four practices said to be paradigmatic of philosophy as theory and practice seem to be strongly derivative from 'Philosophy as a subject'—at least as commonly taught in English-speaking academies since the war. For in two ways they seem *inactivist*: (1) they place a high value on *doubt*; and (2) they relate *reason* to *truth* and *knowledge*. In much philosophy since Descartes these have become philosophical necessities, doubt in the form of philosophical scepticism, and the relation of reason exclusively to truth in the form of the idea that there can't be any such thing as *practical* reason (except in a technological sense)—one manifestation of this latter business being the separation of epistemology from ethics and politics and the centrality of epistemology in Philosophy as a subject. In other words, scepticism and the reason-logic-truth connection since Descartes have put the weight of Philosophy-as-a-subject heavily against *commitment to action* ('Philosophers have so far only interpreted the world; the point however is to change it'). Perhaps this ought to be pointed out, and some mention made of the fact that you reject the *theory-practice* (truth-action) distinction and so avoid subscribing to that inhibition of action induced by scepticism and the theoretical conception of reason. This would perhaps connect with the problem you mention on p. 16, of how self-conscious reflection seems incompatible with spontaneous action. It would also connect with the mention of Feyerabend, p. 25, since Feyerabend's quotation presupposes the very identification of reason with *argument* (whether or not formalised by Aristotelian or any other logic) that is typical of the theoretical conception of reason (see my 'Reason and Violence', *Radical Philosophy 4*, pp. 19–20). [33d, Edgley.]

10ₐ. Compare this quotation from Condorcet's *Mémoires sur l'Instruction Publique* (1791). 'It is necessary that the man and the philosopher cease to be two separate beings, as it were, each with a different language, ideas, and even opinions. Without that, how can philosophy, which is only reason rendered methodical and precise, ever become common and vulgar.' (Cited in 8a, Baker, p. 296.)

10ᵦ. Could it? Is there any important sense in which (say) studying Frege and leafleting a meeting belong together? One of my re-viewers (104g, Anthony Quinton) thought not, finding objec-tionable my proposal for a philosophical practice going beyond the (unobjectionable) aims of promoting truth and rationality to encompass political action.

In this connexion, the *Preface* to Michael Dummett's *Frege* (33a) is instructive. Dummett gave up his work on Frege for four years to campaign against racism in Britain; there's a dis-continuity one can't escape. But in his campaigning, Dummett spoke with the *voice* of a philosopher, and that way of speaking unfroze the thoughts of some, possibly many, who heard him. As a campaigner, he did not deprive us of his philosophical talents, and that is an important continuity.

11. Cf. Marx on appearance and reality: 'Scientific truth is always paradox, if judged by everyday experience, which catches only the delusive appearance of things.' (88, Marx and Engels, p. 209.)

11ₐ. I am unsure now whether an 'interested' work is necessarily a 'political' work in any non-vacuous sense of 'political'; in general, I sympathise with Habermas's position in *Knowledge and Human Interests* (in 48g, Habermas, pp. 301–17).

12. On Kraus, whose work is not available in English, see especially 64, Janik and Toulmin; also 59, Iggers; 67, Kohn, and 116, Steiner. [And see now 67b, 67c, Kraus; 127c, Zohn; 18d, Benjamin.]

13. The following two quotations are from *Extra-Territorial* (117, Steiner):

But one ought not to forget the profoundly disturbing *increase* of actual illiteracy on the world scale. The latest UNESCO estimate puts at almost half the world total that number of primary-school children who drop out before attaining literacy. [p. 160, my italics]

A society with few private libraries and a *sharply diminishing* readership (a survey conducted in 1969 concludes that the *per capita* consumption of books in France is of the order of one per year) ... [pl. 166–7, first italic mine]

Now it is elementary that you cannot prove or even illustrate that something is increasing or decreasing with a non-comparative statistic. Perhaps Steiner has committed a simple logical error, but I would be surprised that he should do so twice in the space of a half-dozen pages. More likely, to me, is that Steiner is working with a suppressed premise that if things look bad in the present, they were better in the past. The enthymemic arguments quoted above are not then illogical. It is just that the suppressed premise, which defines a myth of a Golden Past, is false.

14. Cf. in a different context Feyerabend's remark (36, p. 111, fn. 41):
    ... the current infatuation with 'syntheses' and 'dialogues' which are defended in the spirit of tolerance and understanding can only lead to an end to all tolerance and of all understanding. To defend a 'synthesis' by reference to tolerance means that one is not prepared to tolerate a view that does not show an admixture of one's own pet prejudices. To invite to a 'dialogue' by reference to tolerance means inviting one to state one's views in a less radical and therefore mostly less clear way.
    What Feyerabend does not say (as he should, following as he does Mill: see 91, Mill, pp. 181–3) is that it is those in the one-down, less powerful position who will have to do the real compromising in any 'dialogue'.

15. Cf. the theory that says anyone can achieve their ends through the liberal democratic political system and should only attempt to do so through that system. For part of the critique of such a theory, see 90, Miliband and 7, Bachrach and Baratz.

15a. 'Now it may safely be affirmed that no scepticism, limited to the Absolute, ever did anybody harm, or made the smallest practical difference to any human being', writes J. S. Mill (91c, Mill, p. 426), and the relativism espoused here would be trivial but for the suggestion that even conventional rules may be incommensurable. My reading in the philosophy of social science (e.g., 125b, Wilson, especially the essay by S. Lukes, pp. 194–213) and in resurgent realist epistemology (67d, Kripke and, especially 104b, Putnam) now suggests to me that one can have one's paradigm shifts and commensurability, too. For a criticism of my position in this section, see also the review by Steven Lukes (77b, Lukes).

16. On paradigm shifts, see 68, Kuhn.

16a. J. Buchanan and G. Tullock recognise this possibility as a drawback to the economic theory of politics advanced in their *The Calculus of Consent* (23b, Buchanan and Tullock), writing that 'secure in the knowledge that, regardless of his own action, social or collective decisions affecting him will be made, the individual is offered a greater opportunity either to abstain altogether from making a positive choice or to choose without having considered the alternatives carefully'. In contrast, 'The consumer who refrains from entering the market place will starve unless he hires a professional shopper.' (p. 38.) Joseph Schumpeter accounts for the greater irrationality of people in their political activity on similar lines, arguing that a 'reduced sense of reality accounts not only for a reduced sense of responsibility but also for the absence of effective volition' (114a, Schumpeter, p. 165).

It seems to me that both of these positions can be integrated within the general theory developed by Mancur Olson in *The Logic of Collective Action* (92e), which is briefly discussed in Chapter V, n. 18a.

17. Cf. Lukacs: ' . . . the proletariat *always aspires towards the truth* . . . But the aspiration only yields the *possibility*. The accomplishment can only be the fruit of the *conscious* deeds of the proletariat.' (77, Lukacs, pp. 72–3.)

18. Therefore, I disagree with Marx and Engels: 'All forms and products of consciousness cannot be dissolved by mental criticism but only by the practical overthrow of the actual social relations which gave rise to this idealistic humbug.' (87, Marx and Engels, p. 50.) All? [This remark has been criticised in a review by Jacob L. Mey, who writes:

In the Marx-Engels quotation . . . Pateman actually misinterprets the text. He says that he disagrees with Marx and Engels . . . The trouble with this passage [quoted above] is that its message (the 'comment') is in the repeated opposition 'not . . . but'; cf. in the sequel: 'not criticism, but revolution is the moving force of history' [my translation], and so on. Although its 'topic' part contains the quantifier 'all', the whole passage is not mainly about '*all* forms of consciousness' [my italics] but rather about the opposition between an idealistic view of history and a materialistic one. By querying 'All?' in the topic, Pateman is simply asking the wrong kind of question. If Marx and Engels really had wanted to say that nothing whatsoever in the line of reforming people's consciousness can be achieved by 'mental criticism', then Pateman would have been right in doubting this pessimistic statement which, in fact, would invalidate most of Marx and Engels' work, *post festum et contra factum*! (89c, Mey, pp. 89–90.)]

19. Mill writes that 'the masses' have their thinking done for them
by men much like themselves, addressing them or speaking in
their name, on the spur of the moment, through the newspapers' (91, Mill, p. 195). Who else but the middle classes
read newspapers in 1859?
    [Answer: the working classes! As John Wardle quickly
pointed out (personal communication, 1975 referring me to
125a, Williams, pp. 197–8), the argument that Mill meant 'the
middle classes' by 'the masses' because only the middle classes
read newspapers is pretty obviously false. Though at most times,
Mill includes the middle classes in 'The Many' who stand
opposed by 'The Few' (free-floating intellectuals of a Mann-
ihemian sort), and though it is the middle classes who may pose
the greatest active threat to freedom of thought and discussion,
it is the working classes who pose the active threat to the
economic and political institutions, private property and representative government, which Mill cherished. I addition, the,
arguments of On Liberty should be seen not onn as directed'
against threats 'from below' to the freedom of thly intellectuals
but also as directed 'sideways' against the Comteeans. Mills
arguments for liberty have to do with the conditions of the
possibility of rational authority, exercised by the few over the
many, and as against Comte, Mill believes that liberty is a
condition of the possibility of rational authority. He believes
this because he accepts a dialectical (Platonic) 'theory of the
pursuit of truth' (as he puts it in the introductory notes to his
translation of the Protagoras: 90b, Mill, p. 42), in which the
right to seek to confute (negative dialectics) is held to be a
necessary condition of the possibility of rational belief (or knowledge as opposed to opinion) and hence to the possibility of a
rational authority based on Knowledge. There is further discussion of this aspect of Mill's thought in my thesis, How is
Political Knowledge Possible? (99c, Pateman). See also 91, 91a,
91c, Mill.]

20. Cf. Wilhelm Reich: 'We assert categorically that the fundamental problem for a correct psychological approach is not why
a hungry man steals, but why he doesn't steal.' (106, Reich, p.
25.) Slater writes: 'Most Americans still just want to go about
their business and ignore the problems of their society, and are
willing to pay a very heavy price to be able to do so.' (115,
Slater, pp. 165–6.) [Here is a quotation from Alasdair Mac-
Intyre which expresses an identical thought, 'If we wish to explain the civil rights movement among American Negroes, for

example, we shall do well to pause and ask what needs to be explained. Is it why since 1953 Negro students have acted on beliefs, which they are taught in school, that all American citizens, indeed all men have certain rights, or is it rather why for so long they failed or were unable to act on their beliefs? If the latter we shall expect no general, as it were positive, explanation of the Negro civil rights movement, but only a series of explanations of why the different particular obstacles to such a movement were removed in the early 1950s.' (78e, MacIntyre, p. 257; cf. also the approach to explanation adopted by J. L. Austin, notably in 'A Plea for Excuses' (5a, Austin.) But compare Mancur Olson's account of such situations (92e, Olson, briefly outlined in Chapter V, n. 18a).]

CHAPTER II

Rational Error [0a]

> The trouble ain't that people are ignorant; it's that they 'know' so much that ain't so.
>
> Josh Billings [1]

1. Introduction

Despite my efforts, Chapter I may have given the impression that I think the world could be made a better place by making individuals more rational in thought and action—for example, by getting them to apply more consistently their own standards of logic and argument. I don't wish to deny that getting them to do so is a useful activity, but in this chapter I should like to illustrate one way in which such a strategy alone could not bring about desirable change, not only because of its idealistic misconceptions, but also because one can be rational yet remain in error (this quite aside from the fact that people may think rationally with different and incommensurable premises, concepts and theories). That people are rational does not guarantee that they arrive at true conclusions. In illustrating how this occurs, the focus will shift from thought processes going on in an individual's head to the relation of norms of reason to the social context in which they are used, and the social sources of information which is reasoned about.

Incidentally, if it were the case that on a large scale people were wrong for good reasons, this would tend to invalidate explanations of false consciousness and related phenomena in terms of the irrationalism of the authoritarian personality, brainwashing, etc. Further, it might limit the area of application of what I think are over-hastily applied relativistic explanation: I am a relativist but I don't think that all political disagreements arise from differences which are incommensurable.[1a]

It seems to me that the sociology of knowledge has too often proceeded as if there could be no sociology of rational claims to knowledge and, in equating error with irrationality, ignored the possibility of explaining error as an *effect* of rationality: the consequence of which alternative explanation would be to displace blame from the individual (who weakly and ignorantly, it is supposed, allows his beliefs to be determined by passions and interests) to the sources of error outside the individual and to the social institutions which indicate to the individual that he can rely on these outside sources. More on 'the ways in which error can be socially induced and rationally accepted' (77b, Lukes) below.

The illustrations of rational error are meant to serve other purposes than those indicated in the above paragraphs. I would like to illustrate, for example, how the norms of reasoning actually in use are much more complicated than the rationalities which some Philosophers have constructed or proposed; how it is in terms of the social context that the applicability of norms is decided; how the norms serve other purposes than helping people to get things right and think and act accordingly —that the norms are bound into the social order and serve the maintenance of its hierarchical division of labour.

I raise but scarcely answer questions about what, prior to and in the process of achieving broader social change, can be done about 'reforming' rationality and rational errors, and their sources.

2. Knowledge Claims

I think that in standard use—i.e. in terms of what is conventionally acceptable—one is justified in claiming to know many empirical things (though not, perhaps, anything at all) despite the fact that what one justifiably (because reasonably) claims to know may turn out to be false. If it was insisted that one should not claim to know anything except where it was impossible that one should be in error, then one would never (or almost never —see below on 'seemings') be able to make a claim to empirical knowledge. For in its usual sense 'empirical' implies 'that which might be other than it is' (it is a matter of fact that whoever is Prime Minister is Prime Minister but it could be otherwise, and this in turn implies that any empirical claim made by a person could be mistaken: I could be wrong in claiming to know that so-and-so is Prime Minister, but if I satisfy certain requirements, I am justified in claiming to know that they are Prime Minister.

(In the case of 'seeming' claims such as 'It seems blue to me' it is not clear whether substantive as opposed to verbal mistake is possible, though it might also be doubted whether 'seeming' claims are claims to knowledge.) Could one not claim to know except where there was no possibility of error, society would be impossibly sceptical.

Individuals may be called upon to justify their claims to knowledge and can do so by producing sufficient reasons for them. But what makes a reason or reasons sufficient for a claim to knowledge? My essential point is that in practice this question cannot be answered simply by referring to the reason, the claim and their logical relation. Such is true only of a formal system, not everyday knowledge claims where the acceptability and strength of reasons depends on other factors such as (a) the sort of person who is appealing to the reason, and the sort of person to whom the reasons are being given; (b) the kind of claim involved—whether common or esoteric, whether or not there is a presumption in favour of its truth; (c) the circumstances of the claim.[1b] Perhaps in addition to the study of *natural* logic alongside *formal* logic (see, for example, 73, Lakoff), there is a place for a sort of *socio-logic*, of which this chapter would form an elementary sample.

Let me illustrate the (a), (b) and (c) of the previous paragraph. For (a) consider that in situations with which we are all probably familiar, that something seemed to me to be *x* is more often acceptable as a good, necessary or sufficient reason for the claim that it was *x* if I was not drunk at the time, or an infant or idiot. Reciprocally, it may be that what counts as a good reason depends in some cases on the person *to whom* the claim is being made. For (b), that something seems to me to be blue is always a good and sometimes a sufficient reason for the claim that it is blue, but that something seemed to me to be the voice of God is only in special restricted circles a good or sufficient ground for the claim that it was the voice of God (compare 27, and 28, Chisholm). The justifiability of an isolated claim to knowledge in society at large is inseparably connected with the society's general ontology and theory of the world. As it happens this ontology and theory of the world is such that society is not prepared to evaluate claims to knowledge in terms simply of the clearness and distinctness with which an idea appears to the claimant. The subject matter is always relevant and—for example—to get themselves treated as justifiable, minority claims have to be much better justified than majority ones.[2] Finally, for (c) what is acceptable as a reason in everyday life may not stand up in Court—the law of Evidence must be a mine of epistemological information—and the powerful are able to impose on the powerless the need to be much more circumspect in their claims than the powerful themselves, for otherwise the powerless may find themselves accused of libel, slander, etc. To take an extreme case: if you are a patient in a mental hospital, it is almost impossible to get a claim to knowledge accepted because you are, by definition, unreasonable and therefore not a person who can *know* at all. (See below Chapter IV, section 4.)[2a]

3. Rational Error and the Division of Labour

It is a sufficient ground for claiming to know, and equally for thinking that one knows, that J. S. Mill was born in 1806, to have looked up the date of his birth in the *Encyclopaedia Brittanica*. This is evidently so in TV quiz programmes where the quiz master is right—i.e. justified in his claim to know (better) than the contestant—because the information in front of him is derived from this highly particular source. Of course, things can go wrong: there may have been a misprint or simple error in the encyclopaedia, a typist may have made a mistake in preparing the quizmaster's card, etc., (see 49, Haddon) but these errors are corrigible by reference to other accepted sources of evidence and rules of inference. You can solve disagreement about the date of J. S. Mill's birth by referring to other encyclpaediae or to J. S. Mill experts. But note that the *Encyclopaedia Brittanica* is a socially approved source of knowledge and reference to it justifies a claim to knowledge.

Much, if not most, of our everyday knowledge is derived from and justified by references to institutional sources, including the descriptions other people give us, rather than direct acquaintance. We claim to know something having been told it in school, read it somewhere, seen it on TV or been told it is so by our parents or peers. Some of these sources are unreliable for technological reasons—misprints and the like—but, more importantly, though they are sources which do our information search, retrieval and dissemination for us, they are not in general sources over which we have *control*. Not only is there a division of intellectual labour, but a social division of ownership and control. Now most of the norms of rationality which Philosophers discuss are not designed to apply to everyday situations but to extraordinary situations in which specialists apply norms to themselves and each other in the pursuit of their (paradigmatically natural scientific) enquiries. Philosophers typically have no suggestions to make as to how one can cope with situations in which the sources on which we rely for knowledge disseminate falsehoods or systematically filter information in terms of their world views, that is to say, in terms of their set or sets of concepts and theories. If Philosophers do make suggestions it is in terms of self-reliance, which in practice can only mean a recommendation of scepticism, for reasons given below.

Many people seem to recognise that their lack of control over the operation of information sources makes them vulnerable to being misled or not informed. Why, then, do they not try either to get control over information sources—that is, break down or modify the intellectual division of labour—or, alternatively, take no notice of potentially misleading sources: why go on reading the newspaper if you think that it's 'all lies'? Why continue to accept that the encyclopaedia is reliable? The explanation is bound to be multiple:

For example, you are not normally in a position to find out whether reliance on a particular source is misguided. First, you have to suspect or become interested in the credibility of the source and, second, you have to be able to decide in some way why an alternative source is rationally to be preferred. If you do something, say, which gets into the newspapers, you are able to compare accounts in terms of your own privileged knowledge of the event. I imagine that a great deal of (rationally based) cynicism about mass circulation newspapers derives from the experience of reading reports of, for example, a campaign or strike in which the reader is involved, or which purports to give a description of something with which the reader is personally familiar. But the evaluation of the newspaper may not progress beyond cynicism unless there is a more credible alternative newspaper available: and here it is important to stress that what matters to people is not only that a paper be for them rather

D

than against them, but that it gets its information straighter than the other papers. What is wrong with *The Sun* is both that it is against you and that it says you are earning £35 a week when you are earning £18 (which is, of course, also a way of being against you).

In the absence of a verifiably better alternative source, people can and do invent their own rules for evaluating information. In conversation with relatively unschooled people, I often come across the rule that you can't claim to know anything about a country's social organisation unless you have visited it. (A schooled friend points out to me that the schooled tend to regard a visit as *sufficient* for the most diverse claims to knowledge which only good works of reference could impart). As far as I can tell, this rule is sub-cultural, rather than common to our society as a whole. It is an interesting rule, used in practice either to avoid accepting criticisms of a country (e.g., South Africa) or to suspend judgement on criticisms (e.g., of the Soviet Union). People often say that they'd like to visit such-and-such a country just in order 'to see if it's as bad as it's made out'. The invention of such rules as this implies a fairly high level of self-consciousness about knowledge, and generally it seems to me that the development of such rules involves collective (subcultural or institutional) rather than just individual work. However, the rule in question is sceptical in effect to the degree that visiting the country in question is not a real possibility. It may simply function to avoid political argument.

Scepticism is one practical alternative where different sources of information are not available, but it cuts one off from debate and even action and thus tends to be conservative, as well as being boring to other people. Opinionated people are always more interesting. Another alternative is the retreat to high theory, either used to rewrite information from existing sources into the terms of the theory, or used to exclude the need for information. The latter tends to be inefficient, especially where the theory aims at some kind of action. Some Marxists suffer from having erected around themselves a high wall of impenetrable theory (some of the problems which can arise are discussed in 50, Hallas): they find it difficult to learn anything new, sometimes because they don't want to.

As against these options, reliance on existing sources is encouraged by the provision of legitimations of their reliability. These legitimations are disseminated and the acceptance of them inhibits or confuses criticism. Think, for instance, of the way in which one is encouraged to worship experts and expertise. In Britain, this tendency has been encouraged at an explicitly political level by the leaders of the Labour Party, and I interpret it as part of the process by which they have tried to cut themselves off from or keep themselves free of 'grass roots' pressure and control, and may be one reason why 'unexpert' working class people have dropped away from the party organisation, feeling that they have nothing to contribute. They may have been excluded as well (see 55, Hindess). In the 1970 General Election, the Labour candidate in south-west Islington, where I lived, used as his slogan the phrase 'Let Labour get on with the job', which not only tells people to keep their noses out of politics, but also reifies politics into 'the job' where expertise is clearly what is required for success. [3]

The whole educational system is built around teachers knowing the right answers, and all the right questions to boot. In many cases, there is no possibility of checking what the teacher tells you, if he makes sure that you don't have the same textbook as he is using. (If there's a copy of it in the Library, he may even remove it). If you don't realise what he's doing (and usually you only realise if you become a teacher) you may remain so amazed by his knowledge (as you are by the knowledge of those appearing in University Challenge) that you never get round to asking where he got it from. And with this situation, he's only too happy.

Reliance on sources is more difficult to break (other than by turning sceptic) the more difficult for the layman access to the source's sources becomes. Sometimes, it is quite easy to get hold of the sources your source is using: you can sneak a look at teacher's book. Sometimes it is all but impossible, as when appeal is made to classified information (here you have to wait until you find someone willing to leak it). Access is impossible, by definition, in the case of the priest's claim to special access to God or when a parent appeals to age ('When you get to my age ...'). But the more difficult access to the source's own sources becomes, the more difficult it is to see how a person could make a rational decision to rely on a particular source. It becomes a matter of non-rational trust in the person or institution. A person or institution sensitive to this necessarily non-rational basis to the acceptance of their authority may have recourse to the use of signs which will be interpreted as signs of trustworthiness. For example, when the former TUC General Secretary Vic Feather used to report to his fellow trades-unionists on his dealings with the Government, he increased the confidence an audience had in his reports and himself by playing the 'I'm only a common old working chap . . .' tune.[4] I'd rather hear the tape recording of what transpired. Priests and Professors sometimes try to look benign and a politician will have himself photographed with his pipe, wife, children, dog, yacht—or her husband, children, shopping-basket. The ways in which such trust can then be exploited was graphically described nearly 300 years ago by Locke, who writes of the social function of the doctrine of innate ideas that:

> When men have found some general propositions that could not be doubted of, as soon as understood, it was, I know, a short and easy step to conclude them innate. This being once received it eased the lazy from the pains of search and stopped the inquiry of the doubtful concerning all that was once styled innate; and it was of no small advantage, to those who affected to be masters and teachers, to make this the principle of principles: that principles must not be questioned. For having once established this tenet, that there are innate principles, it put their followers upon a necessity of receiving some doctrines as such; which was to take them off from the use of their own reason and judgement and put them upon believing them and taking them on trust, without further examination: in which posture of blind credulity, they might be more easily governed by and made useful to some sort of men, who had the skill and office to principle and guide them. Nor is it a small power it gives one man over another to have authority to be the dictator of principles and teacher of un-questionable truths, and to make a man swallow that for a principle which may serve to his purpose who teacheth him: [75, Locke, Book 1, Chapter 4, section 25.][4a]

In other words not only is the intellectual division of labour always a possible source of rational error, but also acceptance of the division can be made to rest on more or less rational criteria. The less the reliability of sources is open to check, and the less the co-operative relationship between those who do and those who don't perform specialised intellectual labour, the more it is a question of *trust* which is involved for the lay person. Promotion of expertise seems bound to scientific and rationalistic values; but it is promoted by non-scientific and anti-rationalistic means.[4b]

4. Rational Error in non-scientific argument

Manuals of 'clear thinking' and courses in logic and Philosophy all stress the fallaciousness of reasoning from single examples to general conclusions. In Popper's philosophy of science, it is even asserted that it is basically irrelevant to accumulate evidence which confirms a theory; rather one should attempt to disconfirm it (101, 102, Popper). Yet in the everyday discourse of relatively unschooled people (and schooled people much of the time, it would seem[5]) it is treated as perfectly legitimate both to generalise from single or random examples, and to look only for verifying instances.

In creating or sustaining this situation, I would attribute considerable importance to the practice of popular newspapers. For their reporting of events focuses on single examples which form the basis of generalisations. *The News of the World* is not particularly noted for its statistical approach to social issues. It operates with a sort of scandal theory of knowledge, and complements that everyday approach in which argument proceeds in terms of 'I knew a chap who . . .' Complementary to this way of using examples is the ideology which distrusts statistics: 'There are lies, damn lies and statistics' (Disraeli).[6] It would be interesting to trace the history of the anti-statistical ideology and the means whereby it is sustained. It is an ideology of no use to radicals and revolutionaries, even though many of them generalise from their well-founded criticisms of empiricism to an ill-founded critique of statistics. To sanction the use of examples as a decisive mode of argument is to facilitate the transmission of the ideology of the ruling class. All one needs is the right example and a generalisation can be conveyed through it, as is done every day by newspapers. I do not see that an alternative press can hope to alter the structure of people's beliefs just by means of the substitution of different stories. For the generalisation which the Editor of a radical paper intends a particular story to convey may not form part of the tacit knowledge of the reader, as it does in the case of the stories of the established press. The alternative paper has both to articulate its general theory and to defend it with something more than examples, and here statistics have a part to play. It would in fact be interesting to attempt some sort of quantitative assessment of different use of statistics in different newspapers. The *Daily Express* and *Morning Star* could be compared on this basis. I think explicit general argument and the use of statistics is not only necessary for effectiveness, but is in itself a way of treating the reader as a serious cognitive agent and thus contributes to building up the conditions of a cognitive democracy, by which I mean not a situation in which everyone knows the same things as everyone else, but a situation in which everyone has a rough idea of how to evaluate specialists and their knowledges, and where (most importantly) specialist intellectual institutions (such as newspapers) are socially controlled.[6a] (Note that in the present situation, the presentation of statistical arguments would not mean anything to the considerable number of people who do not understand the percentage system).

5. Memory and Society

In the two previous sections, I have dealt with cases of error in the area of 'knowledge by description', and emphasised sources of error which lay in the falsity of others' descriptions, and located these others in sociological terms of the division of labour, rather than abstractly in other individuals as individuals. I was trying to bring out, in a simple way, how there are social and not merely individual obstacles to knowledge.[7] In this and the following section, I try to indicate how, even when the sources of knowledge are 'in' individuals themselves— in the 'mind'—their failings might be connected to external and social causes and not be correctly analysable in terms of personal failings. The clear expression of the difference in the two sorts of case I owe to the comments of Roy Edgley on a draft of this chapter.

In general, it is a sufficient condition for justifying a claim to knowledge that *x* to refer to one's memory of directly performing or witnessing *x*. Thus, I can justly claim to know that I did *x* or I saw him doing *x* if I can also claim that I remember doing *x* or seeing him doing *x*. In practice, the claim and the justification are often conflated: 'I remember doing *x*' standardly asserts both a claim to knowledge and justification for it, though sometimes 'I remember doing *x*' implies 'But actually I didn't do it'. There are also cases where remembering is only partial, not conclusive, justification for a claim to know.

Generally, however, it is rational to base claims to knowledge on rememberings. But just as the encyclopaedia may mislead me, so may my memory. Memory fails me, plays tricks on me, is defective, etc. This implies that as in the previous two cases I can be rational yet in error. For I can make a justified claim to know on the basis of a memory which itself turns out to be false (i.e. the propositional content of a memory claim turns out to be false).

In practice, there are procedures for guarding against error. The strength of an appeal to memory depends on many substantive features of the claim and the claimants involved: How long ago did an event take place? How involved were you with the event? How much are you claiming to remember? What was your emotional relationship to the event, and to me, the auditor of your claim? And so on.

My own view, however, is that these criteria are not stringent enough, from the point of view of excluding error. In Chapter I, Section 6, I have indicated how one could criticise the memory criterion internally. Does this criticism have any practical application? On the one hand, social developments, such as the development of retrievable information have reduced the importance of a good memory; the mnemonic arts have gone into radical decline. On the other hand, it seems to me that people have to cope with ever greater inputs of information, which they do not have the memory organisation to store. My only evidence here is the subjective experience of situations in which people's memories seem to me not good enough for the purpose for which they themselves require them. For example, I was struck by the way in which day-release apprentices, whom I recently taught, wanted to tell me about TV programmes they had seen the night before yet could not even remember some sort of conventional skeleton to the story, usually a documentary. Of course, this is a non-experimental situation and it is difficult to judge (for example) whether the difficulty is verbal rather than one of memory. For whilst on those rare occasions when I 'watch' a TV documentary, I pay most attention to the words spoken, I suspect that my students paid most attention to the images. Next day, I have only to reproduce what I heard, whereas they have to verbalise a visual experience in talking to me about the programme. On the other hand, they seemed to have similar difficulties in recalling details of newspaper stories, and tend to mis-recall.[8]

As indicated, I think such phenomena of false memory and forgetfulness are to be explained by reference to a growing disparity which exists between the increased volume of information to which people are subjected, often in a random way ('dissociated impacting')[9] and the static or declining capacity to process it which people possess. This capacity seems to me deficient in two respects, which may turn out to be one. The first is mainly conceptual, the second mainly verbal. In the first case, people lack theory, that is, interpretive and organising schemes which would allow the appropriation of information in a coherent form. Here I think by way of illustration of the use of the Bible as a source of theoretical interpretation both of political events and communication in families: to put it crudely, people use the Bible when they haven't got anything better to use. If they are schizophrenic they may not have come across the writings of R. D. Laing. In the second case, there is ignorance of substantive or verbal organisation and classification. Thus, for example, most of this book's readers will possess a classificatory scheme for *education* which includes the classificatory subdivision (corresponding to substantive features of organisation) *primary/secondary/tertiary*, and which is further subdivided into, for example, *secondary (selective/comprehensive)*. This classification can be used in interpreting, ordering and storing information contained in a TV programme about education. Someone without knowledge of these subdivisions of classification might have more difficulty recalling details of a programme about education than someone who possessed it. (Compare Chapter V, Section 3 on superordination).

Also relevant to the explanation of forgetfulness and false memory are the medium of communication and the mode of presentation of information, for example, the dissociated impacting mentioned earlier. Gabel, in an interesting book, links together as mutually reinforcing mode of presentation and weakness of memory in the following way:

> The temporality of political news thus tends towards a non-structured succession of present instants ending, at the limit, with a continuum of a spatial type. Taken in isolation, this phenomenon of journalistic sub-temporalisation is not of great importance. But it is inserted in the wider context of the inadequacy of collective memory, expressed in such sayings as 'The French have short memories'. It supplies a sort of consecration for this collective amnesia ... In a general way, news journalism effectively tends to prefer spatial to temporal information, reporting to historical considerations; now, despite appearances, the latter constitutes a surer source of information. [41, Gabel, p. 93. My translation.][10]

Collective amnesia facilitates the rewriting of History by those in power including the denial that policy has changed even when it has. Gabel subsumes both phenomena under the spatialisation, schizophrenic in character, of political ideology (see especially p. 72 ff.). Collective amnesia, including its deliberate variety, *doublethink*, furnishes one of the grand themes of Orwell's *1984*. Amnesia is a means of social control, both because it furnishes a base for the undisputed triumph of official ideology, and also because by weakening the sense of personal identity it deprives people of a sense of efficacity and thus of the capacity to organise and initiate action (a connexion also made strikingly in Beckett's *Waiting for Godot* (18, Beckett)).[11,12]

If the actual situation were as bad as that in *1984*, it would clearly not be a sufficient response to keep Diaries or to learn mnemonic techniques. These individual practices, however admirable, are almost as limited in their possibilities as the scepticism discussed earlier. What at least is needed is that people should have the equipment to cope with the information they receive and that they should be able to retrieve information not only from their own memory but from external stores as well. Consider the following simple suggestion as an illustration: at present, leading politicians have the texts of their speeches distributed to TV and newspapers. A phrase, a sentence or more will be quoted in the media, and at the time we may be impressed by what we read or hear, yet later we may be unable accurately to recall what the politician said, or indeed, that he said anything. We can go to the Public Library and read through newspaper files, it is true. But would it not be more convenient if the Library filed the actual texts of the politician's speeches? It would make quite a few people's lives easier if they could go into their local Reference Library and ask for the Wilson file.

In the end what was originally a philosophical discussion about memory has turned into a suggestion about improving the possibility of information retrieval. Earlier, the discipline of psychology was relevant to what I was writing; now it is information science and librarianship. I would like to say: thinking practically or politically rather than academically in terms of subjects, or objectivistically, necessitates an increasing range of conceptual reference, which eventually makes collective work indispensable. One person can only skim the surface.

6. Rational Error and Repression

Over a large range of mental states, the individual is supposed best to know their own mind. A claim to self-knowledge is *prima facie* its own validation. But what is the range of claims to self-knowledge which is treated as self-validating? And what are the possibilities of error?

Philosophers have reflected at length on the making of such statements as 'I am in pain' and their relationship to the speaker and their pain. In the case of pain, it has been claimed, one can lie but not be in error: what could self-deception or being mistaken mean in this instance? Verbal error (not knowing the meaning of the word 'pain') would seem to be the only possible kind of error.

But there are cases where Philosophers do not agree to the extent that they do over pain, for example, the case where someone asserts 'I want x'. Is mistake of a substantive kind, or self-deception, possible here?

In everyday life, it seems to me, there is much more agreement over the implications of the statement 'I want *x*'. It is generally assumed that people know best what they want so long as they are not children or lunatics. The possibility of being mistaken or self-deceived is ruled out or simply not envisaged. When I have asked apprentices about 'I want . . .' statements I have found very few who think they might find themselves in circumstances where they might want to say 'He thinks he wants *x*, but really he doesn't' or 'He's mistaken in thinking that he wants *x*', always using in such discussions specific examples for *x*. At least in the area of wants, most people seem to have no room for the possibility of mistake or self-deception and operate a unitary conception of consciousness or mind. Wants fall into the same category as pain, as being areas where claims are self-validating.

It is only when we come to *motives* that the possibility of error is commonly admitted, and a dualist theory of mind comes into operation. But nowhere is any objection put up to the legitimacy of claims to self-knowledge, or that they are *prima facie* to be accepted as true. There is just the difference that some areas of self-knowledge are regarded as being areas of possible error, and some are not. Dispute centres on where the dividing line is to be drawn. I have yet to meet someone who says: people's self-ascriptions are more likely to be wrong than right. Therefore, I don't make claims to self-knowledge myself, and don't think others should do so. A person is not the best judge of their own wants, motives, etc.; other people are.

I doubt that such a position could be conclusively argued against the prevailing one: I think a theoretical paradigm shift is involved, that is, a situation in which certain concepts, terms and arguments of the new theory are incommensurable with those of the old theory or paradigm. Furthermore, this may be an area of reality where the way we think we are actually affects the way we are.[12a] In either eventuality, a choice is necessary which, by the usual criteria of rationality, cannot be a fully rational one. To choose the position that because there are social pressures to not know oneself, and social pressures to say the right thing in a way which confuses the perception and even actuality of mental states, and that therefore it is best not to presuppose that people know best their own minds, is to choose an unattractively illiberal position. Yet to accept many theories which involve the concepts of *Unconscious* and *Repression* involves the rejection of liberal-individualist [and Protestant: see 126a Wolin, Chapter 9] theories of privileged access to one's own mind, and thereby of the presumption in favour of the validity of self-ascriptions. How frequently is one going to let self-ascriptions be wrong before one proscribes for oneself self-ascriptions and challenges both the validity of others' self-ascriptions and their right to make them?[12b]

7. Conclusion

In this chapter, I have tried to illustrate the thesis that error is not an individual but a social problem, and that the reduction of error requires social change. Individual and collective 'tactics' of opposition to error have their part to play, prior to and in the process of achieving social change. But this alone is not enough.

A passion for logic will save no one from error, the truth of which assertion is made clearest by the example of certain paranoias, where from false premises false conclusions are deduced with impeccable logic. (An outstanding case is 114, Schreber.)

NOTES TO CHAPTER II

0ₐ. Highly relevant to this whole chapter is Stephen Toulmin's *The Uses of Argument* (119a), which I have only subsequently read.

1. Josh Billings. Pseudonym of H. W. Shaw (1818–85), American humourist. I have borrowed this epigraph from 103, Postman and Weingartner, p. 140.

1ₐ. But see fn. 15a to Chapter I. The following is a nice statement of a similar point to that originally made here: 'The grand consideration is, not what any person regards as the ultimate end of human conduct, but through what intermediate ends he holds that his ultimate end is attainable and should be pursued: and in these there is a nearer agreement between some who differ, than between some who agree, in their conception of the ultimate end. When disputes arise as to any of the secondary maxims, they can be decided, it is true, only by an appeal to first principles, but the necessity of this appeal may be avoided far oftener than is commonly believed; it is surprising how few, in comparison, of the disputed questions of practical morals, require for their determination any premises but such as are common to all philosophic sects.' (J. S. Mill, quoted from his review of Blakey's *History of Moral Philosophy*, in 108a, Robson. On ends—means relations, see however, 35b, Fay.)

1b. Cf. Toulmin, 'Over many questions in everyday life, different people are differently placed; so that we are prepared to trust one man's judgement without demanding grounds for his opinion, where another man would have to produce solid grounds before we should take any notice of him. Sometimes we do not press a man for grounds because we are so sure that he could produce good grounds if we were to ask for them, but in other cases . . . it does not even matter if he is unable to produce any definite grounds when challenged' [p. 242]. As, for example, when asked: 'How do you know your brother's name is "Roger"?'

This argument has a philosophical interest, as pointing to a universal division of knowledge and its consequences, but also suggests a line of sociological or anthropological inquiry into varieties of evidence, standards of proof or assurance, modes of argument, etc.,—what I here call 'socio-logic'. (Compare also S. Cavell's use of 'logic' in 'Must We Mean What We Say?' (26a, Cavell, pp. 1–43); Mey's remarks on 'socio-logic' (89c, Mey); and my reply (99e, Pateman)).

2. One can see that there are practical reasons for this. If, for instance, it was accepted that a clear and distinct idea of something was sufficient to justify any claim to knowledge, either one would have to abandon the implication which is held to exist between a justifiable claim to knowledge and a hearer's attitude towards it—if you claim to know what time the train goes, I must accept what you say unless I can produce reasons for doubt —or else tolerance of contradictory beliefs would have to be radically increased.

2a. In terms of the academic division of labour, philosophers study what count as *good* reasons for knowledge claims, and sociologists what are *acceptable* reasons. The relativist argues that as between 'good' and 'acceptable' there is a distinction without a difference, the position generally adopted in this chapter, but a position I would no longer wish to maintain.

2b. The whole of Part III of Anthony Downs' *An Economic Theory of Democracy* (32b) is highly relevant to this section. He argues, for example, that 'any concept of democracy based on an electorate of equally well-informed citizens presupposes that men behave irrationally' (p. 221), if there is uncertainty and division of labour.

3. Compare Feyerabend's epistemological principle of '*absolute distrust of expert testimony* and of expert morality' (36, Feyerabend, p. 109, fn. 47). Much of what Feyerabend has to say about epistemology has a political application, and he would claim this himself. I would recommend Feyerabend's work as an antidote to whatever narrow-mindedness there is in my own brand of rationalism.

4. I base this remark principally on a speech made by the late Lord Feather to Exeter trades unionists in early 1973 and at which I was present.

4a. J. S. Mill saw formal debate (formal dialectics) as a means of forming thinkers and of preventing teachers ' "principling" their pupils (as Locke expresses it) with ready-made knowledge' (from Mill's review of Grote's *Aristotle* (91a, Mill, p. 510)).

4b. But how can expertise be 'promoted' other than by nonscientific and anti-rationalistic means? In the text, an implicit contrast is drawn between non-rational acceptance of authority and some underspecified notion of democratic accountability. What is not explored is either the possibility of rational acceptance of authority ('rational authority', on which see, for example, 74c, Lewis, and my 99c), or the possibility of disadvantages to democratic, or other, accountability in relation to science and the pursuit of knowledge more generally, on which see, for example, 127b, Ziman, and 36, 36a, Feyerabend, as well as the whole debate on Lysenkoism. See also the interesting book on Mesmerism by R. Darnton (30c).

5. Here is a verifying quotation: 'We find an often overwhelming tendency for our subjects (university undergraduates) to try to verify generalisations rather than try to falsify them' (121, Wason and Johnson-Laird, p. 240.)

6. Roy Carr-Hill told me this.

6a. What does social control *mean* here? What does or might social control of nuclear physicists mean? Is it, or could it be, a good thing? What does 'cognitive' add to 'democracy'? Does it matter if I haven't a clue how to evaluate an Assyrologist and his knowledge? These are some of the questions which are hurried past in this section. For further discussion of them, see references in n. 4b.

7. I derive the idea of 'obstacles to knowledge' from 6, Bachelard, though I reject his teleology—he offers a sort of Whig Interpretation of Science.

8. I have assumed that forgetfulness is on the same continuum as false memory. Could this be mistaken? [On the substantive theme of the preceding paragraph, there has been some interesting research by the Swedish Broadcasting Corporation on recall of TV material presented in different verbal and visual ways (see 36b).]

9. 'The contrast has been made between the *oral dialectic* of the medieval period and the *dissociated impacting* of the contemporary period. In the medieval period, the slowly accumulating stock of MSS literature meant the very considerable working-over and critical sifting and assimilation of this stock of written culture. A slow rate of written input: a high rate of confrontation of opinion and interpretations. In contemporary society, an 'information and publicity explosion' such as to produce a modern man perpetually reeling under a rate of unselected input that he can no longer work over and transform.' (92, Murray and Wengraf, p. 11.)

10. French original (41, Gabel, p. 93): 'La temporalité de l'information politique tend alors vers une succession non structurée de moments présents pour aboutir, à la limite, à un continuum de type spatial. Pris isolément, ce phenomène de sous temporalisation journalistique n'a pas grande importance. Mais il s'insère dans le contexte plus large de l'insuffisance de la mémoire collective qu' expriment les dictons dans le genre "les Français ont la mémoire courte"; il fournit une sorte de consécration à cette amnesie collective . . . D'une façon générale, le journalisme de l'information tend effectivement à preferer le renseignement spatial (reportage) aux renseignements temporels (considerations historiques); or, en depit des apparences, les derniers constituent une source plus sure de l'information.' [An English translation of Gabel's book is now available as 41a, Gabel].

11. Since a weakening of the sense of personal identity usually seems to me a Bad Thing, I quote some remarks made by Aaron Sloman on an earlier paper used in the writing of this chapter: 'Why should it be a *good* thing to think of oneself as having a persistent identity? Isn't this just a case of social pressures arising out of the need to identify property-owners, rights, duties, descendants, etc.? I can imagine a society without contracts, without long-term commitments, where people do one another no ill, where food, etc., are readily available without long-term planning or effort, where people live only for the moment. Questions of personal identity might then be much less important than they are for us: the *miseries* of amnesia [to

which I referred in the earlier paper—TP], I am suggesting, may be simply a result of social pressures.' To this I have only the reply: How does one get to this imagined society?

12. See my article on *Waiting for Godot* (99a; an abridged version of the original).

12ₐ. One general philosophical issue in question here is the distinction between 'original' and 'representative' existences (to use Hume's terms). There are important discussions of this topic in Edgley's, 33b and 33c, some practical consequences being drawn in his 33d.

12ᵦ. This brief discussion of self-ascriptions should be related to the 'Reasons and Causes' debate in contemporary philosophy of action and philosophy of social science. For example, Alasdair MacIntyre writes that: ' . . . although nothing could count as a reason unless it stood in an internal relationship to an action, *the agent's possessing a reason* may be a state of affairs identifiable independently of the event which is *the agent's performance of the action*. Thus it does seem as if the possession of a reason by an agent is an item of a suitable type to figure as a cause, or an effect. But if this is so then to ask whether it was the agent's reason that roused him to act is to ask a causal question, the true answer to which depends upon what causal generalisations we have been able to establish. This puts in a different light the question of the agent's authority as to what roused him to act; for it follows from what has been said, that this authority is at best *prima facie*.' (78d, MacIntyre, p. 117.) MacIntyre goes on to relate this conclusion explicitly to the possibility of using the concepts of 'ideology' and 'false consciousness' in social science (p. 118). Compare, also E. Gellner's example of *'baraka'* in his essay 'Concepts and Society' (42a, Gellner, esp. pp. 45–9).

CHAPTER III

Not so Inquiring Man [1]

Starting from a given theme their minds laboured in unison. They had no conversation properly speaking

Samuel Beckett *Malone Dies*

1. Introduction

I presented Chapter II as a means of destroying an illusion which Chapter I may have created—the illusion of the effectiveness of cognitive individualism. In turn, Chapter II may have conjured up the image of an anxiously rational person led astray by knowledge sources which provide false premises for impeccable arguments. I don't think many such people exist, and I do think that most people are anxiously rational too little of their time.

I make these assertions from the point of view of a conception of the necessary conditions for achieving social change. To assert that most people are not rational enough can only be done from the standpoint of a conception of the purpose of being rational, and my conception is that one of the purposes of being as rational as one can is to transform the irrational society in which we live. As a result, when I describe examples of non-rationality and irrationality, I choose examples of phenomena which seem to be important as obstacles to social change.

Evidence about the rationality or irrationality of people is necessarily drawn from their actions, including their linguistic actions. It is at that level also that interventions in favour of change have to be made. Hence, in this and the subsequent Chapter I write about communication, its 'pathologies' and interventions against such 'pathologies'. The concept of 'consciousness' is displaced by that of 'communication'.[1a]

2. Idle Discourse

I call discourse 'idle' where its determinant function is simply that of avoiding silence between two or more persons. One cannot not communicate,[2] and the message of silence can be alarm-

E

ing to both 'speaker' and 'hearer', perhaps because the message of silence tends to be so thoroughly indeterminate or ambiguous. Talk supposedly for the sake of talk is, I suggest, talk *against* silence; and this talk by setting up a voluntary bond between two or more persons tends to eliminate a whole range of uncertainty, until such time as the talk goes wrong.[3]

Idle Discourse is essentially symmetrical; participants are on an equal footing. There is no question of one party exercising power over the other, or of competition. But neither is there any question of conveying substantive feelings, exhorting, informing or inquiring. Idle Discourse is static rather than dynamic. Once begun it aims only to stay where it is.

In order for it to remain Idle Discourse, the subject matter of a conversation must remain unimportant. The subject matter must be drawn from a range of conventionally non-controversial subjects, of which the paradigm is *The Weather*. The range of permissible material will vary with the persons involved, and other aspects of the context.

Given the function of communication, what is said need not make particularly good sense: the syntax can be poorly organised and the semantics confused. It doesn't matter that the speakers contradict each other, so long as they don't notice that they are doing so, or do not find it disturbing if they do notice. Tone of voice, length of utterance and pauses, exchange of speaker/hearer roles, are likely to be more significant than either syntactic or semantic features. That something is said, and how it is said, dominates considerations of what is said.[3a]

Idle Discourse typically occurs over the garden fence, at bus stops, and in student coffee bars. It can scarcely be objected to except where it finds its way into conversations which ought not to be idle, or where pressures towards keeping discourse idle prevent the discussion of substantive issues. I have in mind the following sort of situation.

On a train journey, you strike up a conversation with a person sitting opposite. The conversation remains chatty. You interpret your companion's pleasure in the conversation as deriving from the fact of its being a chatty conversation, that is, from its being Idle Discourse. But then your companion introduces into the conversation some prejudiced remarks about black people, without thereby seeming to indicate that he wishes to change the nature of the conversation. It appears that for him prejudiced remarks are within the area of non-controversial material. He does not seem to intend or expect his remarks to be contentious. However, if for you, his auditor, his remarks are controversial and incompatible with idle discourse, a threefold choice presents itself: (i) you can challenge the offensive remarks, thereby altering the nature of the conversation (and risking misunderstanding and unpleasantness); (ii) you can preserve the nature of the conversation by going along with what has been said, even though you disagree with it; (iii) you can react non-committally, change the subject, etc., and thereby tacitly indicate that your companion has touched on a subject which is not acceptable to you as a subject of Idle Discourse.[3b]

Which strategy do you adopt? Which do you think you should? And why?

My own experience is that I lapse into strategies (ii) and (iii) even when I feel I should opt for strategy (i). Sometimes, of course, I feel that to try strategy (i) would be inefficacious, even counter-productive, and therefore I fail to adopt it on rational (means-ends) grounds. But at other times, I feel that strategy (i) would be worth a try, but what I lack is courage to adopt it. I require courage, I think, because the bias of conventional conversational norms is against the adoption of strategy (i). After all, we would not have a place for a concept of 'outspokeness' if people always spoke their mind. The fact is, much conversation has nothing to do with speaking one's mind, which means that in a very precise sense much conversation is alienated. For such conversation is clearly not under the control of the speaker. It need not be under the control of the hearer, for both speaker and hearer may simply obey what they take to be social rules but which neither of them accept (cf. the situations in 72, Laing; 71, Laing and Esterson). Such alienated conversation is not without effect. People may think their beliefs remain intact whether they express them or not, but they are misguided in this. In any case, the purpose of holding a belief can scarcely be to hold it to one's bosom, never expressing it or acting upon it. Again, if no one ever broke up an Idle Discourse by challenging a statement made within it, people would have reason for thinking that their beliefs are more widely shared than in fact they are. Thereby, their beliefs would be strengthened; racism could become as unproblematic as the British Weather just because anti-racists kept their mouths shut.[3c]

3. Idle Discourse and the Phatic Functioning of Language

My concept of Idle Discourse at least resembles that of *phatic communion* which Malinowski described some 50 years ago (80, Malinowski, pp. 146–52). Malinowski defines phatic communion as 'a type of speech in which ties of union are created by a mere exchange of words' (*op. cit.* p. 151). This definition is a functional one: the function of phatic communion is to create ties of union. Malinowski also says of phatic communion that 'Each utterance is an act serving the direct aim of binding hearer to speaker by a tie of some social sentiment or other' (p. 151), and again, that phatic communion 'serves to establish bonds of personal union between people brought together by the mere need of companionship' (p. 151). Malinowski makes this last statement within the context of reference to 'pure sociabilities and gossip' and quotes approvingly from Ogden and Richards' *Meaning of Meaning* (to which his essay appeared as an Appendix): 'Throughout the Western world it is agreed that people must meet frequently, and that it is not only agreeable to talk, but that it is a matter of common courtesy to say something even when there is hardly anything to say' (quoted, pp. 151–2). Malinowski also notes that communication in phatic communion 'does not serve any purpose of communicating ideas' and is not the result of 'intellectual reflection', nor does it 'necessarily arouse reflection in the listener': 'Indeed there need not or perhaps even there must not be anything to communicate' (p. 152). These formulations are quite close to those I have given for Idle Discourse.

But my concept of Idle Discourse and Malinowski's concept of phatic communion differ from Roman Jakobson's *phatic function* in being less inclusive than this latter concept. I write this despite the fact that Jakobson treats his own concept as coterminous with that of Malinowski (see 63, Jakobson). Jakobson includes under the phatic function, messages:

. . . primarily serving to establish, to prolong or to discontinue communication, to check whether the channel works . . . to attract the attention of the interlocutor or to confirm his continued attention. This set for CONTACT, or in Malinowski's terms, PHATIC function may be displayed by a profuse exchange of ritualized formulas, by entire dialogues with the mere purport of prolonging communication [*op. cit.* p. 355]. Jakobson derives the phatic function from his model of the 'constitutive factors in any speech event, in any act of verbal communication' (p. 353), for the phatic function is mapped on to the level of CONTACT in that model, where CONTACT is defined as the 'physical channel and psychological connection between the addresser and the addressee, enabling both of them to enter and stay in communication' (p. 353). However, it seems to me that there is an important difference between the profuse exchange of ritualized formulas, serving simply to prolong communication, and messages which aim to establish or discontinue communication or which check whether the channel works. Thus, for example, 'Hello, can you hear me?' over the telephone standardly functions as a genuine question, the response to which is critical to the initiation or continuation of communication of whatever variety. 'Hello can you hear me?' also conveys information and is meant to convey it; the content of the question is highly relevant to the future actions of both speaker and hearer. This is quite unlike the situation in the case of ritualized formulas where, within the frame of reference of non-controversial material, content is irrelevant and *repetition* indicates neither desire to persuade or elicit a response, but the *inconsequentiality* of what is being said.

Of course, it is very rare if not impossible for communication to serve only one function, and one is usually confronted with situations of dominance and subordination. But there does seem to me a clear difference between the messages of Idle Discourse and the messages which refer to the channel, though I am not sure how these latter are best called. One could say they are *metacommunicational*, and only end up under the phatic function in Jakobson's schema because he doesn't have the category of metacommunicational function in his schema, but rather the category of *metalingual* function, corresponding to the category CODE in the model of factors in the speech event.

The description of the metalingual function in Jakobson seems to me too narrow. He describes this function as follows:

Whenever the addresser and/or the addressee need to check up whether they use the same code, speech is focussed on the CODE: it performs a metalingual (i.e. glossing) function . . . Any process of language learning, in particular child acquisition of the mother tongue, makes wide use of such metalingual operations; and aphasia may often be defined as a loss of ability for metalingual operations. [p. 356]

But this does not cover the case where the addressor or the addressee refers to the *functioning* of the code—that is, raises questions about the kind of communication in which they are engaged, for example, asks 'Do you really mean that?' or 'Are you joking?' Such questions about the functioning of the code are not covered by Jakobson's metalingual function, which covers only such questions as 'What do you mean by "x"?' Nor do the questions which refer to the functioning of the code fall under any of Jakobson's other five categories (Referential, Emotive, Conative, Phatic and Poetic). I would revise Jakobson's schema so as to put together under the heading 'meta-communicational function' those types of discourse which Jakobson assigns to the metalingual function *plus* some of those he (wrongly) assigns to the phatic function *plus* some that he does not seem to allow for.[4, 4a]

The category of metacommunicational function then includes all those interventions assigned in Chapter I to a philosophical practice, though not all metacommunications are philosophical, for the philosophical metacommunications I have indicated are all interventions with respect to the *referential* functioning of language. Thus, they comment on or challenge the success of language use in referring, in asserting true propositions or giving accurate descriptions. Other varieties of metacommunicational practice could be classified according to the primary linguistic functions which they promote. Thus, for example, some psychotherapies are metacommunications in favour of the *emotive* function, whilst the Art of Rhetoric is designed to refine both the *conative* and *poetic* functions. One could say that *How to Win Friends and Influence People* is the theory of the phatic function![4b]

4. Evasions of Argument

In Chapter II, the focus of study was the relationship between individuals and their sources of evidence for knowledge claims. In this section, I want to focus on the relationships between individuals discussing the validity of knowledge claims made by either or both of them, as also putting forward and debating more generally about opinions and beliefs. Especially, I want to consider the ways in which individuals *avoid* such discussions and debates, and consider why they might do so. I think it is common practice to engage in such avoidances.

In their book, *The Pragmatics of Human Communication*, Watzlawick, Beavin and Jackson (122) describe in the following terms a case of disagreement over facts:

The phenomenon of disagreement provides a good frame of reference for the study of disturbances of communication due to confusion between content and relationship. Disagreement can arise on the content or relationship level, and the two forms are contingent upon each other. For instance, disagreement over the truth value of the statement 'Uranium has 92 electrons' can apparently be settled only by recourse to objective evidence, e.g., a textbook of chemistry, for this evidence not only proves that the uranium atom does indeed have 92 electrons, but that one of the contestants was right and the other wrong. Of these two results, the first resolves the disagreement on the content level, and the other creates a relationship problem. Now, quite obviously, to resolve this new problem the two individuals cannot continue to talk about atoms; they must begin to talk about themselves and their relationship. To do this they must achieve a definition of their relationship as symmetrical or complementary: for example the one who was wrong may admire the other for his superior knowledge [symmetrical response to the situation— TP], or resent his superiority and resolve to be one-up on him at the next possible occasion in order to re-establish equality [complementary response to the situation—TP]. Of course, if he could not wait until that next occasion, he could use the 'to hell with logic' approach and try to be one-up by claiming that the figure 92 must be a misprint, or that he has a

scientist friend who has just shown that the number of electrons is really quite meaningless ... [p. 82][4c]

The example as presented is relatively unobjectionable,[4d]
but in my mind raises the question (outside the authors' frame
of reference), why should the resolution of disagreement on the
level of content create a relationship problem or a particular
kind of relationship problem?

By way of answer, I want to say that this cannot be explained
just by reference to the situations where an individual's legitimate tenure of a job, office, etc., depends on his knowing the
answers to such questions as, How many electrons are there in
Uranium? or, more generally, by reference to specifically competitive situations in which individuals find themselves. For I
want to say that explanation of the relationship problem must
also, in general, involve reference to generalised attitudes towards, conventions concerning, the appropriation and use of
knowledge—attitudes which are related to the objective competitive situations. These attitudes and conventions specify that
it is not just a fact if someone is ignorant of the number of
electrons in uranium, but that it is a fault, though sometimes an
excuseable one ('He couldn't be expected to know ...'). That
it is a fault justifies the claim that there exists a morality of
knowledge, in which—at the most abstract level—knowing is a
good thing, and being ignorant a bad one. The person who
knows is, *prima facie*, morally superior to the person who does
not know, and thus when someone 'loses' in a factual dispute,
this affects the relationship between the disputants, unless the
losing party is exonerated from blame. Watzlawick, Beavin and
Jackson are discussing some of the things which losers can do on
the relationship front, in acting either symmetrically or com-
plementarily, that is, in accepting or challenging their defeat.[5]

But a person who feels himself to be a potential loser can
avoid getting into the situation where he has to choose between
complementary and symmetrical responses; he can do so by
opting out of factual argument as such—he can avoid getting
into the situation or refuse to respond in a situation where a
statement is expected from him as to how many electrons he
thinks there are in uranium. The statement-imperative 'Don't
ask me' comes to mean 'I'm not saying' rather than 'I don't

know'. The person may indeed know, but prefer not to commit himself.

Such strategies of *evasion* are most often and most importantly, it seems to me, strategies for avoiding the penalties which generally attach to being an *unsuccessful* inquiring man. And I would suggest that the social penalties meted out to those who simply don't inquire are less severe than those suffered by those who try, but unsuccessfully. The paradigmatic situation (though one which involves power relations) is the classroom where the teacher ridicules the child who gets the answer wrong, but does not ridicule (or even comment upon) the behaviour of the child who doesn't answer at all.

I do not see how one could altogether do without a morality of knowledge, and certainly my practical proposals in this book imply that I would not want to even if it were possible. But it does seem to me that many of the existing rules of this morality of knowledge need changing, among them, that rule which makes it effectively safer and more comfortable not to bother about knowledge than to try and fail. The present morality effectively divides people into two categories: those who try and those who don't. The former compete in a power struggle, which has its victims—the latter stay powerless: they renounce intellectual satisfactions, both direct and instrumental, and are free to use language, like the schizophrenic, as described by Sullivan, in 'the pursuit of durable security' (119, Sullivan, p. 7). But there is no durable security in flight from the world.[6]

The prospect of being wrong does not arise in those arguments where what is at stake (in our positivist order of things) is merely a matter of opinion. But that is not to say that to discuss and argue about opinions is free of risk, even when the risk involved is just that arising from the possible imposition of penalties deriving from the morality of knowledge and does not include the possible application of the material sanctions which a powerful person can use against a powerless one. In the case of debate over matters of opinion, the fault of being wrong is replaced by the fault of being out-argued, which generally means being placed in contradiction with oneself: Barthes remarks that the efficacy of Western dialectical argument rests on the intolerability of being in contradiction with oneself: 'It is sufficient to force a partner into self-contradiction to reduce, eliminate, annul him' (13, Barthes, p. 191, my translation).[6a]

But what kind of efficacy is this which treats a *partner* so? Even in competitive sport, you shake hands with your losing partner and commiserate with him. Is argument that much more competitive that in the triumph of your victory you trample underfoot your partner?[7] Sometimes it is, and severely enough so to provoke people into avoiding argument. In these circumstances, 'I don't want to know' may simply mean that the speaker does not wish to be beaten. Some Marxists invite opponents to state their 'viewpoints', knowing in advance that whatever is said, they will knock the 'viewpoint' to smithereens. And the arguer? Battered adults may make good troops to follow a leader; they don't make a liberation movement.

Argument can be avoided in a whole number of ways which do not involve the giving up of talking. People may simply agree with propositions when really they disagree, taking up (to return to a concept earlier employed) a symmetrical position:

A: I don't think much of this Government.
B: Oh, they're not so bad.
A: I don't say they're bad.
B: They're all right.
A: Yes.

In other words, A submits to B in round 3; a negative evaluation of the Government by A has turned into positive evaluation, without a shred of argument changing hands.[8]

Again, argument can be avoided by 'playing' at arguing, that is, by distancing oneself from one's own arguments as a means of self-protection. (The maverick argument, as in the theory and practice of Paul Feyerabend, has a different purpose. It is meant to throw out of gear someone's mental processes, but in a productive way). When people play at argument, their interlocutor can't really catch them. If they are evangelists of some sort, they may easily fail to recognise that in trying to dispel their partners' illusions, they are trying to remove something which their partners have not got. Compare Locke on what happens when words have no fixed meaning:

Men take the words they find in use amongst their neigh-
bours, and that they may not seem ignorant what they stand

for, use them confidently without much troubling their heads about a certain fixed meaning, whereby, besides the ease of it, they obtain this advantage: that as in such discourses they seldom are in the right, so they are as seldom to be convinced that they are in the wrong, it being all one to go about to draw those men out of their mistakes, who have no settled notions, as to dispossess a vagrant of his habitation who has no settled abode. [75, Locke, Book III, Ch. X]

Finally, people can take the position of neither agreeing or disagreeing with an opinion, and thus swell the ranks of those who listen to all sides and commit themselves to none, except in practice.

5. The Hearer Retaliates

I have written the previous section focusing on the hearer who fears the consequences of the established morality of knowledge and who responds by evasion. In other circumstances, she might have as much or more reason to fear the speaker, in a situation of unequal power. But in this chapter I am confining myself to situations where inequalities of power do not come into the picture.

Evasion can, however, take a more 'active' form than the 'passive' responses described in the previous section. The hearer can effectively hit back at the speaker in refusing to argue, using techniques of a different character to those so far described. In terms previously employed, the hearer can make a complementary rather than symmetrical response.

In particular, I think of the case where the hearer metacommunicates about the speaker's utterances, *not* in order to make a genuine query or criticism, necessary to the continuation of any substantive discussion, but rather to delay or avoid altogether such a discussion. If you have the right metacommunicative skills, it is quite easy to tie someone in knots, as in response to your questions, they try to formulate more precisely what they meant etc. Meanwhile, the metacommunicator has not had to make any substantive comment on the substantive argument. The technique is one very commonly used, I think, by academics who use it in order to avoid taking a position when challenged to do so by students, though this example immediately introduces a situation of unequal power. That a speaker can be tied in knots does not prove that he was unclear himself of what he was saying. His mistake may lie in trying to clarify a perfectly clear statement.

The tactical use of metacommunications in order to avoid substantive discussion is a way of *disconfirming* the speaker's utterances, where disconfirmation may be defined as negating the message, rather than the proposition: the hearer, in effect, does not say 'Your claim, that x, is false' but rather 'You haven't yet made an intelligible claim that I could agree or disagree with'.[8a] This may be compared with Watzlawick, Beavin and Jackson's use of 'disconfirmation' with respect to persons.[8b] They write that:

> Disconfirmation, as we find it in pathological communication, is no longer concerned with the truth or falsity—if there be such criteria—of P's definition of himself, but rather negates the reality of P as a source of such a definition. In other words, while rejection amounts to the message 'You are wrong', disconfirmation says in effect 'You do not exist'. [122, p. 86]

Of course, to disconfirm messages and disconfirm people are clearly interrelated. I treat disconfirmation (using the term 'invalidation') and related practices more fully below in Chapter VI.

6. Concluding Remarks

In this chapter, I have been writing about some of the ways in which people can and do dodge significance (meaning) and disagreement about significance (argument). I have concentrated on face to face situations where the statuses of the participants are irrelevant to the explanation of what occurs. I introduce the dimension of power in the following chapter. If widespread through a population, and pervasive in their influence, I think the sorts of evasions I have illustrated can be of considerable political significance. For such evasions sustain, in practice, all existing social institutions, since they stand in the way of any critical (reflective) consciousness. In a situation of prevalent evasion, to attempt to convey information or argue is like trying to talk to a brick wall. The simile seems to me apposite, for the person who refuses information and argument has reified himself into some Thing, which is but which does not think and therefore does not act. H. S. Sullivan writes of the schizophrenic that:

> The schizophrenic, early convinced that since it is unobtainable, satisfaction is not the prime consideration in life, uses language more or less knowingly in the pursuit of durable security. [119, p. 7]

The emphasis here is on the pursuit of and possibility of *satisfaction* as that which leads to dynamic, inquiring uses of language. To the degree that the pursuit of security dominates everyday thought and language use, I think this is because people have decided that other satisfactions are not obtainable. Idle Discourse is the language of the powerless who accept their position.[8c]

What seems to me important is to attempt to establish a morality of knowledge in which being wrong or getting out-argued don't get penalised, or—at least—don't get penalised in the ways which drive people into evasion. Most importantly, I think that instances of being wrong or getting out-argued should not be allowed to lead to ascriptions of a *general* character to the person, of the sort 'You're just stupid', as opposed to particular ascriptions of the sort 'That was a stupid thing to say' (cf. 61, Ingleby). Again, in any reorganisation of social institutions factual or theoretical knowledge and argumentative ability should not be taken as sufficient (or even necessary) criteria for the allocation of non-intellectual statuses, for a brilliant intellectual is not necessarily the best party leader.

NOTES TO CHAPTER III

1. This title is at the expense of an interesting book on George Kelly's Personal Construct Theory: D. Bannister and F. Fransella *Inquiring Man, The Theory of Personal Constructs* (9).

1a. There is surely more to the displacement of 'consciousness' by 'communication' than is indicated in this paragraph. What is here presented as a methodological and practical argument can also be presented as an ontological thesis about the primacy of *social practice* over *individual consciousness*, the latter being seen as the product of the former and not *vice versa*. According to Habermas, 'In the tradition of Kantianism, Cassirer was the first to make the transition from the transcendental critique of consciousness to the critique of language', though 'In a certain way Peirce anticipates Cassirer's philosophy of symbolic forms' (48g, Habermas, p. 331 fn. 13). See also Bar-Hillel's comments on Apel's position, 'what Kant should have discussed under the heading of philosophy of language he, unfortunately, treated as transcendental philosophy, so that Apel's proposed transformation is for me the most natural thing' (9a, Bar-Hillel, p. 119 replying to 4a, Apel. For a statement of Apel's position in English see, for instance, his 4b).

2. This is Watzlawick, Beavin and Jackson's first metacommunicational axiom. See their 122, p. 49. [Unfortunately, it involves a conflation of 'communication' and 'information'. See above Chapter I, n. ob].

3. Silence is avoided for other reasons such as, for example, that silence tends to bring with it self-awareness and awareness of the passage of time.

3a. The characterisation of 'Idle Discourse' in the preceding paragraphs should be compared with Heidegger's treatment of *'Gerede'* in *Being and Time* (54b, esp. pp. 211–24). Heidegger characterises *Gerede* as a species of phatic communion, which contrasts with the referential use of language: 'The primary relationship-of-Being towards the entity talked about is not "imparted" by communication; but Being-with-one-another takes place in talking with one another and in concern with what is said-in-the-talk.' (54b, p. 212.) Furthermore, idle talk is self-guaranteeing, and Heidegger characterises this in a similar manner to the way Adorno treats the 'jargon of authenticity' (1a, Adorno, esp. p. 100 quoting Karl Kraus 'the phrase gives birth to reality'), writing that 'The Being-said, the *dictum*, the pronouncement—all these now stand surety for the genuineness of the discourse and of the understanding which belongs to it, and for its appropriateness to the facts. . . . Things are so because one says so.' (54b, p. 212.)

However, in terms of explaining *Gerede*, Heidegger and Adorno part company, the former rejecting any account of it as a historical phenomenon which can be historically transcended (p. 220; the remarks here could be aimed at Lukacs, if Goldmann is right: 43c, Goldmann), whereas the latter argues (1a, pp. 101–2) that *Gerede* 'is forced on men by a social structure which negates them as subjects long before this is done by the newspaper companies' (p. 102).

3b. The nature of this tacit indication is characterised and explained by H. P. Grice as an implicature generated by flouting a maxim of Relation (47a, Grice).

3c. J. S. Mill makes the same point, in *Representative Government*, 'Any prejudice whatever will be insurmountable if those who do not share it themselves truckle to it, flatter it, and accept it as a law of nature' (91d, Mill, p. 271).

4. Compare Watzlawick, Beavin and Jackson's procedure. They divide every communication into a *content* and a *relationship* aspect (122, pp. 51–4) 'such that the latter classifies the former and is therefore a metacommunication' (p. 54).

4a. One reviewer, Thomas Kochman, thought that the distinctions I draw in the above paragraphs between Malinowski's 'phatic communion', Jakobson's 'phatic function' and my own 'idle discourse' (to which I have now added Heidegger's *Gerede* in n. 3a above) are 'self-indulgent and perhaps aggrandising ("academic")' and 'could quite reasonably have been omitted' (66d, Kochman, p. 124).

Now the distinctions are drawn in as detailed a fashion as they are because I wanted to try to distinguish a category of alienated and alienating communication in which power relations played no part, at least, immediately. This then clears the ground for the analysis in Chapter IV where power relations are introduced into the analysis and further categories of alienated and alienating communication are distinguished. However, as is indicated by the quotation from Adorno in n. 3a above, power relations enter mediately into the explanation of *Gerede*, which in itself seems not to involve any immediate power relationship between those engaged in idle discourse.

4b. My partial ignorance of, and hostility towards, contemporary analytic philosophy prevented me in 1973 from making any explicit use of Searle's speech act theory or Grice's theory of conversation, even in a simple comparison with Jakobson. I now think that speech act and conversation theory, that is, the theory of language use (pragmatics) as developed by Searle and Grice from the beginnings pioneered by Austin (114b, 114c, 114d, 114e, Searle: 47a, 47b, Grice; 5b, Austin) offer a powerful way of approaching the kinds of questions raised in this chapter, certainly much more powerful than is provided by Jakobson's schema. See further the new notes added to Chapter IV. There are some interesting criticisms of Jakobson's schema in 104a, Pratt, Ch. 1.

4c. Compare the analysis offered in the course of Brown and Levinson's important paper on politeness (23a, Brown and Levinson). They treat contradictions, challenges, etc., as a threat to the positive face wants (the desire to be desired) of the original speaker (p. 71).

4d. Though a textbook of chemistry is an *authoritative* source of information, whatever relation exists between rejecting authority and being illogical it is unlikely to be one of *identity*.

5. Roy Edgley comments:
   You make what appear to be two assumptions here: (a) that the connection between 'Snow is white' and 'It's wrong to think that snow is not white' is contingent; and (b) that 'It's wrong to think that snow is not white' is a moral appraisal. I reject both of these in my book *Reason in Theory and Practice* [33b, esp. Ch. 3]. In my view, *criticism* of (actual or possible) beliefs and assertions is one of logical implication, or at any rate a *necessary* connection. If I'm right, this is a counter example to the fact-value distinction as it's usually interpreted, i.e. as implying a 'logical gap' between factual and evaluative judgements.
   [Response: I accept that the relationship is non-contingent (on which see also 114b, Searle, Ch. 8) but think that the appraisal can be a moral one. For this is one way in which the non-contingent relationship can be, as it were, *realised* in concrete social practices. Whether it *has* to be realised in a moral way is another question to which I don't know the answer.]

6. Roy Edgley comments: Does your discussion fail to distinguish the question 'Is it right to think that p.?' from the question 'Is it worth finding out (having an opinion on) whether p.?' It looks as if it subscribes either to the idea of knowledge for its own sake or to the idea that the value of knowledge is overriding. My view is that some bits of knowledge are more worth having than others, i.e. some questions are comparatively not worth asking

('How many children had Lady Macbeth?', 'What did Princess Anne have for her wedding breakfast?', etc.): not bothering about knowledge of this sort is not 'the pursuit of durable security'—on the contrary, a typical way of pursuing security and avoiding reality is precisely by a single-minded pursuit of useless knowledge, whether of the trivial gossipy kind or of the scholarly academic kind.

6a. Barthes' account of dialectics is surely polemical. One object of Socratic dialectics is to convince the person who thinks he knows that really his knowledge is only opinion, on the basis of his own commitment to standards of evidence and argument. In moving from opinion to knowledge through dialectics, the substantive position he asserts may, but need not, change. The slogan *credo quia absurdum* is the last resort of someone trying to evade the force of reason, for as Searle writes, 'he who states (i.e. he who is willing to engage in statement making) is committed (*ceteris paribus*) to avoiding self-contradictions. One does not first decide to make statements and then make a separate evaluative decision that they would be better if they were not self-contradictory. So we are still left with commitments being essentially involved in facts' (114b, Searle, p. 191; cf. n. 5 above). To what *use* these commitments are put is another matter. On relations between logic and rhetoric, see for instance 35a, Evans, and 57a and 57b, Howell.

7. J. S. Mill has some remarks (91, pp. 181–3) on what he calls 'the morality of public discussion' (p. 183) by which he means that such things as 'want of candour, or malignity, bigotry, or intolerance of feeling' (p. 182) ought to be condemned and 'merited honour' given 'to everyone, whatever opinion he may hold, who has calmness to see and honesty to state what his opponents and their opinions really are, exaggerating nothing to their discredit, keeping nothing back which tells, or can be supposed to tell, in their favour' (p. 182).

8. The behavioural theory used by Watzlawick, Beavin and Jackson does not, as far as I can see, allow one to say whether the agreement which A and B arrive at in the above example involves genuine or pseudo agreement on A's part. To establish whether agreement is genuine or artificial one has to go beyond the behavioural sequences and impute mental states to the speakers. It is not enough to refer to other stretches of behaviour, for there still remains the problem of which stretches of behaviour to privilege as representing the 'real' A or B. Gramsci deals with a similar problem when discussing the contradictions

F

between thought and action—see 46, Gramsci, pp. 321–43.
[Though he is not concerned with individuals but social classes.
See further 81a, Mann, on the theory of dual consciousness, and
77a, Lukes, p. 47 f. on the passages in Gramsci referred to here.]

8a. But what is to count as an 'intelligible claim' and what not?
This question is of practical importance in relation to how we
react to the discourse of the insane (cf. Chapter IV, section 4
below). It has also been discussed theoretically in the philosophy
of language, philosophy of social science and philosophy of
religion (where Wittgenstein's theory of 'language games' has
provided the basis for a reply to the logical positivists' onslaught
on theological uses of language). One way into the issue is
through the question of 'Radical Translation' (on which see,
for example, 104e, Quine, Ch. 2; 30d, Davidson; 74b, Lewis;
104c, Putnam).

8b. Compare also 48f, Habermas.

8c. Compare 81a, Mann, Ch. 3, on Fatalism.

CHAPTER IV

Repressive Discourse

He speaks to me as if I were a public meeting.
Queen Victoria, of Mr. Gladstone (alleged). [0a]

1. Scope and Definitions

In the previous chapter, I considered some forms of communication where the power relations obtaining between speaker and hearer were irrelevant to their interaction. In contrast, the forms of communication which I shall discuss in this chapter depend upon and sustain inequalities of power. In fact, I shall deal only with cases in which the speaker is more powerful than the hearer.[0b]

However, I want to distinguish between *repression* and *oppression* resulting from the exercise of unequal power. Further, I want to distinguish between repressive *forms* of discourse, repressive *content* and repressive *context* of discourse though it is only with repressive forms of discourse that I shall be concerned. How do I draw these various distinctions?

A relationship is oppressive when 'naked' power or force is used to prevent those who are oppressed by the relationship from satisfying some of their needs, wants, desires, where these could be satisfied without preventing other people's equal satisfaction of the same needs, etc. In an oppressive relationship, nothing is disguised, either explicitly or implicitly (I use the idea of implicit disguise to cover the cases of repressive *omission* discussed below). This lack of disguise does not exclude that the oppressed may fail to see their oppression, but if they do fail, it is for reasons external to the oppressive relationship immediately in question. In contrast, essential to a repressive relationship is the element of *disguise*. Either the oppressive nature of a relationship is disguised, so that it is no longer a question of 'naked' but of 'clothed' power or force ('the velvet glove'), or the relationship aims to disguise or has the effect of disguising from the oppressed either their own power or their needs, or both. To give a crude example: armies generally oppress people purely and simply, though if armies start saying that what they are trying to do is 'win the hearts and minds of the people', then the relationship army/people has acquired a repressive aspect. Governments, in contrast, generally are involved in repressive and only subordinately oppressive relations with those they govern.

Here I am only concerned with one form of repression, namely, repressive discourse, and in turn with only one aspect of it: its form, rather than its content or context. What are the distinctions here? (The chapter itself will have to demonstrate that this very narrow focus is justified.)

The context of a discourse is repressive when its real nature is disguised; thus a police situation may be disguised as a therapeutic one[1] (needless to say, this is not necessarily a question of conscious intent.) The idea of a repressive content of discourse is roughly equivalent to that of *ideology*. For example, Kings do not merely assert their Power but their Right: often, their Divine Right. Of course, disputes over the truth and falsity of propositions render the application of the term 'ideological' as disputable as the terms 'true' and 'false' themselves. For 'ideology' usually stands in opposition to 'science' and this opposition is itself often transformable into the opposition False/True. Thus, Marxist theory of ideology often dissolves into the theory of truth, as in the work of Louis Althusser (2, 3, 4).

On the other hand, there are a number of well-established paradigms of ideological discourse. For example, (1) a concept-word (e.g. 'nation') is promoted against another concept-word (e.g. 'class') which would be more accurately descriptive of a state of affairs. Thus, 'national interest' is more accurately replaced with 'ruling-class interest' and what is typically ideological in the use of 'national interest' is the attempt to generalise what is in fact a highly particular interest. Marx himself stressed the importance of this particular ideological method (87, Marx and Engels.) Again, (2) that which is social or conventional is reified into something natural (see 77, Lukacs).

This still leaves the category of repressive discourse, where the repressiveness resides not in the context or content but in the form itself. It seems to me that there are two ways in which the form can be repressive: either in so far as it disguises the *status* of the message carried by the discourse, or in so far as it disguises the *social relationship* which makes possible the discourse in question.[1a] The same stretch of discourse may do both of these things at once.

Examine the following case. If an Army sergeant says to a corporal, 'As your sergeant, I order you to get your hair cut' this is not, by my criterion, an instance of repressive (form of) discourse, even though the Army context of the order may be repressive and the content of the order is. But the form in which the order is given does not disguise the social relationship which makes the legitimate giving of such an order possible. Equally, the order does not disguise its status as an order. There is explicit reference both to the social relationship ('As your sergeant . . .') and the status of the discourse as an order (indicated by the explicit performative 'I order you to . . .').

In contrast, if the same[2] order is given in the form 'Get your hair cut!' then I think that this is repressive in form because it omits reference both to the social relation which allows such an order to be legitimately given and to its own status as an order. Of course, in the Army context, the order given in this abbreviated form is *in practice* no more repressive than the order given in the expanded form, and this shows that repressiveness in practice cannot be regarded as a consequence of form.[3] On the other hand, I think there are contexts where it makes a practical difference whether orders are given in contracted or expanded form.[4]

Thus consider a family situation in which orders are habitually given in the contracted form (Shut up!). I think this form of communication of orders makes it more difficult for the recipient of orders to become aware of the power relations which permit one member of the family to say 'Shut up!' to another, but do not permit that second member to say 'Shut up!' to the first. I think he is more likely to take for granted the power relations—that is, be unaware of their existence—than if orders were explicitly given. Power relations will only be revealed to the second member of the family if to a 'Shut up!' he replies 'Shut up yourself!' and finds himself cuffed round the ear. But if he isn't spontaneously cheeky, the power relations will be naturalised, and the form of the utterance compounds such naturalisation. The effects of this may well spill over into attitudes towards social institutions other than the family.

Consider three more examples, in which the emphasis is on

disguising the nature of the utterance rather than of the social relationship.

(1) An order disguised as a request is repressive, for if the disguise is not seen through, the recipient of the request/order will respond to a request and thereby remain in ignorance of the real nature of the social relation between himself and the person giving the request/order.

(2) Somewhat similar to the above case is that situation which has acquired the name 'Double Bind' and which I discuss in detail in Section 3 below. Here, the meaning of the discourse is formally undecidable, but at the same time the discourse contains 'instructions' *not to recognise this fact*. The Double Bind provides the most striking evidence for the claim that the *form* of discourse is important; for the effects of double binding can be of pathological proportion, and can be so *independently of the contents of the messages transmitted*, though not of their context, since there can be therapeutic Double Binds, which entails that the pathological consequence of Double Binds are not just the effect of the form.

(3) Whilst a speaker may innocently make a meaningless statement and have this pointed out to him, a speaker in a position of superior power can attempt to strengthen his position by presenting meaningless utterances *as* meaningful, and this is more easily effective if the hearer does not even have a chance of replying. Professional politicians very rarely have to persuade their audience but have to make a show of communicating with their publics. They can get away with material which is poorly organised, syntactically and semantically, and which may well approach to meaninglessness. The audience which then fails to understand is consequently further convinced of its incapacity for 'high' politics, and the power of the professional politician is further increased, especially when using the medium of TV he can convey a favourable 'analogic' image of himself at the same time as he presents his meaningless 'digital' information.[5]

In considering the repressive content of discourse, I linked this to ideology. Similarly, I think the repressive forms of discourse of the sort listed above can be linked to *mystification*.[5a] If the critical concept of 'ideology' arises from a preoccupation with *truth* or *logic*, that of 'mystification' arises directly from concern with *freedom*. The repressive forms of discourse reduce a person's freedom in so far as they reduce the possibility of rational appraisal of either social institutions or utterances or both. Hence, the possibility of rational action is curtailed and there is scarcely a definition of freedom which does not make that possibility a component of freedom.

Ideology produces misunderstanding of the world; mystification produces apathy, fragmentation and disorientation—and, if Reich is correct (see his 106), vulnerability to irrational appeals. Apathy, etc., have a real foundation in lived experience, but they are compounded by mystification. It is not people's clear and distinct understanding of false ideas which alone keeps them down, but also their inability to clearly and distinctly distinguish and think about truth or falsity, partly as a consequence of the repressive forms of discourse to which they are exposed (for other possible reasons, see Chapter V below). Radicals and revolutionaries encounter the effects of mystification when they find that people do not so much disagree with them on substantive issues but rather don't see how they can do anything to change the world.[5b]

The following sections seek to illustrate and substantiate some of the points and claims made in this section.

2. I and We[5c]

Typical in academic discourse is the use by the author or speaker of 'we' or 'our' as opposed to 'I' or 'my': 'thus we see that . . .'; 'we use x to mean . . .' 'we realise that . . .' and so on. This little 'we' functions to bring the reader or hearer into the shared world of the writer or speaker often without giving that reader or hearer reasons for coming in and always in a way which disguises the inequalities between them. The use of the 'we' is repressive when it disguises an absence of argument (but converting a subjective judgement into an objective claim), or when it disguises an existing social relation of inequality (between speaker and hearer), or when it does both of these things. Throughout this book, I have tried to use 'I' not 'We' except where I am making an empirical claim about what I think we (you and I) in fact do, and even in such cases I have often prefaced the 'we' with an 'I think' to make clear the status of the statement. If this book appears unduly tentative, then I would say it does so because I have tried to give my statements the status they deserve. I think that many speculative books attempt to give themselves a status they don't deserve simply by the suppression of the 'I think'.

Discussion of the difference between the use of 'We' and 'I' generally takes place in the context of work on claimed social class differences in linguistic codes (though even if there are not different *codes*, differences in *usage* would still be significant.) Thus, in Basil Bernstein's division between *restricted* and *elaborated* codes, 'we' is claimed to be characteristically used by speakers of the restricted code, and 'I' (in such phrases as 'I think') by speakers of the elaborated code.[6] Members of the lower working class are thought to be confined to the restricted code (see 21, Bernstein *passim*; for criticisms of Bernstein's work, see 30, Coulthard; 69, Labov; 109, Rosen; 32a, Dittmar).

Bernstein explains the differential usage of 'We' and 'I' (which I agree exists) as several other differential usages (such as the greater usage of impersonal pronouns by restricted code speakers) by reference to the major function of the restricted code, which Bernstein states to be the following: 'The major function of this code is to reinforce the form of the social relationship (a warm and inclusive relationship) by restricting the verbal signalling of individual response.' (21, Bernstein, p. 78.) In another formulation: 'The major function of this code is to define and reinforce the form of the social relationship by restricting the verbal signalling of individual experience.' (21, p. 128.)

Now I would say that the need to define and reinforce the form of the social relationship, if this need does exist, itself needs to be explained. I would suggest that the explanation has to be sought in the fact that the social class which makes more use of 'we' and 'it', etc. is an oppressed class which is in a defensive relation to the dominant culture and class. The use of 'we' and 'it', etc., serve a solidaristic function and this is genuinely possible in so far as the adult individuals participating in communication occupy roughly equal social statuses. In this context, Bernstein's use of the expression 'sympathetic circularity' is apposite to characterise the defining and reinforcing functions of language use: it is *sympathetic* since people are co-operating together linguistically in opposition to their social and cultural subordination, and it can be *circular* since individuals share the same social status—their own relations are not *hierarchised*. In such cases, the solidaristic use of language in sympathetic circularity may be confused with the Idle Discourse described in Chapter III—at least, I fell into such a confusion in the first draft of that chapter and of this.[7]

On the other hand, if the focus is shifted to the use of such devices as 'we' and 'it' in the process of *socialisation*, then I think they are distinctly unsympathetic, for it seems to me that they serve a determinately repressive function. Statements employing such devices as 'we' and 'it' *presuppose* a shared world and implicitly deny that their subject matter might be a matter of reflection, inquiry and dispute, or even that they have a subject matter: the statements are naturalised, that is, deprived of their cognitive and consequently provisional status. Further, as used in socialisation, such presupposing of a shared world functions as an unexplicated conative[8] of the sort 'Think (or Be) like me!' Such statements consequently disguise a power relationship, which is covered over (as in academic discourse) by the egalitarian 'we' and by the omission of any explicit sign of the conative function which the statements are performing.

Similar criticisms apply to the use of simple imperatives by adults addressing children. If simple imperatives (and likewise physical coercion) on the model 'Do this! Do that!' constitute the determinant mode of verbal socialisation, then the child is deprived of the knowledge that the norms etc. into which it is being socialised can be the object of cognition and rational dispute. I imagine that socialisation by imperative discourse is effective in producing *reified* ways of thinking in which the world just is—either you like it or you lump it, but you don't change it. If it does work like this, then as discourse it is *reifying*. (Equally, knowledge that the norms can be the object of cognition and rational dispute is not effectively conveyed by those middle class methods of 'person-oriented' (see 21, Bernstein, especially Ch. 8) socialisation which create an over-developed sense of guilt, which functions as an internalised social control mechanism. There must be other ways of socialising children than the two mentioned in this paragraph.)

Child socialisation is the subject of an ample specialist literature and I am sure the deficiencies of imperative control have been commented upon elsewhere, and not only by Bernstein. I would just like to note in passing that, in comparison to the inherently conservative nature and effects of imperative control, socialisation which employs reason-giving permits, and perhaps encourages, disagreement and demands for change from those socialised.[9] This suggests to me that the classical forms of bourgeois ideology, with their emphasis on reason giving, invited disagreement and hence social instability. The classical forms of bourgeois ideology have been ineffective as social stabilisers because of their form. Indeed, in origin they were intended as social destabilisers.[9a] In our own time, several authors (notably 83, Marcuse and 48, Habermas) have commented on the new forms of bourgeois ideology, such as one dimensionality and the use of science and technology as ideology, which limit the role of reason giving and argument to *means-end* reasoning.

A caricature of this shift away from rational argument—that is, away from forms of ideology whose structure permits an internal critique—is provided in a little book by Mr. (now Professor) Thomas McPherson (81, McPherson; for criticism see 95, Carole Pateman). McPherson argues that the very *question* 'Ought I to obey the Government?' (central to classical bourgeois political theory) is illegitimate because meaningless: he writes that 'to seek a general justification for our being obliged at all in political society is to pursue a meaningless question' (p. 65). It is clearly a much more effective form of social control to abolish fundamental questions than to answer them in the affirmative. For affirmative answers can always be challenged, with reasons. To follow the advice of Professor McPherson would be to deprive oneself of the knowledge that there was anything which could be challenged—incidentally, the goal of the State in *1984*.[10] Professor McPherson's work is the clearest example I have come across of a reflection in Philosophical work of the process described by Habermas in the following terms:

Old-style politics was forced, merely through its traditional forms of legitimation to define itself in relation to practical goals: the 'good life' was interpreted in a context defined by interaction relations. The same still held for the ideology of bourgeios society. The substitute programme prevailing today, in contrast, is aimed exclusively at the functioning of a manipulated system. It eliminates practical [where 'practical' is used as in 'practical reason'—TP] questions and therewith precludes discussion about the adoption of standards; the latter could emerge only from a democratic decision-making process. The solution of technical problems is not dependent on public discussion. Rather, public discussions could render problematic the framework within which the tasks of government action present themselves as technical ones. Therefore the new politics of state interventionism requires a de-politicisation of the mass of the population. To the extent that practical questions are eliminated, the public realm also loses its political function. (48, pp. 103-4)[10a]

In other words, the *State* is depoliticised and it is to the legitimation of this process that McPherson contributes in his *Philosophy*.

3. The Double Bind

The Double Bind hypothesis was first formulated in a 1956 paper by Bateson, Jackson, Haley and Weakland (reprinted in 15, Bateson, pp. 201-27). It sought to explain the genesis and nature of schizophrenia in terms neither of genetic constitution or infantile trauma but, rather, in terms of a continuing pattern of communication between parent and child, resulting in schizophrenia for the child.

Classically, schizophrenics have been described as having 'weak ego' functioning, whether this is the terminology used or not. For the authors of the Double Bind hypothesis, the relevant ego function is to be characterised in terms of 'discriminating communicational modes [literalness, metaphor, etc.—TP] either within the self or between the self and others' (p. 205), and the schizophrenic is to be seen as exhibiting weakness in three areas of such an ego function:

(a) He has difficulty in assigning the correct communicational mode to the messages he receives from other persons.
(b) He has difficulty in assigning the correct communicational mode to those messages which he himself utters or

emits non verbally. (c) He has difficulty in assigning the correct communicational mode to his own thoughts, sensations and percepts. [p. 205]

Thus, for example, the schizophrenic uses metaphors as do other people, but he uses unlabeled metaphors: 'He has special difficulty in handling signals of that class whose members assign Logical Types to other signals' (p. 205). In terms previously used in this book, the schizophrenic has difficulty in *metacommunicating*.[11]

How are the schizophrenic's difficulties[12] to be explained? Bateson and his associates sought to find repetitive sequences of communication to which the schizophrenic was exposed which could account for the acquisition of the mental habits which are exemplified in schizophrenic communication. They argue that the essential characteristics of such communication would be the following:

1. *Two or more persons* . . .
2. *Repeated experience* . . .
3. *A primary negative injunction.* This may have either of two forms: (a) 'Do not do so and so, or I will punish you' or (b) 'if you do not do so and so, I will punish you' . . .
4. *A secondary injunction conflicting with the first at a more abstract level, and like the first enforced by punishment or signals which threaten survival.* This secondary injunction is more difficult to describe than the primary for two reasons. First, the secondary injunction is commonly communicated to the child by non-verbal means . . . Second, the secondary injunction may impinge upon any element of the primary prohibition. Verbalization of the secondary injunction may, therefore, include a wide variety of forms; for example, 'Do not see this as punishment'; 'Do not see me as the punishing agent'; 'Do not submit to my prohibitions'; 'Do not think of what you must not do'; 'Do not question my love of which the primary prohibition is (or is not) an example'; and so on . . .
5. *A tertiary negative injunction prohibiting the victim from escaping from the field* . . . (though) if the double binds

are imposed during infancy, escape is naturally impossible . . .

6. Finally, the complete set of ingredients is no longer necessary when the victim has learned to perceive his universe in Double Bind patterns . . . [pp. 206–7]

The authors continue:

We hypothesize that there will be a breakdown in any individual's ability to discriminate between Logical Types[12a] whenever a Double Bind situation occurs. The general characteristics of this situation are the following:

(1) When the individual is involved in an intense relationship . . .

(2) And, the individual is caught in a situation in which the other person in the relationship is expressing two orders of message and one of these denies the other.

(3) And, the individual is unable to comment on the messages being expressed to correct his discrimination of what order of message to respond to i.e. he cannot make a metacommunicative statement.

We have suggested that this is the sort of situation which occurs between the preschizophrenic and his mother, but it also occurs in normal relationships. When a person is caught in a Double Bind situation, he will respond defensively in a manner similar to the schizophrenic. [pp. 208–9]

How do schizophrenics themselves respond? The authors characterize three possible strategies:

If an individual has spent his life in the kind of Double Bind relationship described here, his way of relating to people after a psychotic break [why not before?—TP] would have a systematic pattern. First, he would not share with normal people those signals which accompany messages to indicate what a person means. His metacommunicative system—the communications about communication—would have broken down [would he ever have had a metacommunicative system?—TP], and he would not know what kind of message a message was . . . Given this inability to judge accurately what a person really means and an excessive concern with what is really meant, an individual might defend himself by choosing one or more of several alternatives. He might, for example, assume that behind every statement there is a concealed statement which is detrimental to his welfare. He would then be excessively concerned with hidden meanings and determined to demonstrate that he could not be deceived . . .

He might choose another alternative, and tend to accept literally everything people say to him; when their tone or gesture or context contradicted what they said, he might establish a pattern of laughing off these metacommunicative signals . . .

If he didn't become suspicious of metacommunicative messages or attempt to laugh them off, he might choose to try to ignore them. Then he would find it necessary to see and hear less and less of what went on around him, and do his utmost to avoid provoking a response in his environment . . . This is another way of saying that if an individual doesn't know what sort of message a message is, he may defend himself in ways which have been described as paranoid, hebephrenic, or catatonic. These three alternatives are not the only ones. The point is that he cannot choose the one alternative which would help him to discover what people mean; he cannot, without considerable help, discuss the message of others. [pp. 210-11]

Comments[12b]

As stated by Bateson and associates, lack of metacommunicative skills is seen as both cause (p. 208) and consequence (p. 210) of Double Binding. This is consistent with a simple learning theory that metacommunicative skills are, indeed, learnt as skills in childhood and through adolescence, and that Double Binding, which is effective because such skills have not yet been learnt, also inhibits or prevents the learning of the skills—not least because the tertiary negative injunction can forbid the victim to leave the *conceptual* as much as the *physical* field. A good case history of such a tertiary negative injunction applied to the conceptual field is that of Judge Schreber, whose *Memoirs* (translation 109, Schreber) formed the basis of one of Freud's most famous case studies (40, Freud). In a recent study, Schatzman (108) has pointed out that in committing 'soul murder' on his son, Schreber's father forbade his victim to correctly identify his murderer. In this he was completely successful: to the end Judge Schreber claimed that his persecutor was God, and never saw that behind God stood his earthly Father. One could say: forbidden to leave the conceptual field in which his Father had placed him, Schreber could only comprehend his persecution in an insane way. (On Schreber's fascinating case, see also 70, Lacan and 125, Wilden, Ch. X).

To return to Bateson and his associates, I would qualify their analysis at one point, and argue that it cannot be *after* the 'psychotic break' that the victim's way of relating to people acquires a systematic pattern. Logically, the victim cannot previously have *possessed* a metacommunicative system which could have 'broken down'. That the absence of such a system is observed only after a psychotic break is to be explained by the fact that it is only after such a break that the schizophrenic individual will come to the attention of a psychiatrist. As for the break itself, from the literature I have read, it would seem that this must at least sometimes be construed as a desperate attempt to *generate* a metacommunicative system, rather in the same way that the first signs of madness noted by the parents of 'schizophrenics' studied by Laing and Esterson (71) must be construed at least in part as explicably *gauche* attempts to establish a self-created identity: *gauche* because the child has been obstructed by its parents from learning how to create such an identity. Such an interpretation is consistent with those theories which see the psychotic break as essentially an attempt at self-healing, not to be interfered with. What has to be cured is the illness which *preceded* the break, the illness which consisted in adjustment or submission to the pathological family world. Freud was probably the first modern psychologist to suggest the positive aspect of the break.[13]

It is the *power* of parents over children in our society which permits Double Bind situations to be created and sustained in the family. It is a heretic against the familial ideology who believes that children should be free to vote with their feet—and as soon as they can walk (see 47, Green and 56a, Holt).

The Double Bind is repressive in many ways, most importantly in that it precludes the child from conceptualising and acting upon what is going on in the family situation and, eventually, in all situations. The effects of the Double Bind are compounded by the fact that Double Binding is not confined to parent/child interaction, as Bateson and his associates themselves indicate (p. 209, cited above). Some ideologues of the populist Right have managed to articulate for the 'ordinary man' what Bateson, R. D. Laing and others have articulated for the schizophrenic. Formally speaking, Enoch Powell in the following account is describing some of the ingredients of a Double Bind situation, but in this case it concerns the relation of the mass media to their public:

> The power of the minority, which though still only in its infancy, we have watched being exerted here and elsewhere during the last few years, derives from its hold on men's minds. The majority are rendered passive and helpless by a devilishly simple, yet devilishly subtle, technique. This is to assert manifest absurdities as if they were self-evident truths. By dint of repetition of the absurdities, echoed, re-echoed and amplified by all the organs of communication, the majority are reduced to a condition in which they finally mistrust their own senses and their own reason, and surrender their will to the manipulator. In all war the objective is to break the opponent's will. Our danger is that the enemy has mastered the art of establishing a moral ascendancy over his victims and destroying their good conscience. [Speech at Northfield, Birmingham, 12 June 1970; reprinted in 104, Powell, p. 108]

And again:

> The whole power of the aggressor depends upon preventing people from seeing what is happening and from saying what they see. [104, Powell, p. 109]

From these quotations one can extract point by point equivalence with the original Double Bind model. In place of the two or more persons, one has the relation of the media to their public, engaged in a continuing relation which produces for the public repeated experiences of repressive communication. The equivalent of the Double Binding conflict between primary and secondary injunctions lies (in the first quotation) in the assertion of 'manifest absurdities *as if* they were self-evident truths' (my italics). Just as much as in the Double Binds described by Bateson and his associates, this 'as if' assertion involves confusion in logical typing, and confusion, moreover, which specifically involves the metacommunicative level, for the way in which a proposition is asserted is a *comment* on that proposition. Thus, to say 'He says the most outrageous things in the mildest way' is to say that he says them *as if* they were not outrageous, but rather mild. Thus he confuses and perhaps eliminates one's perception of the proposition *as* outrageous.[14]

In the case of the relation of media and public, the equivalents of the tertiary injunction not to leave the field, would be such phenomena as the assertion that one is threatening the 'freedom of the press' if one criticises the press. Again to say that TV is addictive is to say that it works like a tertiary injunction, in preventing the victim from leaving the field.[14a]

The reactions which Powell ascribes to the victim of the mass media are not, however, comparable to the reactions ascribed to the Double Bound schizophrenic. For whereas schizophrenia is the *unwanted* product of parental socialisation, Powell describes what results when those who broadcast through the media are *successful* in their 'brain smashing' (p. 110) enterprise. The reactions Powell ascribes to the victims of the media would presumably only be found in the children of schizophrenogenic parents who surrendered their will and autonomy to their parents, and I assume that it is not such people who psychiatrists generally encounter, but rather those who revolt.

The therapeutic solution to people's metacommunicative problems is to educate them in meta-communication (and metacommunication includes those interventions which were characterised as philosophical in Chapter I). Education in metacommunication involves both giving support to people's own tentative explorations in metacommunication and the actual teaching of metacommunicative skills, as a sub-class of cognitive or communicative skills in general. As defined in Chapter I, philosophy is a sub-class of the class of meta-communicative skills.[15]

The solution to repressive communication in the case of the mass media, of which Double Binding is only one aspect, finally lies in a change of ownership, control and technical organisation—something which Powell does not envisage. Prior

G

to this change-over there are forms of knowledge, such as the critical semiology pioneered by Roland Barthes (11, Barthes) which are similar to communication oriented psychotherapies, in that they aim to equip individuals with cognitive skills they have not got, but which they need just in order to get-by and as a necessary condition of doing anything more than just getting-by. The characteristics of critical semiology are not all that different from those of the radical therapy of schizophrenia, in which the therapist attempts to build up the schizophrenic's understanding of how his/her parents operate and does so as a way of weakening the schizogenic parental hold over the child. The therapy of the psychoses is obviously *ego* building—but in radical therapy, the *ego* is built up to increase individual independence of the *environment* (including the family environment) and not, in the first place, of the *id*.

Barthes has said that he once considered a career as a psychotherapist; I would like to add here a brief indication of the relevance of his semiology, in the shape of a review of his book *Mythologies* (11, Barthes).

3a. Roland Barthes' Mythologies[16]

The development of publicity, of a national press, of radio, of illustrated news, not to speak of the survival of a myriad rites of communication which rule social appearance makes the development of semiological Science more urgent than ever. In a single day, how many really non-signifying fields do we cross? Very few, sometimes none. [11, *Mythologies*, p. 112, fn. 2[16a]]

[E]verything, in every day life, is dependent on the representation which the bourgeoisie *has and makes us have* of the relations between man and the world. [p. 140]

The development of a mass culture, dominated and determined by the growth of a mass media, has been opposed, if unequally, by attempts to understand or destroy or transform it. That these attempts have been made by those to whom mass culture is least directed should not cause surprise; and the interest of certain intellectuals in the process is easily explained by a conviction that mass culture poses a political threat: it threatens to stabilise or generate a massive, generalized false consciousness, against which radicals and revolutionaries will batter in vain.

In terms of understanding, it is the workings of medium as message and the manipulative aspects of mass culture that are most familiar, thanks to the work of Marshall McLuhan and Herbert Marcuse. In the case of the latter, central to his theory of manipulation (82, Marcuse) is the concept of *repressive desublimation* (though I would like to think that the validity of this concept is relatively independent of the problematic in which it has its present place). Repressive desublimation is characterized, in quasi—if not strictly—Freudian terms, as a manipulation and partial satisfaction of the claims of the id, necessarily involving a diminution in the scope and strength of ego-dominated activities, and hence of the ego itself. In this process, it seems to me, the super-ego can either be weakened or re-shaped: there are now people walking about guilt-ridden about *not* getting sexual pleasure. Either way, the weakening of the ego is synonymous with a psychotization of culture, of which the statistical increase in the diagnosis of schizophrenia may be symptomatic and of which talk about 'identity crises' certainly is. Within such a perspective common, I think, to all members of the Frankfurt School, the finding of techniques of resistance to repressive desublimation and ways of building up the ego become strategic imperatives. This is spelt out particularly clearly in Reimut Reiche's *Sexuality and Class Struggle* (107a, Reiche).

Though it has never, to my knowledge, been inserted within the problematic of the Frankfurt School, I would suggest that we can usefully view the development of semiology in France and elsewhere as being, in part, a resistance to repressive desublimation or, more generally, to manipulative mass culture: semiological knowledge is itself ego-building, whilst effectively semiological resistance-techniques are being taught nearly every time a Liberal Studies' teacher gets students to look 'critically' at advertisements—to isolate the desires and ideologies which they invoke but generally do not name. This critical semiology is, to use Barthes' term, a *semioclasm*—the shattering of a petrified universe of signs.

Of course, to name a desire or an ideological concept does not generally diffuse or destroy its power, any more than (in the case of a desire) it satisfies it—which makes it possible for the *avant-garde* of ad-men to *name* that to which they are appealing without thereby destroying the effectiveness of their appeal. On the other hand, naming is a necessary condition of exorcism—which is why the bourgeoisie is immovable so long as it succeeds in ex-nominating itself (see *Mythologies*, p. 138).

In an older vocabulary, one speaks of *demystification* and *ideological critique*, and Barthes places his work explicitly as a development of these (p. 9). The danger in both cases is not simply the ever-present one of 'overlooking' the necessity for political action, for there is also the danger that in sighting their object exclusively at the cognitive level they ignore the insertion of the relation between consumer and mass culture (the *Spectacle* of Situationism) within an economy of desire. Any attempt at a purely cognitive demystification and assumption of reality without attention to the need for a struggle to reappropriate alienated desire is misguided, though this is not to deny that desire may only exist as conceptualized, as symbolically organised.

What then is semiology? What is this knowledge which I think can be used, in self-defence in everyday life and in political combat?

The short mythologies, of which just over half are translated in Dr. Lavers' selection (there are some surprising omissions—mythologies of Billy Graham and Poujade, for instance), are examples of the kind of 'practical criticism' in which semiological science is embodied. Barthes' method is to take, one by one, events (the trial of a certain Dominici), institutions (striptease, steak and chips), products (a Citroën car), performances (a wrestling match) as well as books, films, articles and advertisements and attempt to show what they intentionally connote as opposed to what they obviously are or denote: a wrestling match is a wrestling match, yes, but also a spectacle of suffering, defeat and justice in which every hold, throw and gesture signifies these concepts. Of course there is more than one concept of justice; in wrestling, the concept signified is that which demands an eye for an eye. One might say that the match offers a sort of ostensive definition of this justice.

Certain themes of Barthes' short mythologies are insistent:

the transmutation of the historical into the natural; the elimination of historical specificity and promotion of universal, necessary and therefore empty, useless concepts such as birth and death (as in *The Great Family of Man*, pp. 100–2); the inability of the petty bourgeois (and the mythologies are predominantly critiques of the world of that class) to imagine an Other, not here a Lacanian Other but the otherness of other people, eliminated by the petty-bourgeoisie when it reconstructs them in its own image (as with the peasant Dominici) or cages them in the zoo of the exotic. And so on.

The essay *Myth Today* which forms the second part of this volume represents an ex-post attempt to construct a theoretical framework for the critique of the signs of our time, in this instance, myth-signs. Barthes says that he finds this essay, dating from 1956, hardly re-readable today, but it has scarcely been superseded, even by his own *Elements of Semiology* (12, Barthes). Therefore, I shall concentrate on an exposition and critique of *Myth Today*.

Barthes summarizes his theory of myth, couched in terms derived from Saussure, as follows:

> In myth, we find . . . the tri-dimensional pattern [of] the signifier, the signified and the sign. But myth is a peculiar system, in that it is constructed from a semiological chain which existed before it: *it is a second-order semiological system.* That which is a sign (namely the associative total of a concept and an image) in the first system, becomes a mere signifier in the second. [p. 114]

This might be more easily understood if read for a moment as a linguistic definition of *connotation*, or if read alongside Barthes' diagrammatic representation (p. 115), reproduced on the next page:

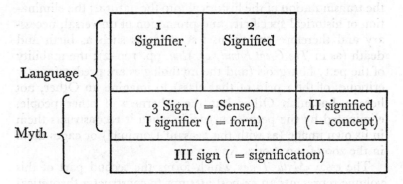

An example may further clarify matters:

> I am a pupil in the second form in a French lycée. I open my
> Latin grammar, and I read a sentence borrowed from Aesop
> or Phaedrus: *quia ego nominor leo*. I stop and think. There is
> something ambiguous about this statement: on the one hand,
> the words in it do have a simple meaning: 'because my name
> is lion'. And on the other hand, the sentence is evidently
> there in order to signify something else to me. In as much as
> it is addressed to me, a pupil in the second form, it tells me
> clearly: I am a grammatical example meant to illustrate the
> rule about the agreement of the predicate. [pp. 115–6]

In other words, 'because-my-name-is-lion' is the first-order
sign or sense, which becomes the signifier or form for the second
order signified or concept 'I-am-a-grammatical-example'. So
far so good.

For Barthes, myth is a form of speech (*parole*) in a language
(*langue*), but very clearly the procedures of the mythologist will
not be identical with those of the linguist of 'natural' languages.
For example, the standard procedures of the linguist when
constructing a dictionary of a language is to use native speakers.
It is in this way that he establishes relations between signifiers
and signifieds. But could one hope to construct a dictionary of
myth-language in the same way—could one establish the connection between the forms and concepts (Signifier I and Signified II) by asking the seeming equivalents of native speakers,
namely, those engaged in the *production* of mass culture?

The difficulties at first appear to be of a practical order, and there is nothing in Barthes to suggest they might be theoretical. The practical problems are quickly listed. First of all, any given concept can be represented by an indefinite number of forms, even though these, in contrast to natural languages must be relatively motivated (p. 126). There are an indefinite number of ways of connoting 'sex appeal'; exuberant synonomy is the rule in the field of myth. Secondly, any dictionary would become rapidly out of date; the world of myth is fast-changing in comparison to language; myths wear out even more rapidly than the new cars or clothes which are their substances. Thirdly, it seems likely that the concept of a given form is context-bound much more generally than with words, that is to say, the concept is subject to structural determination of meaning: the same photograph will not connote the same concept in *The Times* as in the *Morning Star*, and not solely in virtue of their different readerships—I am tempted to say: the meaning of a photograph is its *use* in the newspaper. (Could some myth forms be pure indices or 'shifters', in the sense that their concept changes with each instance of their use?)[16b]

For Barthes, however, there is no need to consider the obstacles to a linguist's approach, for to him the enterprise of going to the producers is strictly unnecessary. (I shall suggest below some of the theoretical limitations of such an approach). According to Barthes, the language of myth is immediately comprehensible in virtue of the fact that, far from hiding its concept 'behind' its form, 'myth hides nothing' (p. 129). And when Barthes writes this, he seems to mean what he says: for him, the concept is immediately audible or visible. The theory of knowledge at play here is a philosophy of sensibility which is naïvely empiricist: a theory in which even connotative meanings are immediately given to the ear or the eye. For example, Barthes writes of the example of Latin grammar, cited above: 'It *tells* me clearly: I am a grammatical example' (p. 116; my italics). Again, of his second example (a photograph of a Negro soldier saluting the French flag) he writes: 'whether naïvely or not, I *see* very well what it signifies to me: that France is a great Empire . . .' (p. 116; my italics). In these examples, the translator is rendering literally the original French. In short, though there are possibly contradictory statements, the determinant statements are those which specify the immediate availability of the signification, and this is surprising. For one would have thought that a science of myth was necessary precisely because in this as in other cases of capitalist daily life, appearance and reality (here, ideological reality) do not coincide. How can a science of myth be necessary if appearance and reality do coincide?

Barthes' answer is that in being evident the concept or signification is not in consequence inefficacious, the 'principle' of myth being to transform History into Nature. And it is *this* transformation which has to be exposed by science:

> ... in the eye of the myth consumer, the intention ... of the concept can remain manifest without however appearing to have an interest in the matter: what causes mythical speech to be uttered is perfectly explicit, but it is immediately frozen into something natural ... If I read the Negro saluting as symbol pure and simple of imperiality, I must renounce the reality of the picture ... if I decipher the Negro's salute as an alibi of coloniality, I shatter the myth even more surely by the obviousness of its motivation. But for the myth-reader, the outcome is quite different: everything happens as if the picture *naturally* conjured up the concept. [pp. 129–30]

In short, the essential function of myth, which it is the task of mythology to disrupt, is the naturalization of the concept, the classic way in which a crime can be both recognized and accepted. In an important later article (14b, Barthes), Barthes has described with respect to the use of photographs in advertising one mechanism of such naturalization: the symbolically coded connotation of the photograph has to 'pass through' the naturalistic filter provided by the photograph itself as a non-coded (iconic) re-presentation of an object.

The option of the visibility of myth is forced upon Barthes, for he poses as the only possible alternative that the myth is hidden and therefore useless. In positing the creation of meaning and the relation between concept and form within a pre-structuralist psychologistic theory of *intention* (see, for example, pp. 119–20 and the discussion of Basquish chalets, pp. 124–5), he explicitly rejects any recourse to an unconscious: 'There is no latency of the concept in relation to the form: there is no need of an unconscious in order to explain myth.' (p. 121.)

But if everything passed at the level of conscious intentionality, one could justifiably approach myth producers as if they were native speakers. It is, I suggest, because there is an unconscious intentionality—as with natural *grammar*—that one would be theoretically unjustified in any such attempt. Further, in the light of the claims of structuralism, it is probably in principle wrong to seek a one-to-one correlation of form to content, whether the latter be conscious or not. Rather, one should constitute the system of a given category of forms (e.g., the faces of women in men's magazines—and note that here I have had to make reference to a context as well as a category; compare the earlier remarks about structural determination of meaning) in opposing them to each other, and in this way elucidate their concepts.[16c] The immediate problem then arises: how does one constitute a 'given category'? Can it be circumscribed independently of the concepts it hides? And this is a general problem of structuralist methodology.

In the present case, it seems to me that the introduction of an unconscious is the obvious solution to the paradox that something entirely transparent should require a science devoted to its study. Thus, I would say that the 'concept' exists, for the most part, as an unconscious generative-interpretative schema: generative for the myth-producer, interpretative for the myth consumer. (In the work of the mythologist the schema becomes wholly or partly conscious). On the side of production, the 'concept' acts as a *selector* between suitable and unsuitable forms —though it does not define a unique choice, for reasons indicated above; on the side of consumption, the 'concept' determines the reading (generally unconscious) of the form. The myth is still able to perform its function of transforming History into Nature *given* certain interpretative schemas among myth-consumers.

But how does the mythologist manage to discover and criticize (put into crisis) the unconscious deep structures of myth emission and reception? I think it is because he too is a native speaker in the world of mass culture: that is to say, that he too has lived or lives its ideological[16d] depths and can speak its forms. Ask a native speaker and he cannot tell you the deep-structure of his ideology; search within yourself—that is, within your culture—and you will find them. Is this not what

Barthes is doing in the short mythologies? And if he is able to do this, could he not also have been a successful ad-man? But he chooses to work on the other side, revealing myth in order to shatter it—if not after the fashion of Laszlo Toth.[16e] And because mythological description and critique is in consequence internal or immanent, it seems to me that it may have an answer to questions concerning the ontological status of the structures it uncovers, but which, some might say, it invents. Semiology is not a science of 'As If'; it is about how we work and are worked upon.

In *Elements of Semiology*, Barthes rewrites the schema of *Myth Today*, reproduced above, as a schema of connotation, and if we apply to this latter schema the concept of the 'immanence' of language which Barthes uses in the same text (p. 24) then we get an approach not all that different from the one I have proposed in the preceding paragraphs. The same seems to be true of the article 'Rhetoric of the Image' (14b) though neither text is as explicit as one would wish.

Barthes's readership is probably confined to teachers of literature, persons with an interest in mass culture and left-wing intellectuals. I should just like to note in this section one possible application of the semiological approach of *Mythologies* to a different field, that of Philosophy.

Analytical Philosophers apply themselves directly, in conceptual analysis, to the concepts (in Barthes's sense), the ideological signifieds of discourse; they began directly with the study of justice, democracy, etc. These concepts are not *produced* in analysis, as are Barthes's (recall, for example, the study of a wrestling match), but form the starting point for it: specifically, one studies actual occurrences of 'justice' and 'democracy' in ordinary discourse. It hardly needs to be said that the results of this method are frustratingly dissatisfying, for the *words* tend to occur in speech and writing as mere boo-hooray words. Their conceptual content is light. But this does not entail that we do not have or operate one or several concepts of justice, democracy and so on. I suggest that we do indeed have such concepts, but that if we want to find them, we shall have to follow a Barthesian method of analysis—starting from a discourse which does not necessarily contain the word 'democracy', but rather producing a concept of democracy lying at the back of, or generating, the discourse. The concept thus derived could become the object of further critique.

In this way, I suspect we could convincingly illustrate and justify the claim, for example, that the scope of politics is much wider than that which it gets when its scope is defined by reference to the surface occurrence of the word 'politics'. One could, I think, show how political (in the narrow sense) concepts lie behind representations in the most diverse fields of everyday life, where the word 'politics' or any immediately recognizable political reference does not occur. Once this is shown, it is a short step to justifying the surface use of the word 'politics' in such contexts as the well-known title *The Politics of Experience.* For myself, I am certain that at the back of our discourse about experience, reason and knowledge, the machines of justice, equality and democracy are at work. And those of production, consumption and commodity?

4. Sanctions, Real and Ideal

Who do you think you're talking to?
In Sections 2 and 3 above, two different forms of repressive discourse were described and their consequences briefly indicated. These repressive communications disguise their own nature, disguise social relations, and inhibit the possibility of becoming aware of that nature and those relations.

But repressive discourse is not always effective in these forms. What happens when a hearer succeeds in commenting upon or acting against such repressive communication, the message it bears, the social relations it hides or the effects such communications are having?

Consider some possible responses in different contexts to such behaviour.

In the parent-child relationship, the parent can respond to 'cheekiness' with physical coercion or verbal threats or prohibitions on the use of such metacommunications (as in 'Don't be cheeky', which is itself a metacommunication). Each of these strategies reveals more of the social relation than had been visible before (and in this sense represents a failure, as is recognised in confrontationist political theories which recommend actions which will force the system to show its true oppressive character). At the same time as they reveal the relation, such responses none the less reinforce it. For example, the child's response is not taken up at a substantive level, but treated just as cheekiness; the particular parent-child relation is not modified, as it would be if the child's 'cheekiness' was treated as the legitimate basis for a parent-child debate. One of the defining characteristics of a particular sort of childhood is that the child's utterances are *commented upon* rather than *replied to*. The child's utterances don't count, and nor does the child. A response such as 'Don't talk to your Mother like that' is simultaneously a metacommunication and a prohibition, imperative in mode and positional in style—it refers to family positions (Mother) and thus to the form of the social relation. (See further 21, Bernstein, Ch. 8).

As a second example, consider how in the work situation phrases such as 'Who do you think you're talking to?' (which contains an implicit threat to sanction you if you continue talking as you are) reveal the existence of social relations which determine who can (legitimately, effectively or freely) say what, when and how—that is, which reveal the existence of political relations of discourse or, in other terms, of a politics of communication. 'Free Speech' understood as speech protected from the sanctions which can be imposed in situations of unequal power, and the possibility of 'dialogue' as conversation between equals in power, are the exceptions rather than the rule. In the family, at work, and in relation to the mass media either there is no 'Free Speech' or there is no possibility of 'dialogue' because power is unequal. To speak as if 'Free Speech' or 'dialogue' are or could be actualised in these situations is to talk ideologically, to propagate a myth. I am writing this on the 6th June, 1973 and the newspapers report that Professor Samuel Huntington has been prevented by chanting students from lecturing at the University of Sussex. The students get a newspaper report because they were using the power which superior numbers give in a *remarkable* way, remarkable because usually they do not exercise this power. The unequal power which parents and bosses habitually use to stop children and workers from speaking their mind is unremarkable, because habitual. In other respects, the two situations are not comparable. For example, it is doubtful whether Professor Huntington has been harmed by his experience, though the students who took part in the demonstration possibly will be. But children are seriously and sometimes permanently harmed by the fact that they are forbidden 'Free Speech'. I want to ask, however, what good reasons are there for not analysing the cases of Professor Huntington, children and workers in the same conceptual and evaluative framework? Of course, the cases are different. But don't they all involve questions about the right to speak, for the analysis of which a single set of concepts and values should suffice? (see below, Chapter VI, for further discussion and also Mepham (89)).

Physical coercion and threats to one's job are real sanctions; prohibitions of the sort 'Don't be cheeky' are ideal ones. 'Don't be cheeky' avoids the necessity of confronting the child's substantive response, and in that sense *disconfirms* or *invalidates* it. I would generalise and define ideal sanctions in terms of the way in which they *ex-communicate* the hearer (initial speaker). Sending someone to Coventry is the ideal type of such ex-communication. As a third example of sanctioning in different contexts, I want to examine the situation which I think prevails to a greater or lesser degree in many if not most Western mental hospitals.

5. Reduction to Silence: the Mental Hospital

Patients in Western mental hospitals are not forbidden to speak, either to each other or to staff or visitors. They are generally 'free' (in the negative sense) to say what they wish, and in this negative sense, their discourse is tolerated: by the staff, by the other patients—more precisely, by the institution. However, whilst not to my knowledge anywhere inscribed as an explicit rule, it is common and perhaps standard practice for staff (and, equally, other patients and visitors) to invalidate what patients say, the form of invalidation depending on context and content of the patient's utterance and also the status and idiosyncracies of the staff member.

The most obvious form of invalidation is that of *ignoring* what the patient says. If, for example, a patient asks a nurse or Doctor on his rounds 'When am I going to be released?', the question will commonly be ignored by the addressee: he will avert his

gaze, stare through the patient or walk on, according to circumstances, status and style. Even if he does not employ these
means of para- and extra-linguistic invalidation, the nurse or
Doctor may begin or continue to talk to the patient as if the
question had not been posed. (For some supporting evidence,
see 110, Rosenhan).

The message of the official behaviour is something like this:
the patient has not posed a reasonable question (and the
patient is thus confirmed in the status of unreasonable, that is,
outside reason), or else the patient has not asked a real question,
but has merely produced a *symptom*, possibly to be noted by the
staff member but clearly not capable of being replied to: you
cannot talk to symptoms. Or both processes occur, in which
case both the status of reasonable question has been denied and
the status of symptom imputed.

This ordinary, commonplace, everyday action of ignoring a
patient's question cannot be conceived as a regrettable lapse
from the ideal of mental hospital practice; for it is clearly coherent with the general theory and practice of asylums and
psychiatry as developed from the beginning of the nineteenth
century. Thus, Foucault tells us in *Histoire de la Folie* (translated as 39, *Madness and Civilization*) that at the beginning of the
nineteenth century, the insane were for the first time separated
rigorously (in a *Nouveau Partage*) from the other confined groups
of society, with whom they had hitherto been mixed together—
in prisons, houses of correction, etc. Simultaneous with the birth
of the asylum is the birth of a new institutional psychiatry. For
the first time, Foucault claims, the insane as well as being ex-
communicated from society were ex-communicated from the
community of discourse. Foucault says that madness was
'reduced to silence by positivism'. He expands on this as
follows:

> Silence was absolute; there was no longer any common
> language between madness and reason; the language of
> delirium can be answered only by an absence of language,
> for delirium is not a fragment of dialogue with reason, it is
> not language at all. [39, p. 262]

This general statement of Foucault's can be compared with
contemporary mental hospital reality. Consider, for example,

the diagnostic situation in so far as it subjects the patient's discourse to a particular fate. Suppose, for example, that a patient claims 'My letters are being opened'. In a diagnostic situation, will this statement be treated as making an empirical claim which, after investigation, could be shown to be true or false? Is it the sort of claim which a diagnostician would promptly proceed to investigate? Clearly not. The diagnostician does not so much simply assume that the claim is false, for this would leave open the possibility that it might be true, and that sometimes he ought to check out such claims. Rather, the diagnostician will treat the claim as neither-true-nor false, but *nonsense*, meaningful only at the behavioural level of *symptom*. As a good positivist, he knows that nonsense statements are those which cannot be proved either true or false, and therefore it could not possibly be relevant to check out the statement in question. Instead, the nonsense statement goes down in the case file as (say) a paranoid symptom. I want to ask: why should a claim ('My letters are being opened') which would be regarded as empirical in an everyday context, cease to be so regarded in the mental hospital context? If it is said that the justification for the different treatment is that such statements always turn out to be false when investigated, this is simply not so, as Laing and Esterson have shown (71, Laing and Esterson): one of their more striking cases concerns the girl who believes her parents are trying to exert telepathic control over her thoughts. It turns out that they are. Again, if it is said that, whether true or false, such statements don't have the function of making referential statements, even though this is the form in which they appear to us, this can only be demonstrated (and the person thereby shown to be ill or joking) by acting *as if* such statements were performing their normal function and seeing if a patient responds to a standard response in a standard way.

There is a further argument to be disposed of. Suppose, says an opponent (a real one, met in a discussion), that the patient says something like 'I've been in this hospital a million years'. This also has the form of an empirical claim, capable of being true or false. But are we really to check it out? Is there really any point in looking up the date of admission on the patient's file? And is not the statement so blatantly false as to suggest that the function in the patient's discourse of such a statement is not an empirical one? Two points in response: first, that since so many ordinary statements look blatantly false to mental hospital staff, when they are quite possibly true, it might be prudent to treat all seemingly empirical statements as empirical until they are proved otherwise; second, that it seems to me that the best way to discover the real nature of the statement is to respond initially to the apparent nature of the statement. Thus, how is one to make a decision as to whether the statement 'I've been in this hospital a million years' really is an empirical claim (in which case, I think one would be justified in imputing a 'disordered sense of time' to the speaker) or whether it is an unlabelled metaphor, or whether it is just a metaphor lacking in any prefatory indication of the sort 'It seems to me as if . . .', *except by* carrying on a dialogue with the person making the claim? And what other starting point to choose than the apparent nature of the statement? (Of course, this is already to move outside a positivist frame of reference, and restore the patient to the realm of communication. Once again, one comes up against a paradigm shift).[16f]

When it comes to behaviour as opposed to discourse, the equivalent to the ascription of 'nonsense' status to discourse seems to me the ascription of 'bizarre' status to acts. But if the context of the behaviour is excluded from the frame of reference, exactly nothing is left to check the wilder flights of fancy of nurses and psychiatrists in their observation of the 'bizarre' behaviour of a person whom they just know to be mad.

Here, then, are a few examples of 'reduction to silence' or invalidation in one special institution of Western society. I think similar patterns can be found in other special institutions (compare the mental hospital reduction with the way in which teachers find so many questions *unreasonable*), and I would also argue that the separation of asylums and the insane from the rest of society does not mean that the procedures of the other institutions of society are of a totally different order from those of the asylum. Consider how the insane were treated before the age of positivism and the asylum. They remained part of the community of discourse and great efforts—often desperate, often unthinkable today—were made to recuperate them for sanity. Could this have been without a basis in wider social practices? What generally operative theories and practices might have made possible the following technique of cure, described by Foucault and dating from the eighteenth century:

> Zacatus Lusitanus describes the cure of a melancholic who believed himself damned while still on earth because of the enormity of the sins he had committed. In the impossibility of convincing him by reasonable argument that he could be saved, his physicians accepted his delirium and caused an 'angel' dressed in white, with a sword in its hand, to appear to him, and after a severe exhortation this delusive vision announced that his sins had been remitted. [39, p. 188]

Nowadays, such things only occur in films, as farce; more exactly, in the film *M*A*S*H*.

6. Conclusions

It seems to me largely futile to address moral imperatives to those responsible for repressive discourse, demanding that they change their ways. In addition, the people with the greatest moral right to issue such imperatives, namely the victims of repressive discourse, have either been forbidden to issue such demands or have been rendered incapable of doing so. Even if they were able to make demands, these would be unenforceable.

I would explain this futility by saying that for a large number of cases the repressive forms and use of discourse is built into the existence and exercise of unequal power. It is not that the institution has a repressive skin, which it could slough off. It *is* repressive, and language is one of its repressive media, along with physical coercion and economic sanction. Crudely, what is wrong with the parent-child relationship is not a repressive 'side' or 'aspect'; it is the parent-child relationship itself. Similarly, for the worker-boss situation, and patient-asylum relation. Another example which may help to make the point for some readers: its style is a *defining* and not accidental characteristic of the Socialist Labour League (now called the Workers' Revolutionary Party).

I fear that my formalistic analysis may itself give some support to the idea that one can do away with the repressive *aspects* of a social institution. For I have not articulated as well

H

as I would like how the forms of repression are specific to, generated by, and functional to a particular repressive institution. In practice, the repressive forms carry only certain messages because it is only certain messages which require this form. It is logically possible that science or truth should be communicated in a repressive manner, but it is unlikely. Science and truth do not require repressive forms of communication, though scientists and holders-of-truth may. In which case, it is not science that is to be criticised, but another institution parasitic on it.[17]

Yet if it is futile to demand that those in power cease engaging in repressive discourse, it is very important that the use of such forms of discourse should not be carried over into movements aiming at radical social change, as has certainly happened.

Further, I think it is important to combat repressive discourse and its effects. In the family situation, this means fighting among other things for the right of children to leave home, and providing support for those who do so. In the work situation, factory or industry newspapers can combat the repressive discourse of management apologists, as well as the repression of management. Faced with the mass media, individuals can do a bit of critical semiology (without necessarily ever having heard of 'semiology') and they can support alternative media. People working in established media can try to demystify their medium as well as change the messages they are sending out. A precondition of all such struggles is a sensitivity to the fact that there is a lot more to be struggled against than 'bourgeois ideology', or rather, that bourgeois ideology has many more unacceptable faces than we are accustomed to see.

NOTES TO CHAPTER IV

0ₐ. But Disraeli treated Victoria 'like a woman' (120a, Wallas, p. 192) which puts a different light on Mr. Gladstone's behaviour.

0_b. Where the hearer is more powerful than the speaker, self-censorship (for instance) will be found.

1. Another example would be that of TV, where the context, in which *reply* to messages is impossible, is repressive.

1ₐ. Compare 48a, Habermas, p. 140 on the omission of dialogue constitutive (pragmatic, illocutionary) universals and the effect of this on locutionary meaning.

2. It is the same in so far as it shares the same logical form with the first order. 'It is clear that sentences like "I order you to go home" in which there is an overt performative verb, namely "order", enter into the same logical relations as a sentence like "Go home" in which there is no overt performative verb in the surface form.' (73, Lakoff, p. 166.) In other words, both orders have the same logical form. The repressive form of discourse is a question of the style of an utterance. Now style is the subject matter of rhetoric or poetics, and I think that the developed study of repressive forms of discourse will have to draw its concepts from these sciences, as has already occurred in communications oriented psychotherapy and in semiology (see 10, 11, 12, 13, Barthes).

[Unfortunately, the generative semantics theory of illocutions espoused by Lakoff has been devastatingly criticised in recent years. For an introduction, summary and references, see 78b, Lyons, p. 778f, and for a thoroughgoing critique, 41c, Gazdar, Ch. 2. However, that said there still remains the need for a pragmatics (theory of use) which will account for the choices referred to here as 'stylistic'. Brown and Levinson's paper is important in this respect (23a). See also 73a, Lakoff. In the semiological tradition, see Benveniste's 'La Découverte Freudienne' (18c, Benveniste, pp. 75–87, esp. pp. 86–7) for a discussion of the relationship between motivation and intention).]

3. None the less, I think investigations can show the use of certain forms to be 'guilty until proved innocent', and therefore generally to be avoided by anyone intent on not repressing other people.

4. Roy Edgley comments:
  ' "Get your hair cut" may *omit reference* both to its own status and to the social relationship, but does it *disguise* these things? Isn't there a difference? Austin could be interpreted as saying that you don't *understand* the form of words "Get your hair cut" unless you recognise it as an order, and though he referred to this as *force* rather than *meaning*, it might be argued that force (thought not performatively referred to) is disguised only when the form of words is not the *standard* form for conveying that force (e.g., perhaps—to quote one of my own military experiences of the order "Get your hair cut"— "Who do you think you are, Mozart?"). Otherwise, it might follow that ordinary statements *disguise* their force, rather

than performatively omit reference to it, simply by being in the form 'Snow is white' rather than "I assert that snow is white".'
I accept this objection, for I don't want to be committed to the view that 'Snow is white' involves disguise, whilst my argument in the text requires that I do accept it as involving disguise. What I need to say is something like this: repression can be achieved by omission, but not all omissions are repressive. In other words, repression cannot be made just a matter of form. (In the case of the Double Bind, that there can be therapeutic as well as pathological Double Binds illustrates the truth of this.)

[Keith Graham observes that I confuse illocutionary force and perlocutionary effect, to use Austin's terms (5b, Austin). Though my distinction between oppressive and repressive discourse has been taken up by other authors (e.g. 89b, 89c, Mey), the way it is drawn in the text is surely unsatisfactory, since one consequence is that 'Can you pass the salt?' must be counted as repressive since it 'disguises' a request for assistance as an inquiry after your abilities, and, in general, has the consequence of equating 'repression' with 'indirection'. It now seems to me that the whole issue can only be satisfactorily analysed in terms of speech act theory. See, for example, the papers in 29c, Cole and Morgan, all of which bear directly on the question. (See also App. 6, 'Is there Power in Words?')]

5. Compare Wilden: 'Functionally, the politician may employ the analog context of his digital text to obscure or replace the text, as we saw in the television campaign for the 1970 US elections, for example. He may in other words be apparently conveying denotative information about issues and events when in fact he is actually talking about his relationship to his audience and their relationship to the image and images he projects. In such a context, the 'conceptual' value of the digital information is zero.' (125, Wilden p. 164.)

5a. The concept of 'mystification' has been most fully developed by R. D. Laing. See what is said in 122 Watzlawick, Beavin and Jackson, p. 213, and the reference given there.

5b. Colin Barker (personal communication, 1975) suggests that what I need here is a concept of 'class confidence' alongside the traditional concept of 'class consciousness':

> The case I think is most interesting is that of the person who makes such a rational calculation [as I suggest] and is disappointed by his conclusion. He says to the revolutionary, in effect, 'of course, it's all right in theory but no good in

practice'. . . . It is what is commonly called cynicism—a form of disappointed hope. The phenomenon is, in my experience, of considerable importance. I find that there are far more would-be revolutionaries than revolutionaries, especially amongst the working class. It's a phenomenon which is also important in explaining why, as I think Lenin once said, revolutions are the festivals of the oppressed, and why all important revolutionary movements start 'spontaneously'. The change consists in previous impossibilities suddenly becoming possible. The phenomenon is found in strikes, too, of course. (See my narrative of the Pilkington strike for an example [9b, Barker]). The categories of sociology . . . are quite useless for discussing this kind of thing—sociologists talk about it as if it were a measurable and static phenomenon, when the real problem is, perhaps, not class consciousness in that sense but *class confidence*, which is a very practical sort of reasoning. The distinction is something that I have found it very hard to convey . . . when for example discussing why in some ways a mass meeting is a more democratic forum than a secret ballot —because at a mass meeting each individual 'voter' is able to make two judgements more easily than he can in a secret ballot, namely (1) *should* we strike/continue to strike (2) *can* we strike/continue to strike? The response of his fellow workers is a crucial element in his decision about question (2), which is, of course, a decision about collective and not individual action.

5c. Cf. J. S. Mill, *Autobiography* (91b, pp. 72–3):
I may observe by the way that this book (Condorcet's *Life of Turgot*) cured me of my sectarian follies. The two or three pages beginning 'Il regardait toute secte comme nuisible', and explaining why Turgot always kept himself perfectly distinct from the Encyclopedists, sank deeply into my mind. I left off designating myself and others as Utilitarians, and by the pronoun 'we' or any other collective designation, I ceased to *afficher* sectarianism. My real inward sectarianism I did not get rid of till later, and much more gradually.

6. In general, of the restricted code, he writes ' . . . individual qualification is implicit in the sentence structure, therefore it is a language of implicit [particularistic, context dependent—TP] meaning. *It is believed that this fact determines the form of the language*' (21, p. 43).

7. Compare an editorial footnote in Burns and Burns (25, p. 194):
' "Phatic" communication consists of utterances or symbolic

communication which serves to create or maintain interaction, or, more positively, consensus, rather than to convey meaning or denote objects.' My point is that 'interaction' and 'consensus' are not on the same level, and so the latter is not a more positive version of the former.

8. The conative function of language consists in orientation towards the addressee and 'finds its purest grammatical expression in the vocative and imperative' (63, Jakobson, p. 354).

9. I recall joining with some sixth-form friends at school to demand that the School Rules be rewritten with *reasons* given for each rule. We would then have had something to *argue* with. Our request was refused. Obviously the Headmaster was a restricted-code user. [See the argument in 29e, Cooper, that in both regulative and instructional contexts, teachers are 'restricted code' users.)

9ₐ. Cf. 77, Lukacs, p. 226.

10. Professor McPherson does not follow his own advice. At pp. 61–2 of his book he produces '. . . a general theory of obligation, according to which obligation to a system is entailed by having chosen it.' McPherson then proceeds to empty 'choice' of any meaning by equating 'choice' first with 'being a citizen' and subsequently with 'being a social creature', thus obliging everyone, at all times in all places. Well done, Professor McPherson!

10ₐ. For a discussion of the 'political function' of the 'public realm' (*Öffentlichkeit*), see 48b, 48j, Habermas.

11. Compare Jakobson's account of aphasia (62, Jakobson).

12. In using the word 'difficulties', I make schizophrenia an instance of incompetence rather than deviance, and treat it as failure rather than self-conscious rebellion. What is weakness or difficulty from the psychotherapist's point of view, is often seen as health by the parents (see 71, Laing and Esterson). Schizophrenics only get labelled schizophrenic, I am tempted to say, when they try to stop being schizophrenic, that is, when they do actually rebel. It is not the rebellion which is the schizophrenia, but rather any precedent adaptation. [J. M. Hinton criticises my account of schizophrenia, writing: 'There is a bad moment when he seems to be saying that the illogic of severe schizophrenia is just a failure of formal education.' (55a, Hinton, p. 235.) I am not saying this; though I am accepting a social account of the origins of schizophrenia.]

12ₐ. I am not sure that the theory of logical types is the most helpful apparatus to employ in formulating Double Bind theory. Laing writes: 'It is doubtful if the logical type theory, which arises in the course of the construction of a calculus of propositions, can be applied directly to communication', 72b, Laing, p. 148). See also 122, Watzlawick, Beavin and Jackson, pp. 192–6. I think that what Bateson did using Logical Type theory could be redone using speech act and conversation theory concepts.

12_b. See also the discussion in 29b, Collier, p. 109 f.

13. In the following quotation (from 40, Freud, p. 71; Freud's italics): '*The delusional formation, which we take to be the pathological product, is in reality an attempt at recovery, a process of reconstruction.* . . . we may say, then, that the process of repression proper consists in a detachment of the libido from people—and things—that were previously loved. It happens silently, we receive no intelligence of it, but can only infer it from subsequent events. What forces itself so noisily upon your attention is the process of recovery. . . .'

14. Such Double Binds can have an educational or therapeutic function. 122, Watzlawick, Beavin and Jackson discusses this.

14_a. There are some very interesting ideas on the nature of addiction in Bateson's essay, 'The Cybernetics of "Self": A Theory of Alchoholism', in his 15, pp. 280–308.

15. This tie-up between therapy and philosophy is a characteristic feature of contemporary analytic philosophy, deriving from Wittgenstein. See his 126. [See also 48g, Habermas, esp. p. 287 where psychoanalysis is described as both theory and therapy. Habermas is influenced by Fichte who equates reason and the interested employment of reason *via* the notion of self-reflection.]

16. This is a version of a review which appeared in *The Human Context*, 1973 (98, Pateman). It was written during tenure of a Leverhulme European Studentship. Jay Caplan, Annette Lavers and John Mepham commented on drafts of it. In his *Leçon*, Barthes now describes the subject of this 'first Semiology' of his as '*La langue travaillée par le pouvoir*' (14d, Barthes, p. 33).

16_a. On the semiological significance of footnotes, see 40, Freud, p. 22, fn. 1.

16_b. As Barthes writes in 'The Photographic Message', 'a photograph can change its meaning as it passes from the very conservative *L'Aurore* to the Communist *L'Humanité*' (14e, Barthes, p. 15).

See also 49a, Hall and App. 5. There is a confusion in the paragraph to which this is a footnote between 'context' and 'structure'. The concept of 'structural determination of meaning' is *semantic* in character; the concept 'context' belongs to *pragmatics*.

16c. This is how C. Lévi-Strauss put it in a lecture at the Collège de France in 1972. But once again 'structural determination of meaning', a semantic field concept, and 'context' (e.g. 'men's magazines'), a pragmatic concept, are conflated. This is characteristic of most semiology, and of analytic philosophy of language before the rise of truth-conditional semantics and Gricean conversational theory.

16d. In 'Rhetoric of the Image' (14b, Barthes), Barthes explicitly equates the field of the signified of connotation with ideology, as also in *Elements of Semiology* (12, Barthes, p. 92). But compare the position in *S/Z* (14a, Barthes), and the remarks in 16, Baudrillard, pp. 191–2. In *L'Empire des Signes* (14c) Barthes suggests there can be connotation-free signification. See Appendix 4 to this book.

16e. Who attacked the Vatican's *Pietà* in 1972.

16f. What is at issue here is the 'proper' way of computing the illocutionary force assigned to an utterance. The designation of a speaker as a 'hospitalised schizophrenic' is something which goes into the computational index used to determine illocutionary force on the basis of meaning and (in the broadest sense) context. The 'normal' computation produces the result that 'I've been in this hospital a million years' either has the force of an assertion (in which case it follows that the speaker's sense of time is disordered) or has no decidable force at all (and hence doesn't count as a speech act in a language). If the speaker index was 'normal', then the utterance would be computed as a joke, since it involves the apparent assertion of a proposition which it is common knowledge cannot be true (compare Labov's account of ritual insults as insults which cannot possibly be believed to be true by speaker or hearer: 69a, Labov). On computational indices see 74a, Lewis. On speech-act assignment, see 41d, Gazdar.

In the paragraph following that to which this note is appended, I recommend the very inclusion of context in determining meaning or force which I exclude in the preceding paragraph. Context is always relevant; what matters is how it is used in computations.

17. Roy Edgeley comments:

'Science and truth do not require repressive forms of communication . . .' Doesn't science as it at present exists in our capitalist technocracy require forms of communication that at the very least don't invite free and open discussion. Historically specialised by a process represented ideologically in philosophical demarcation disputes, it requires institutions manned by experts speaking a technical jargon embodying a highly specialised conception of rationality and perhaps significance. Of course it might be argued that this is the fault of 'another institution parasitic on it', but this way of putting it seems idealistic and essentialist, i.e. it suggests that science could change radically and yet remain essentially what it is. In particular Kuhn might be interpreted as suggesting that science needs to be 'repressive' in a certain way, since normal science schools scientists in the acceptance of a paradigm that makes it extremely difficult for a new paradigm to replace the old.

CHAPTER V

Impossible Discourse

> Most people think that nothing but this wearying reality of ours is possible.
>
> Nietzsche

> The boundaries of the possible in the moral [social] realm are less narrow than we think; it is our own weaknesses, our vices and prejudices that limit them.
>
> Rousseau *The Social Contract*

> It is often said that men are ruled by their imaginations, but it would be truer to say that they are governed by the weakness of their imaginations . . . We have no slaves to keep down by special terrors and independent legislation. But we have whole classes unable to comprehend the idea of a constitution.
>
> Walter Bagehot *The English Constitution*

1. Introduction

Already, in the previous chapter, it has been indicated that some forms of repressive communication make it impossible for the 'victim' to learn the skills which they need if they are to comment on or escape from the repressive communication to which they are subject, or the context in which it takes place, or both. In this chapter, I explore further ways in which I think it can be said that people are socialised *out of* certain linguistic and cognitive skills, and in this way socialised *into* a necessary acceptance of particular substantive ideologies and social systems. 'Thought control' and control over possible action can be achieved not just by the unvaried repetition of the same ideological message, but also by making it impossible for a person to *understand* certain sorts of message. What the mind can't know, the heart can't grieve over.

2. Confessions of a liberally educated Englishman

I cannot talk about sub-atomic physics, atomic physics, or even physics. Nor can I understand a discussion between physicists, and I should be equally uncomprehending should a physicist try to talk directly to me about physics. I might get a vague idea of what he was talking about if he translated his message into metaphor. When it comes down to physics, I am ignorant.

But in what does my ignorance consist? Simply, in never having done physics properly and in having forgotten, to all intents and purposes, what I learnt in four 'years' of school Physics. It is not just that I am ignorant of the meaning of certain words (and of almost the whole of the language of mathematics), and of the existence and meaning of certain theories. It is also that I have never done laboratory experiments in physics, apart from the most elementary (memories of magnets and iron filings . . .). I very much doubt that I could learn physics now just by reading textbooks from elementary to advanced, and by learning mathematics. I should also need to do experiments, and under supervision. Even if I could teach myself, with a Home Physics set, it would be quicker and easier to be taught.

Physics is effectively unintelligible to me, I want to say, because it is the theory of a practice in which I have never seriously been engaged. But whilst I think that I could now learn physics, by doing it, it may be that I would find some of it very difficult to master and some of it impossible: I may not have the intelligence (capacity to learn) to master some of its higher reaches. Possibly, I am too old for it. Possibly, I lack certain more abstract abilities which would make it possible for me to understand physics (just as I lack certain more general practical abilities which make it possible for some people to take things apart, repair them, and put them together again).

I wonder whether this situation that I am in with respect to physics (and most other subjects) is comparable to that situation in which some adults seem not to *understand* the discourse of radical and revolutionary politics, not to be able to *think* in radical or revolutionary terms, and where sometimes this situation seems intractable in the face of strenuous efforts by skilful political propagandists, agitators and educators.[0a] It does seem to me that many people have not made a conscious and rational choice of political perspective, and that they *could not* make such a choice. Rather, they are *confined*, quite literally, to some variety of conservative 'world view', either through *ignorance* of alternatives, or through *incapacity* to understand them. It is with the possibility and existence of the latter that I am especially concerned in this chapter. No more than I can choose rationally between Newtonian and Einsteinian physics (ignoring questions of paradigm shift), both because I don't know what they involve and wouldn't understand if I was told, no more than this do I think that some people have chosen or can choose rationally between competing political perspectives. I am ruling out an incommensurability which would prevent a fully rational choice from behing made, and I am ruling out that an existing substantive commitment, a material interest, or psychological prejudice, bar the way to understanding. I am concerned to investigate the possibility of a simple incapacity to understand, an incapacity which might be described as *formal* in character.[1]

If there is a similarity between physics and the discourse of radical and revolutionary politics, or even, as Bagehot suggests, the discourse of liberal-democratic politics, such questions arise as: What are the similarities? Can one learn to engage in these political discourses as one learns to do physics? Are some people incapable of learning either physics or these discourses?

At a concrete level, I am particularly interested in the phenomenon of 'working-class conservatism', and the general discussion derives from thinking about that. This point could be kept in mind in reading what follows.

One of the stimuli to writing this chapter was dissatisfaction with orthodox Marxist discussions of working-class false consciousness. I came to the conclusion that emphasis on the ideologies transmitted by the school, family or mass media could not alone explain the content and structure of working-class conservatism (and here I don't mean party-political Conservatism). I came to the conclusion that the approach via the critique of substantive ideological transmission at least needs complementing with a critique of formal, abstract incapacities for thought, equally the product of the socialisation process but less frequently remarked. I am suggesting, in other words, that the problem for radicals and revolutionaries is not simply that people have got idea A rather than idea B, but that at least some people lack the means to understand, think with or believe idea B, even when it is presented and argued for in a non-antagonistic way and even when acceptance of idea B would allow people more successfully to satisfy their material inter-

ests than does idea A. This thesis may be compared to the situation of the psychotherapist, who is interested not just in the
substantive content of a paranoia (for instance), but also with
formal features, such as incapacity to metacommunicate, which
the paranoia may reveal. (Compare Chapter IV).

My 'liberal' education played some part in closing my mind
to physics, perhaps irreversibly. I think that the socialisation in
which other people are involved effectively closes their minds to
certain sorts of political idea, where by 'closes their minds' I do
not mean that it makes them prejudiced, emotional, etc., but
that it does not give them, or prevents them from developing,
the intellectual equipment which would allow them to be open
to (to accept or reject) such ideas. They are socialised out of this
possibility. That some people may defend themselves against
their own lack of understanding by resort to prejudice, etc.—
rather as frightened humanists despise physical scientists—is
not my immediate concern. (I illustrate one form which such
defence can take when in Section 3 below I discuss the transformation of 'not understanding something' into 'understanding
that it is nonsense'.)

3. Language and Logic

I don't understand physics because I don't know the language
of physics. This is partly a question of *vocabulary*, partly one of
concepts, partly one of the mental *organisation* of vocabulary—and
the last two aspects are inter-related, as I shall try to show.
These are some of the obstacles to my understanding physics.
Do some people face comparable obstacles to understanding
radical or revolutionary politics?

Is it, first of all, that some people lack the vocabulary with
which they could understand and within which they could
think certain thoughts? Though not of central importance, the
absence of vocabulary is, I think, of more importance than the
logical possibility of paraphrase might make it seem. It is
plausible for Orwell in *1984* to attribute considerable significance to the removal of words from the lexicon, for though
paraphrase remains logically possible, to actively engage in it
requires a greater commitment to thought than does the simple
use of a ready-made word-concept. Words are things to think

with, and without them one is obliged to produce the means of
thought as well as thought itself.[1a]

However, even if a vocabulary is known, the concepts belonging to each word may not be fully or accurately known.
'Trotskyism', 'Anarchism', 'Soviet', 'commune', etc., are
known to many people (though how many?) but perhaps in the
majority of cases they will be known as the *names* of desirable or
undesirable practices. They name objects, institutions and practices and they direct or discharge considerable emotional
energy, but their conceptual content in use is small; they are
used as *proper names*, which do no more than designate or refer.
The words (no more than a proper name) cannot be used to
think with about the practices to which they are used to refer.
(This is perhaps what people are getting at when they object to
labelling, that is, the use of an emotionally-loaded proper name).
In addition, such words may be used inaccurately to refer,
though this is not entailed by their being used as proper names.[1b]

The way in which descriptive words are emptied of their conceptual content, and thereby become purely referential expressions, has been amply commented upon, for example, by
Marcuse. I think that Anglo-American philosophers have compounded rather than counteracted this process in their analysis
of political terms, since they have taken as the starting point for
their analyses the actual occurrence of such words on the surface of discourse, where they are used as mere naming and
'boo-hooray' expressions. The results of such analysis are bound
to be as disappointing as the discourse being analysed. The
results of such analysis for political philosophy have been disastrous, but no more so than such a use of words has been for
the possibility of everyone's political thinking.

If not by suppression, or emptying of content, then by other
means can potentially critical concepts be rendered practically
useless for critical thought. Marcuse has commented on such
means in *One Dimensional Man* (83). There he writes of the role
of combining contradictory thoughts in a single expression.
This occurs, for example, when a policy described in terms
which would justify its designation as 'reactionary' is then
named as 'revolutionary'. This could be a simple case in which
'revolution' has been emptied of meaning and is used simply to
express an attitude or name an object, without giving rise to

formally contradictory predication. On the other hand, there do appear to be more subtle cases (and it seems that Marcuse has these in mind) where one can speak of genuine contradiction, since the conceptual content of each of two terms is simultaneously predicated and denied. That is to say, the effectiveness of the statement made by A in persuading B to adopt an attitude towards *x* involves simultaneously evoking in B his understanding of the conceptual content of (say) 'revolution' whilst describing *x* in terms which indicate that it does not possess the properties which would justify the predication 'revolution'.[1c]

I think I can make this clearer with a concrete example from the sphere of trade names. In one sense, the trade name '*Belair*' for a brand of cigarette is an arbitrary proper name possessing a reference but lacking a sense. If I ask for a packet of *Belair*, I use the name as a proper name and do not think of the name as having a conceptual content. On the other hand, the name '*Belair*' contributes to the task of selling the cigarette to the degree that the conceptual meaning (here, the literal meaning) and also the connotations of meaning (such as 'Frenchness') are known to the buyer.

But, with regard to the literal meaning, it might be questioned whether this would work as a selling force if the buyer became explicitly aware of the meaning. For if someone were to become explicitly aware of the literal meaning of *bel air*, would this not equal awareness of a characteristic so 'obviously' the opposite of the real characteristics of the product as to lead the potential buyer to ridicule the product? (In Orwell's *1984*, *Victory* is the brand name for the products with which a defeated population is drugged).

Against this interpretation, consider what could happen if the potential buyer does not accept as 'obviously' true that 'Smoking can Damage your Health', that is to say, does not accept as obviously true the content of H.M. Government's Health Warning printed on the side of the packet. In such circumstances, conscious awareness of the meaning of *Belair* would produce a situation which could be characterised as follows: the packet of cigarettes carries, printed on it, two statements which both purport to be true of the contents of the packet. One says that what you inhale when you smoke *can* damage your health; the other says that what you inhale when you smoke is *bel air*, and 'good air' *cannot*, by definition, damage your health. (I am expanding and interpreting the two statements to put them in formally contradictory form, but I don't think that my expansion is far from the truth.) Now, all students of philosophy know that if two statements are formally contradictory, then they cancel each other out. No meaning is 'produced'. Unless the buyer privileges either the Government statement, or the meaning *Belair*, the formal effect of giving the name *Belair* to the cigarette is to cancel the Government's message. Of course, the meaning of the proposition implied by the name *Belair* is also cancelled. *Belair* remains as a name, and a set of connotations, that is all, though the cigarette manufacturer, like the Government, can try to get the buyer to privilege its statement against that of its opponent, in which case no cancelling of meaning occurs. But, apart from this, giving the cigarette the name *Belair* is an attempt to repulse and reduce the critical discourse of the Government.

Marcuse also refers to *telescoping* and *abridgement* of discourse as a means by which rational thought with critical concepts is rendered difficult. He writes of this process of telescoping and abridgement that it 'cuts development of meaning by creating fixed images [which "militates against the development and expression of concepts", p. 95] and which impose themselves with an overwhelming and petrified concreteness' (83, p. 91; compare 11, Barthes, passim). Perhaps the best example of this process is the photo-journalism in which one is presented with the 'picture which sums it all up'. Of course, the picture is captioned to make sure that there is no misreading of it. But, literally, meaning is reduced to an *image*. In political thinking, I think that this sort of photo-journalism encourages the reduction of structurally very complex situations to the level of exemplification of very general, a-historical and non-operational concepts, such as 'trouble', 'violence', 'fear', 'hunger', 'bewilderment', etc., all of which have their Faces. Such photo-journalism never improved anyone's understanding of the realities or complexities of political life. Its images fix understanding at the level of surface appearance.

Such practices as those discussed above can become important social phenomena because language, though the socially produced means of thought, is not socially controlled. Increasingly, control over the development of language and its use is held by State institutions, including mass media and monopolistic private enterprise, as in journalism and advertising. Orwell's *1984* developed the possible consequences of the State's domination over language. The semiologists, who have studied the same kind of linguistic developments as those which interest Marcuse, have sometimes failed to appreciate the possibility and existence of class or other minority control over language, whilst recognising that minority groups are responsible for the creation of sign systems and fixed combinations of signs in such fields as furniture and clothing. Even Barthes, on whose work Marcuse draws extensively, can write:

> In the linguistic model, nothing enters the language without having been tried in speech, but conversely no speech is possible . . . if it is not drawn from the 'treasure' of the language . . . But in most *other* semiological systems, the language is elaborated not by the speaking mass but by a deciding group. In this sense, it can be held that in most semiological languages, the sign is really and truly 'arbitrary' since it is founded in artificial fashion by unilateral decision. [12, p. 31, my italic][2]

But isn't the situation of 'most other semiological systems' also true of natural language? Is the language of politics really elaborated by the 'speaking mass'?[2a]

Beyond the question of vocabulary, and the effects on it of the way in which it is used, there is the question of how a given vocabulary is organised in the individual's mind, and how this in turn affects the possibilities of thought. What I mean by this can be illustrated by an example from Vygotsky's psychology. In his *Thought and Language*, Vygotsky (120) points out that: 'A child learns the word *flower*, and shortly afterwards the word *rose*; for a long time the concept "flower", though more widely applicable than "rose", cannot be said to be more general for the child. It does not include and subordinate "rose"—the two are interchangeable and juxtaposed. When "flower" becomes generalized, the relationship of "flower" and "rose", as well as of "flower" and other subordinate concepts, also changes in the child's mind. A system is taking shape.' (pp. 92-3.) Vygotsky

I

has already indicated what he takes to be the significance of this development: 'To us it seems obvious that a concept can become subject to consciousness and deliberate control only when it is part of a system. If consciousness means generalization, generalisation in turn means the formation of a superordinate concept that includes the given concept as a particular case' (p. 92).[3]

Two further points need to be made before the significance for political thinking of such phenomena can be indicated: (1) that relations of superordination and subordination develop as a result of socialisation and not as a result of some inner maturation process, proceeding independently of the particular social environment. Vygotsky himself stresses the significance of formal instruction in school subjects, arguing that through school instruction concepts are learnt from the start in relations of superordination and subordination, and that this catalyses a similar development of the organisation of concepts which the child has learnt 'spontaneously': 'It is our contention that the rudiments of systematization first enter the child's mind by way of his contact with scientific concepts and are then transferred to everyday concepts, changing their psychological structure from the top down (p. 93).' This also implies that there is nothing inevitable about the development of conceptual organisation. (2) The second point to be made is that not all the words of a natural language are organisable into the 'trees' which can always be constructed for scientific words, and which makes them scientific. Lyons (78, Lyons) who calls subordinate words 'hyponyms' (thus, 'scarlet' 'crimson', 'vermilion' are co-hyponyms of 'red' (pp. 454–5)) writes that:

> The main point to be made about the relation of hyponymy as it is found in natural languages is that it does not operate as comprehensively or as systematically there as it does in the various systems of scientific taxonomy. . . . The vocabularies of natural languages tend to have many gaps, asymmetries and indeterminacies in them. [p. 456]

—something which is explored at length in Wittgenstein's later writings (126 Wittgenstein).

I think that these psychological and linguistic theses are relevant to the question of the possibility of different sorts of political thinking. I think that even if relevant political words are learnt, they need not be organised hierarchically or systematically, even in an adult's mind. In consequence, they can remain wholly or partly a-conceptual. If this is the case, it necessarily affects the possibility of understanding discourse which employs them as concepts. Lyons seems to make the same point in a 'neutral' context, though it depends on how one reads the 'as for instance':

> It may be impossible to determine and perhaps also to know the meaning of one word without also knowing the meaning of others to which it is 'related'—as for instance, *cow* is to *animal*.[3a] [p. 409]

Let me now try to illustrate this line of argument with an example from the realm of political discourse. Suppose that the concept of *anarchy* or *anarchism*, which would be involved in any proposition about the possibility or features of an anarchist society, is (partly) defined as being a *society without a government*. A verbal or conceptual tree[10] built up from the elements 'anarchy', 'society', 'government' and expanded to include the co-hyponyms of 'government', looks like this:

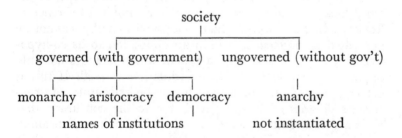

Within the hierarchy presented by the diagram, the higher up the tree you go, the greater the degree of abstraction, though all of the concepts above the level of the names of institutions are abstract ones: they are concepts rather than complexes in Vygotsky's sense of 'complex', which is that a complex word is one for the application of which there is no finite set of necessary or sufficient defining characteristics: in Wittgenstein's terminology, the members of a complex possess no more than a *family resemblance* (126, Wittgenstein, paragraphs 66–7).

Now, I think that though the word 'society' is generally learnt, it is frequently not organised in a person's mind into the kind of tree given in the diagram; it can be and is learnt and retained a-conceptually. The understanding of 'government' which such a person would then have would not be one which related 'government' to 'society' but one where the concepts of types of government or the names of instantiations of governments were used to give it meaning. This would entail that 'government' was understood not as a concept, but as the family name of a collection of particulars. It would be understood as the name of a complex.[5]

Consider now what is required for 'anarchy' to be adequately understood. My theory is that it cannot be adequately understood except when organised within a tree which extends up to and including the level of 'society'. For, first, the concept of 'anarchy' cannot be understood by reference to its own instantiations, since there are none. And, second, the definition of 'anarchy' includes reference to both 'government' and 'society' and it cannot be understood on its own level as a simple *absence* of monarchy, aristocracy, etc. Monarchy, aristocracy, etc., are linguistic co-hyponyms, but I do not see how the concept of 'anarchy' can be produced by opposing these concepts to the word 'anarchy' unless there is already an implied reference to 'society'. In other words, the meaning of 'anarchy' cannot be generated or understood within an opposition to its co-hyponyms. It requires placing in a system which includes not only oppositional features, but superordination as well. If this is correct, my understanding (which may be inaccurate) of structuralist theories of meaning leads me to the conclusion that their account of the generation and understanding of meaning requires revision. For, as I understand such theories, their oppositions are made at only *one* level—indeed, the idea of *opposition* implies that of being on the same level (see 112, Saussure).[5a]

But this point is an aside to my main object in this section, which is to suggest a theory of the following sort:

I am suggesting that adults can possess, and that some do possess, a vocabulary in a particular area (I am using the case of political vocabulary) without having that vocabulary conceptually organised, with consequences similar to those which psychologists report for the non-conceptual organisation of children's vocabularies. Not only would the existence of such non-organisation explain failure to understand the meaning of terms, though those terms might be known, and thus explain failure to understand or generate the relevant sorts of discourse, but it would also explain such phenomena as insensitivity to contradiction which has frequently been remarked in adults for specific areas of discourse. Thus, in their case studies, Laing and Esterson remark the insensitivity of schizogenic parents to their own self-contradictions.[5b] Studies of the 'authoritarian personality' report the same thing (see 106 and 107, Reich) as do McKenzie and Silver in their study of working-class Conservatism (79, especially pp. 120–1). In this last case in particular there are other possible explanations of apparent self-contradiction. Thus, limitations of vocabulary may lead a person to use contradiction as a means of conveying meaning for the explicit conveyance of which they lack the necessary vocabulary. There is no self-contradiction in the bad sense when I say of a taste difficult to define 'It's sweet and yet it isn't.'[5c]

Classical cognitive defect theories of schizophrenia also comment on insensitivity to contradiction in schizophrenics, and I think these studies are particularly valuable. (See 52, Hanfmann and Kasanin, and 65, Kasanin). For whilst, as Eluned Price told me, these studies have largely been discredited as studies of phenomena specific to *schizophrenic* cognition (see, for example, 121, Wason and Johnson-Laird, Ch. 18),[6] this discrediting takes the form of showing that what is allegedly related to schizophrenia is, in fact, related to level of formal education received. It was possible to think that features of schizophrenia were being described simply because most hospitalized schizophrenics have a low level of formal education. Theories about the 'schizophrenisation' of culture thus turn out to have a firmer basis than simple analogy. For the features of 'schizophrenia' which originally prompted such analogies turn out to be non-specific to that state; they are features to be found in the thinking of a large proportion of the population.[7]

There may be objections to my procedure of using material from child psychology and psychopathology to understand sane, adult people, who are neither children nor schizophrenics. But there is no reason why they should not share characteristics with children and schizophrenics, and if the latter are better studied than the former (most psychological studies of 'normal adults' in fact use undergraduates as subjects), this is an added reason for using such studies as a jumping-off point. There may be theoretical objections to such a procedure, but this is different from a simple dislike of it, which can only be founded on a contempt for children and 'schizophrenics'. That is simply the chauvinism of the man in the street, defined as sane, adult, white, male and middle class. So I am not too worried by this dislike. I may well be wrong in thinking that some adults, as a result of their socialisation, have important characteristics in common with children and schizophrenics. I am bound to think that the theory is at least worth testing.[8]

To return, then, to Vygotsky. In the report of an experiment, Vygotsky tries to show how children regard the name of an object as a property of that object, and thus lack a fully formed appreciation of the nature of symbolism: writers like Cassirer (26) and Goldstein (44) would say that the child lacks the *abstract attitude*.[9] To demonstrate this point, Vygotsky confronts the child with a situation in which the name of an object is arbitrarily changed: a dog is henceforth to be called a 'cow'. For most adults, I presume that such an arrangement would produce no substantial difficulties, and about the first thing a Philosophy student learns to recognise explicitly is the arbitrariness of the word-sign. I doubt that an average adult would respond to Vygotsky's questions as does the typical child, who, having been told that a dog is henceforth to be called a 'cow', responds to questions in the following way:

(Experimenter)—Does a cow have horns?
(Subject)   —Yes
(Experimenter)—But don't you remember that the cow is really a dog. Come now, does a dog have horns?
(Subject)   —Sure, if it's a cow, if it's called a cow, it has horns. That kind of dog has got to have little horns. [120, Vygotsky, p. 129]

Even if this particular experiment was badly designed and conducted, I don't think it follows that the value of such an experiment is destroyed by the claim (made by objectors to the above argument) that the child is more intellectually sophisticated than the experimenter.[10]

I presume that most adults asked whether a dog, arbitrarily renamed 'cow', would have horns, would reply that it would not (Is that your reply?), but I also presume that it does not follow that they would get the answer right whatever the *kind* of word change involved. I think that the ability to perform this kind of intellectual operation or the ability to perform it easily could be content-specific. And where the situation is a non-experimental one, from which the motive either to please or displease an experimenter is absent, I think that sane, adult people do sometimes perform operations like those of the child in Vygotsky's experiment. I suggest that in some areas, some adults do treat a word as the property of an object. Aaron Sloman remarked, in comments on draft material for this chapter, that people can be conceptually agile in some domains and straight-jacketed in others. [See now his 115a]. I assume this is so. I shall illustrate the kind of phenomena which the assumption covers, and I shall take two examples from the realm of political discourse and understanding.

(1) Consider the following case.[11] I come across a person who argues in such a manner that it is clear that he believes that if something is conventionally called a system of Justice, then it must have the property of being Just, again as conventionally defined. This entails such consequences as that, confronted with empirical evidence that an existing institution of Justice contravened in its practice the *conventional* norms of Justice (that is, it is unjust in its own terms), such a person could not admit that such evidence *might be true*. The possibility of empirical evidence being relevant is ruled out *a priori*, and this entails that for this person it is tautologically true that if something is called a system of Justice, then it must be Just. This is not quite the same kind of case as that where the practice of existing institutions, whatever it may be, *defines* what is right, for I am not denying that this person has a concept of Justice defined independently of practice.[12] I am claiming that this person cannot admit that the word 'Justice' could be erroneously applied. This seems to me analysable as a case in which the arbitrariness of the word-sign 'Justice' is not recognised, that is, a case

where the word-sign is treated as a property of the object. Hence, any discussion which contrasts Reality with an independently defined Ideal is impossible, which means that any rational discussion is impossible. Though this example, based on a single conversation, may seem extreme (and does leave many questions unanswered), I think there is a widespread tendency to use political concepts in the above fashion. Marcuse sensed it and produced an analysis in terms of one-dimensional thought.

(2) Take another example, a little easier to describe and substantiate from experience. To me it seems that some people are unable to understand, or argue in terms of propositions involving explicit counter-factual conditionals, though again such inability need not be across-the-board; it can be content-specific. What I mean is that some people respond to arguments of the sort which begin 'Suppose you had . . .' with a straightforward 'But I didn't . . .' It has been put to me that this *genre* of response does not show people's cognitive limitations, but rather their cognitive sophistication. They refuse to be drawn into the kind of hypothetical argument in which the most skilled in dialectical debate necessarily wins. Now, whilst I agree that some people use the response 'But I didn't . . .' as a refusal, I don't accept that this is always the case. My reasons are two-fold. First that one elicits the response 'But I didn't . . .' even in circumstances where the respondent recognises that it is in his interest to understand the hypothetical argument (as in direction giving: 'Imagine you're standing at the corner of Charing Cross Road and Oxford Street, with Centre Point on your right . . .'). Second, that I find it inconsistent that people should be so intellectually sophisticated as my opponents' argument makes out, yet so frequently be taken for a ride by all sorts of con-men, from politicians upwards.

I have produced only two examples, but I am sure others can produce further instances of linguistic or logico-linguistic ways in which adults with little formal education and no experience of other relevant learning situations, can be inhibited or prevented from thinking certain thoughts and understanding certain sorts of discourse or argument. Such incapacities are content-specific and can be given a social explanation. The incapacities may not always be apparent, not least if the person consciously or unconsciously seeks to hide them. Thus, for

example, when he does not understand an idea, he may say
that it is 'Nonsense'. Roland Barthes has commented on this
particular mode of response as a characteristic of petty-
bourgeois thinking (11, Barthes, especially the essay *Blind and
Dumb Criticism*, pp. 34–5). Enoch Powell seems to employ this
strategy of labelling as 'Nonsense' that which he does not
understand (104, Powell, especially *The Enemy Within*, pp. 104–
12) though here it is difficult to distinguish the use of 'Nonsense'
as an emotive synonym of 'False' from the use of 'Nonsense' to
disguise lack of understanding.[13]

The reader could try to add their own examples and analyses
to my list. Why is it, for example, that some people reply to
Why? questions about causation with restatements of facts?

4. Theory

Part of my ignorance of physics consists in not knowing the substantive theories of physics. It is out of the question that I
should re-invent such theories myself. Quite aside from the
material resources needed to set-up and conduct experiments,
one person does not have the time or intelligence to re-invent
the product of centuries, if not millenia, of collective work.
There is no alternative to reading other people's books, going to
other people's lectures, and using apparatus under other
people's supervision.

There are many theories of politics, both scientific and
normative. Most people have never had any formal instruction
in any of them, let alone the ones, like Marxism, which can
help them understand and act upon their own political situation
in the world. The *omission* of political education in *theory* from
the curriculum of schools is more important, I think, than any
substantive instruction they administer to their pupils, such as
'British Constitution', the ideology of which seems to consist in
presenting the abstract formal description of institutions as a
model of their actual functioning. Again, such political theories
as the media present seem to me either to be of too high a level
of abstractness, or to be trapped in the concrete example. It is
the middle range of theoretical concepts which is *missing*, and
this quite aside from any overt *bias*. The abstractness of media
concepts consists in the use of reified 'forces' such as 'progress',

'reaction', 'order', 'disorder', etc., as explanatory concepts; the concreteness of the media consists in the description of social reality at the level of isolated *events*. Of course, it is at the most abstract and most concrete levels that there is least disagreement (at least overtly so) and the resort to abstract and concrete may be the means whereby they discharge their obligation to be overtly unbiased. The middle range of concepts (which include concepts like 'class', 'status', etc.) is the area of greatest overt controversy and it is therefore *excluded*. (The exclusion of substantive *contents*, perhaps the most important way in which bias operates, is a different issue.)[13a]

Professional politicians are possibly even worse as sources of theoretical understanding of political reality. Their position depends on limiting understanding of politics and their own role within it. The fact that the speeches of very few politicians bear reprinting is some indication of the absence of theoretical (even informational) content from what they say. The reading public has nothing to learn from them, only about them: the Collected Speeches of Harold Wilson could be used only to damn.

To the degree that people feel the need for explicit political theories, I think they are left very much to their own devices. The vocabulary of politics is determined externally, and certain ideologies of voting are propagated at election time, but for the rest, politics, far from being the field *par excellence* of deliberately propagated ideology, is left to a great degree to be occupied by *spontaneous ideologies*.

These spontaneous ideologies reflect closely the immediate circumstances of daily life and do not transcend them; they take appearance for reality and concrete incident for theory. They reify the existing order of things. Thus, racism and working class conservatism. Reification involves at least three processes absent from radical and revolutionary theories. First, there is no theoretical recognition of the historical character of the present social order. Even if there is an awareness of the historical emergence of the present system, that system is seen as the culminating goal of the historical process beyond which no substantial change is possible. Second, there is no conscious awareness of the dependence of social change on human action, whether collective or individual. This is true of religious conceptions in which 'God has his plan', of technocratic conceptions in which technology has its own immanent plan, and in deference views in which 'You've got to have the people with money'—where a contingent feature of society, that wealth is the dominant source of power, is reified into a necessary feature of social existence. Third, the needs, wants or interests which might stimulate action to change the social order are repressed and sublimated. Wilhelm Reich theorises in detail about the mechanisms by which this is accomplished (106, 107, Reich).

Now the argument of this chapter has been that many people are linguistically inhibited from thinking theoretically about politics, and if this is correct it helps explain the weakness of spontaneous ideologies. For essential to theory (which is what such ideologies aspire to) is the employment of elaborate causal and functional concepts and the corresponding vocabulary. In my teaching, I noticed that when asked for explanations of social phenomena, apprentices often redescribed the phenomena or restated the question minus the interrogative (e.g., Why is there a housing shortage? There aren't enough houses. Compare 51, Halliday, p. 35)[13b] There was, at least, a lack of readiness to volunteer causal explanations, though no lack of readiness to offer answers.

In terms of theory, I have read and been influenced by the work of Basil Bernstein, but I do not think that my arguments depend for their validity on acceptance of his theory of restricted and elaborated linguistic *codes*. For Bernstein, it is a defining feature of the restricted code, to which the lower working class (at least) is allegedly confined that it lacks 'elaborate causal conceptions' (21, Bernstein, p. 47). I agree that elaborate causal conceptions are lacking, but doubt that the lack is necessarily or empirically systematic enough to merit the use of the concept of 'code'. If there is such a thing as a restricted code, lacking in elaborate causal concepts, then I think its existence would have to be explained by reference to the fact that some people think they have no *use* for elaborate causal conceptions. They may have reconciled themselves, for example, to their real exclusion from politics (see Section 5 below). Such privatisation would explain the use of a restricted code, as Bernstein himself indicates (21, p. 147), though I would expect a dialectical relationship between code and circumstances: that

is to say, that whilst the circumstances produce the code, the
code strengthens the grip of circumstances.

5. Practice

I don't think explanations are needed of people's conceptual
limitations. What is needed is an explanation of how such
limitations are ever broken out of. [Aaron Sloman, in remarks on draft material for this book. (Compare 123,
Wertheimer, and 115a, Sloman)]

If I were to make the attempt to learn physics, I should need a
motive (and a pretty strong one) if I were to make any progress
in the subject. I might be driven by ambition, pure or idle
curiosity, or necessity. It is unlikely that I shall ever be strongly
enough motivated to learn physics.

Could the relation of people to the understanding of politics
be similar? A motive is needed equally for someone to set out
to understand politics, but it would seem, at first glance, that
such a motive is always and universally present. For the life of
every person is inescapably a political life, and prospects of
being happy and free depend in direct and important ways on
the form of society within which a person lives. Failure to
'recognise' such facts is precisely what constitutes the psychological side of real alienation and political exclusion, a position
I argue in 'The Experience of Politics' (see Appendix 1).

Because of real and psychological alienation, the ever-present
motive for understanding politics does not 'surface' in the form
of an interest in politics, whilst alienation does surface in the
'flight'[14] from politics into 'private' modes of existence, doomed
to defeat because based on belief in what is, in fact, a non-
existent possibility of privacy. Rather than challenge a real
state of affairs, or the psychological states which it generates,
people try to escape them both. Perhaps they can conceive of
no other way out. Certainly, their attempted solutions only
compound their powerlessness and sense of powerlessness; but
why might they not be able to conceive of any other way
out?

On the one hand, I am sure that some people make a rational
calculation and conclude that change is practically impossible.

On the other, I am sure—as indicated in previous sections—
that there are people who can't or don't envisage radically
different situations, let alone believe that it is possible to bring
them about. The non-existence of fully acceptable alternatives
elsewhere in the world is a potent factor in confirming both
these perspectives, which is why it is far from irrelevant for
left-wing organisations to devote a great deal of intellectual
effort to analysing the structure of the Soviet Union, China,
Cuba, etc.

Again, it is not as if the work or the family situation provides
alternative experience which might be applied critically to the
political realm from the point of view of changing it. If anything, work and family are less democratic situations than is
politics. Interestingly, the family situation produces reactions
in children structurally very similar to the reactions of adults to
the political situation in which they find themselves. (Compare
Chapter IV, Section 3). For example, in their studies of the
families of schizophrenics (many of the characteristics of which
must be regarded as typical rather than deviant, at least of
practice if not of ideological norms), Laing and Esterson (71)
show how children respond to denial or prohibition of their
practice, or invalidation or negation of their own self-defini-
tions, by *withdrawal* (which becomes catatonia in the clinical
stage). When there is no way out through the door, or there
seems no way out, or where they lack the means to fight back
(including the cognitive means), children may withdraw as the
only alternative to complete submission. It resembles political
apathy or privatisation in being a *fugitive* practice in response
to a denial of the *need* for self-determination.[15]

Last but not least, changing the world demands a great deal
of time, effort, strength and courage. Serious efforts to change
society frequently encounter severe repression. Who'd be a
revolutionary?

The powerful, over-determined character of the obstacles to
political action and knowledge does illustrate the meaning and
realism of the Marxist perspective which emphasises not an abstract political-educational effort as that which generates a
political movement, but, instead, the force of economic circumstances, and the needs and interests which economic developments simultaneously generate and frustrate. But if this is so,

then the greatest of the obstacles to political action would then appear to be those practices which encourage people to accept frustration, or make them fearful of fighting for their needs, or lead them to repress their self-knowledge of their own frustrations. In Chapter I, Section 6, I discussed and criticised the established assumption that people *will* act to satisfy their needs and further their interests. The most difficult problem facing radicals and revolutionaries is that where people do not or will not act to satisfy their needs, where they accept frustration or repress their knowledge of it.[16]

This is why I think the writings of Wilhelm Reich deserve such careful study, and also why I think that any political movement today must itself be a source of satisfaction to its members and not purely a sacrifice. There should be nothing 'religious' about a political movement.[17] Activities like theatre, film and music should be neither decorative features of a political movement or narrowly instrumental. For in them people may come to know their own desires and become willing to act collectively to satisfy them.[18,18a]

6. Conclusions

I have compared politics to physics, but I do not wish to encourage the technocratisation of politics in the sense that that phrase is understood by writers like Habermas. That is, I do not wish to regard politics as a sphere in which exclusively instrumental problems arise; nor do I wish that political control should be vested in 'experts'.[18b] On the other hand, I do believe that theory is needed to understand what is going on in political society, and I come reluctantly to the conclusion that people will always remain unequal in the level of their theoretical sophistication, and that, in consequence, there will be theoretical leaders. But they need not be leaders in everything else as well: and if they claim to be, and enforce their claim, the effects are often enough disastrous. Leaders can also be subject to greater control and enjoy less permanence than they now do.[19] Yet it still remains true, I think, that people cannot spontaneously generate the range and depth of political knowledge required for them to function effectively as political agents. In this sense, I think my heuristic analogy between physics and politics is not so misleading, and I have to come down, against some of the anarchists, on the side of Lenin.[19a]

My ignorance of physics is historically explicable and of no importance. Comparable ignorance about politics is common, explicable and important. I think that the theories I have sketched in this chapter are relevant to political activists in their daily work, and that the effort to confirm or refute them would be worthwhile. This book would more than have achieved its purpose if some of its remarks were found useful by those engaged in the nitty-gritty work of achieving radical social change.[19b]

NOTES TO CHAPTER V

0a. In *Reflections on Language* Chomsky argues for regarding 'the properties of mind that underlie the acquisition of language and common sense as biological properties of the organism, on a par in this respect with those that enable a bird to build a nest or reproduce a characteristic song; or, for that matter, comparable to the properties that account for the development of particular organs of the body . . . Humans are not specially adapted in the same way, to the learning of physics' (29b, Chomsky, p. 155). Granting the concept of 'Special adaptation', my question is whether 'politics' is more like physics or common sense, and I suggest that it is more like physics. This puts me in the same camp as (for instance) Comte, Mill and Marx, opposed by anarchists, moral sense theorists, and maybe others. If one replaced 'politics' with 'sociability', then on one side would stand, for instance, Hobbes, Freud and Marcuse, arguing that humans are not specially adapted to social existence, but rather have to be compelled to it, and on the other Aristotle, assorted anarchists, and (possibly) Rousseau. In a review of the first edition of this book Keith Graham criticises the leading ideas of this chapter at some length (45a, Graham).

1. I am using the economic idea of rational choice between competing alternatives as a heuristic device; I do not believe that society could ever be so organised that beliefs could be chosen in a *Which?*-type way. Note that theories of prejudice or of the authoritarian personality presuppose equal capacity for understanding and choice-making. If what I write in this chapter is true, it undermines the legitimacy of such an assumption.

1ₐ. Compare this editorial comment in 64a, Johnson-Laird and Wason, p. 445, 'if language has no effect on thought processes [as they are suggesting] then what cognitive advantages accrue to those who possess it? It seems most plausible that language can provide an economic notation for conceptual "Computations" (see [36c] Fodor ...). Mental arithmetic with Roman numerals would be taxing; it would be impossible with an Aboriginal language in which explicit numbers cease at five.'

1ᵦ. My concepts of 'proper names' were formed before I became aware of the Rigid Designator Revolution, very simply expressed in 67d, Kripke, and 104b, Putnam.

1ᵧ. Compare Ernest Gellner's delightful discussion of the concept of *'Bobility'* in his essay 'Concepts and Society' (42a, Gellner, esp. pp. 41–5). *'Bobility'* is a concept with self-contradictory (*not* ambiguous) applications; its incoherence is functional, for it serves to mystify.

2. This passage was published in 1956. But in his seminar of 1971–2, Barthes was still speaking of the 'social contract' of language.

2ₐ. The answer 'No' is plainly intended to this rhetorical question, which hides an equivocation in the use of 'language' in the preceding passage, where concepts of both *langue* and *parole* (or 'competence' and 'performance') are in play. It could be said, for example, that while *langue* or competence is common property, the right to *parole* is unequally distributed, allowing those with the right or power to speak to code utterances in cognitively limiting ways. However, this cannot be the whole story either. At one level, the syntax of a language is the common property of all speakers of the language, Chomsky (for instance) stressing the equifinal character of language acquisition (29b, Chomsky): whatever sentences go into the human infant, more or less the same grammar comes out. But this happily egalitarian situation is not paralleled by equifinality in the development of other cognitive capacities: both 'semantic competence' ('The Dictionary'; see 30b, Cresswell on the concept 'semantic competence') and world-knowledge ('The Encyclopaedia') are unequal between persons: what goes in affects what comes out. Compare n. 0ₐ above.

3. If 'flower' and 'rose' are not hierarchically ordered, then there is no contradiction for the speaker in such statements as 'It's a rose, not a flower' or 'If it's not a flower, is it a rose?'. Note that the speaker is not contradicting himself; there is no contradiction for him, only for the hearer.

3ₐ. For his more recent treatment of this topic, see now 78b, Lyons, Ch. 9.

4. Not all trees are alike. Whorf (124, p. 136; see also the whole of the essay *The Relation of Habitual Thought and Behaviour to Language*, pp. 134–59) suggests that the word 'stone' logicolinguistically implies 'non-combustibility'. However, this implication seems to exist only as the result of belief in a particular theory, namely that stone is non-combustible, and even to this theory there are exceptions (e.g. brimstone). The link between 'monarchy' and 'government' is different in nature. Here, the link *is* logico-linguistic. One could say that is a synthetic truth (or falsehood) that 'stone' and 'non-combustibility' have the link they do or are supposed to have, whereas it is an analytic truth that 'government' and 'monarchy' have the relationship which they do. Whorf fails to come to terms with the fact that different theories can be developed within the same language (by speakers of the same language) and this, I presume, because of his identification of thought and language. [Compare the discussion of Yorick Wilks' ideas in 21b, Boden, pp. 171–2. My notion of an educational practice which leaves open the possibility of accepting or rejecting a given position commits me to the view that within a single language an indefinite number of theoretical positions can be expressed].

5. If I am correct in thinking that the conceptual understanding of a word requires reference to a superordinate term, then the most abstract words—those at the tops of trees—with no superordinate words of their own, would be doomed to remain the words for complexes; they could not be concepts. This seems to me paradoxical, for it is my conventional view that the most abstract words ought to be the most rigorously conceptually definable. [This looks like a 'semantic marker' theory, for criticism of which see 104b Putnam and 74a Lewis. The 'paradox' I encounter seems to resemble what Peirce regarded as the dilemma of scholastic realism: if 'Society' (for example) cannot be defined upwards or downwards, must one intuit its meaning? Peirce's solution is to propose that 'Society' is to be understood in relation to 'laws of society' (i.e., as a theory-laden term): 'To Peirce, it seemed that this relational character of all properties, or the fact that every property is essentially a term in some law and unintelligible save in the context of some law, was the most important logical lesson that modern science has to teach.' (41b, Gallie, pp. 153–4)].

5ₐ. Maya Arnestad (Personal communication, 1976) disputed this

K

criticism, but I have mislaid her letter and cannot recall its contents, though I recall agreeing with her.

5b. See also 122, Watzlawick, Beavin and Jackson, p. 91 f. on *imperviousness.*

5c. Compare 78b, Lyons, p. 418, who says that whereas tautologies can be taken at face value 'what are at first sight contradictions (e.g. *Is he married? He is and he isn't*) are usually reinterpreted in such a way that they are seen as merely paradoxical rather than as logically inconsistent. In both cases, however, their interpretation, in context, is subject to the application of procedures, or strategies, which derive from the assumption that the speaker must have had some reason for uttering a platitude or a paradox'.

6. To a large degree, this was recognised by the students of schizophrenic thought being criticised. Thus, for instance, Kasanin writes that abstract or categorical thinking (the absence of which was regarded as a trait of schizophrenia) 'is a property of the educated adult person' (65, Kasanin, p. 42). And Hanfmann and Kasanin write that 'the difference in [test] scores of this [group, largely composed of attendants at a state mental hospital] and of the college-educated group is sufficiently striking to warrant the conclusion that the highest performance level in the concept formation test is the prerogative of subjects who have had the benefit of college education' (52, Hanfmann and Kasanin, pp. 59–60).

7. The question then arises, What are the specific features of schizophrenia? Some have concluded that there are none, that schizophrenia as a disease-entity does not exist.

8. Many of Wason and Johnson Laird's undergraduate samples do appallingly on reasoning tests. This cannot just be put down to the nature of the tests, for some do well on them. It could be put down to differential reactions to the test situation. Hudson has explored this (58, Hudson).

9. The opposition abstract/concrete helped me a great deal when I started in 1970 on the lines of thought developed here, though it has fallen into a secondary place in this chapter. I would still recommend the books which originally helped me, namely 26, Cassirer and 44, Goldstein.

10. Compare from a different context the following criticism of Cameron: 'In our opinion all explanations [of failure on the Vygotsky blocks test] in terms of evasion or projection of blame on the task etc., misrepresent the situation of those patients who perform to the best of their ability but are unable even to con-

ceive of the performance required from them' (65, Kasanin, p. 96).

11. Based on a discussion in an evening class I once taught.

12. Vygotsky's child has an adequate understanding of both 'cow' and 'dog', otherwise he would not be able to make the particular mistake that he does.

13. This point was brought home to me by Chris Arthur.

13a. Compare now the treatment of television news in 43a, 43b, Glasgow University Media Group.

13b. So much for my understanding! That there is a 'housing shortage' *because* 'there aren't enough houses' is a perfectly good explanation, though one which is as it stands false, since there are lots of empty houses around the country.

14. Some people seek to solve political problems by spatial displacement, that is, by *emigration*. It would be interesting to study the political ideology of emigration.

15. In contrast, Reich construes apathy as a defence mechanism against recognition of one's class position and interests (106, Reich, p. 201).

16. 'The masses' class consciousness does not consist of knowing the historical and economic laws which rule the existence of man, but: (1) Knowing one's own needs in all spheres; (2) knowing the means and possibilities of satisfying them (3) knowing the hindrances which the social order deriving from private enterprise puts in their way; (4) knowing which inhibitions and fears stand in the way of clearly recognising one's vital needs and the factors preventing their fulfilment ..., (5) knowing that the masses' strength would be invincible in relation to the power of the oppressors if only it were co-ordinated.' (107, Reich, pp. 68–9.)

17. 'If one wants to lead the mass of the population into the field against capitalism, develop their class consciousness and bring them to revolt, one recognises the principle of renunciation as harmful, stupid and reactionary. Socialism, on the other hand, asserts that the productive forces of society are sufficiently well-developed to assure the broadest masses of all lands a life corresponding to the cultural level attained by society.' (107, Reich, pp. 23–4.)

18. Reich, in contrast, has a manipulative concept of song, dance and theatre: '... we must secure the emotional attachment of the masses. Emotional attachment signifies trust, such as the child has in its mother's protection and guidance, and confidence in being understood in its innermost worries and desires in-

cluding the most secret ones, those relating to sex'. (107, Reich, pp. 58–9.) Apart from the last nine words, this reads more like Stalin than Reich.

18ₐ. Since writing these paragraphs, I have read and been impressed by Mancur Olson's *Logic of Collective Action*. (92e, Olson; see also 40a, Frohlich, Oppenheimer and Young; 119b, Ullman-Margalit; and, for criticism of Olson, 53a, Heath), which I believe casts a good deal of (not entirely welcome) illumination on problems which exercise all radicals and revolutionaries. Olson argues that rational self-interested individuals will not act to achieve common or group interests in providing collective goods, of which interests they are aware, unless (1) the group to which they belong is small or (2) some form of coercion is employed to get them to act in their own interests or, alternatively, unless (3) an organisation which mobilises the group in pursuit of the group's own interests can offer selective incentives to participation which directly benefit individuals. Now satisfaction of condition (1) is not sufficient to overcome the problems to which Olson draws attention, which is that it is not (economically) rational to contribute to the provision of a good, if you can enjoy that good without making such a contribution and 'collective goods' are precisely those which have to be supplied to collectivities and cannot be withheld from individuals (street lighting is a simple example).

Olson's arguments satisfactorily explain the 'apathy' of groups who have a common interest but don't organise to satisfy it, and the 'free rider' behaviour of individuals who seek to evade taxes or remain outside Trade Unions whose activities benefit them. He is also able to explain both coercion (by Governments, Trade Unions and Nationalist guerilla movements) and the tendency of lobbies and pressure groups (such as motoring organisations) to provide individual incentives.

Olson explicitly spells out the relevance of his ideas to Marxist theory: 'It is *not* in fact true that the absence of the kind of class conflict Marx expected shows that Marx overestimated the strength of rational behaviour. [Olson is justifiably treating Marx as arguing that capitalism *produces* economistic reasoning in the proletariat—TP]. On the contrary, the absence of the sort of class action Marx predicted is due in part to the predominance of rational utilitarian behaviour. *For class-oriented action will not occur if the individuals that make up a class act rationally* ... a worker who thought he would benefit from a 'proletarian' government would not find it rational to risk his life and resources to start a revolution against the bourgeois government.' (92e, Olson, pp. 105–6.)

If Olson's account is true, it can explain both the tendency of revolutionaries to overestimate the benefits of revolution in Utopian fashion (thereby altering the pay-off matrix) and the tendency of vanguard parties to substitute themselves for the class, since the prospect of office in a revolutionary Government provides a selective incentive to the participation of their members, which lessens as the party grows in size.

In contrast, using Olson's theory one could argue that the relative success of women's organisations in recent years is to be explained by the fact that such organisations offer immediate, selective incentives to each woman who participates, in the form of advice, mutual help, friendship, and useful knowledge (medical knowledge, for instance). The revolutionary party cannot offer such benefits without running the risk of slipping into reformism or the risk of the organisation becoming an end in itself—the Movement which moves nowhere (cf. 89d, Michels). In seeking to retain 'purity', revolutionary groups are insensibly led to adopt coercive methods of getting and keeping members, a familiar aspect of Trotskyist and Maoist groups.

18b. Compare 48e, Habermas, esp. p. 75.

19. The Maoist criticism of Stalin, that he made mistakes, is no criticism at all. For it does not challenge his right to have held the kind of power which *permitted him* to make such mistakes. [As Hume puts it, 'if the Minister be wicked and weak, to the degree so strenuously insisted on, the constitution must be faulty in its original principles, and he cannot consistently be charged with undermining the best form of government in the world. A constitution is only so far good, as it provides a remedy against maladministration, (58a, Hume, p. 25).]

19a. Or should I say 'one of the Lenins'? Martin Barker (personal communication, 1975) draws a distinction between the 1902 Lenin and the 1905 Lenin; the 1905 Lenin believed that 'the working class is instinctively, spontaneously social-democratic (communist)'.

Bob Dent (personal communication, 1975) says my conclusion is 'lazy': 'The Lenin theory of political practice is none other than the bourgeois theory of education adapted to politics.' (To which I'd add that Vygotsky's theory of education is very much an adaptation of Lenin's theory of politics.) See also criticism of my position in 45a, Graham.

19$_b$. After completing the revisions to this chapter, I read Jerome Bruner's essay, 'Culture and Cognitive Growth', reprinted in his *Relevance of Education* (Penguin Education, Harmondsworth, 1972), which is directly relevant to Sections 3–5 above. See also A. R. Luria's *Cognitive Development: its Cultural and Social Foundations* (Harvard University Press, 1976), drawn to my attention by Svend Erik Olsen. Luria presents fascinating data, gathered in the Soviet Union in the nineteen thirties, and argues a Vygotskyan case for the causal role of social change and formal education in cognitive development.

However, it now seems to me that the strong thesis of this chapter, that 'many people are linguistically inhibited from thinking theoretically about politics' (p. 139) probably has to be replaced with a weaker thesis that many people are inhibited from thinking theoretically about politics, the explanation of any such facts being overdetermined. And any explanation would almost certainly have to avoid Bernstein-type accounts, which are now pretty much in tatters.

CHAPTER VI

Tolerance

> As a rule my mind is as true as a sphere and my character as
> honest as the day: never false if I have the slightest interest in
> being true, never true if I have the slightest interest in being false.
> I say things as they come to me; if sensible, all to the good, but if
> outrageous, people don't take any notice. I use freedom of speech
> for all it's worth.
>
> Diderot *Rameau's Nephew*[1]

1. The Study of Tolerance

Undergraduate students of Philosophy at some time in their
careers probably will write an essay on Tolerance. Most likely
they will deal with the problem of establishing a criterion which
will distinguish those acts of Individuals which the State (or
other Individuals) ought to tolerate from those which it (or
they) may legitimately prohibit and punish. Almost certainly
the student will take as the object of discussion the criterion
proposed by J. S. Mill in *On Liberty* that:

> ... the sole end for which mankind are warranted, indi-
> vidually or collectively, in interfering with the action of any
> of their number, is self protection. That the only purpose for
> which power can be rightfully exercised over any member of
> a civilised community, against his will, is to prevent harm to
> others. His own good, either physical or moral, is not a
> sufficient warrant [91, p. 135]

—and nor is any repugnance which the action may provoke in
others. It is only harm, in a material sense, which justifies interference and it does so because it is truly immoral (57, Honderich; 127, Wollheim).

Of course Mill's criterion is meant to govern the conduct of
individuals and voluntary organisations as well as of the State
and its agencies. Indeed, Mill thinks that the threat to liberty
is greater from individuals (especially when operating as
masses) and from voluntary organisations than it is from the
State. Such concerns as these of Mill are unlikely to dominate

the student's essay. He will put himself in the position of the State confronting the Individual. He thinks like a Legislator and overlooks that he himself is an Individual. Interestingly, under the heading of Tolerance he will never consider what the Individual ought to tolerate from the State. Either the State is not thought of as capable of causing harm to others not outweighed by any greater good, or, if it is, the discussion is not subsumed under the heading and criteria of Tolerance (which it could well be) but shifted to the rubric of Political Obligation, where the student will discuss a different set of criteria, such as *consent*. (I wonder why this should be so?). In this chapter, I hope to focus on some of the problems of Tolerance which the student's essay is unlikely to tackle.

First, since I do not expect to find myself in the position of Law-giver but as an Individual in my society, I consider the application of Mill's criterion (which I largely accept) in the case of the Individual. Concretely, the real context in which like many others I first encountered the problem of Tolerance was that where a reactionary speaker was scheduled to speak at our college or University. In my own case, it was in 1969, when Enoch Powell was due to speak at University College, London, that I first seriously had to confront the problem of Tolerance. For I had to establish on what grounds, if any, I was justified in trying to stop his visit or stop his meeting taking place if his visit went ahead. The harm criterion is very relevant here, and I try to indicate how it could be applied to the analysis of the case of Professor Samuel Huntington, who was physically prevented (by noise) from speaking at the University of Sussex in June 1973 (see below, Section 5).

Second, Mill's criterion specifies in what circumstances power or force may be used against an individual or group. Where power or force is legitimately used there is no intolerance, properly speaking; the harm criterion implies that some things ought not to be tolerated just as much as it implies that some things ought to be. 'Intolerance' in its proper sense only exists where an individual, group or the State is applying a criterion more stringent than that favoured by the critic who stigmatises a policy as intolerant. For someone who favours a policy of *indifference*, even the correct application of the Millian criterion would appear intolerant. Further, it should be noted that in specifying the circumstances in which power or force may be used, Mill does not imply that *only* these can be used, nor that if there is no case for the application of power or force, there is no case for the application of anything else. Mill, indeed, is quite explicit that other pressures may be brought to bear even where power or force may not. Thus, he writes:

> Though doing no worse to anyone, a person may so act as to compel us to judge him, and feel to him, as a fool, or as a being of an inferior order: and since this judgement and feeling are a fact which he would prefer to avoid, it is doing him a service to warn him of it beforehand as of any other disagreeable consequence to which he exposes himself. It would be well, indeed, if this good office were much more freely rendered than the common notions of politeness at present permit, and if one person could honestly point out to another that he thinks him in fault, without being considered unmannerly or presuming. [91, pp. 207–8]

One of the themes of this chapter is to point to some of the consequences of a general prohibition on the kind of non-coercive interventions which Mill favours. In many ways, what I shall be doing in this chapter is to measure contemporary ideals and realities against the Millian ideal. The criticisms of Mill which I shall offer are subsidiary in comparison, though I do try to face the problem of what can and should be done when the presuppositions of Mill's theory are not actually realised.

To conclude what has become a guide to the reading of this chapter, let me say that much of it refocuses the material of the first five chapters and that though there is no elaborate cross-referencing, this assertion could usefully be kept in mind.

2. The Practice of Tolerance

To adopt Mill's criterion is to be committed to the view that intolerance exists wherever behaviour is prohibited and punished by the State, or against which power is exercised by private individuals and voluntary organisations, but where no fairly direct and material harm is caused to others. On this criterion, what kinds of intolerance exist in Britain today?

At the level of Law, laws against blasphemy and the possession of cannabis are as clear examples of intolerance as one is likely to find. Neither causes fairly direct or material harm to others. Most evidence suggests that laws against obscenity are equally intolerant, for arguments of the sort that a person committed a crime because of exposure to obscene material fall down against the counter-argument that millions have read or seen a particular piece of obscene material or obscene material in general without committing a crime.

But what of laws against sedition? Or the police harassment of the seditious and their publications, even if this does not lead to prosecution? Doesn't the Millian criterion justify this intolerance, for—if successful—sedition is going to cause harm to others: very few capitalists can be convinced that they would be better off by being expropriated. How could a would-be social revolutionary argue within the Millian frame of reference? Doesn't Mill, in the following passage, show where his criterion inevitably leads in practice?:

> ... even opinions lose their immunity (from counter-action) when the circumstances in which they are expressed are such as to constitute their expression a positive instigation to some mischievous act. An opinion that corn-dealers are starvers of the poor, or that private property is robbery, ought to be unmolested when simply circulated through the press, but may justly incur punishment when delivered orally to an excited mob assembled before the house of a corn-dealer, or when handed about among the same mob in the form of a placard. Acts, of whatever kind, which, without justifiable cause, do harm to others, may be and in more important cases absolutely require to be, controlled by the unfavourable sentiments, and, when needful, by the active interference of mankind. [91, p. 184][1a]

My criticism of this passage is that Mill applies his own criterion *erroneously*. Harm to others can be justified, as Mill says; harm becomes justifiable when it is necessary to prevent greater harm to others. If it is the case (as it probably was in Mill's time) that corn-dealers *are* starvers of the poor (they can hoard corn and push up the price to a level at which people cannot afford enough even to survive), then it is certainly the case that their actions are causing direct, material harm to others. If the corn-dealers can be forced to release their corn, or the Government forced to intervene to make corn available, by such acts as people storming their houses or even burning them down, not to mention waving hostile placards before the corn-dealer's house, then it follows (since the harm done to the corn-dealer is clearly less than the harm done to those who would otherwise starve) that the lesser harm is justified. That is to say, it ought to be a defence against a charge (e.g. of trespass, damage or arson) that the harm caused was in the public interest, that is, that the act did more good than harm. Such a defence was no doubt quite unacceptable to nineteenth-century British courts (it is today a necessary part of any defence against a libel action); which is not to say that Mill's criterion might well require that such a defence be permissible.[2] In a juster social order, the Government would be responsive to popular needs, without people having to resort to force; or else there would be no corn-dealers, but rather a socialised system of food-distribution, immediately sensitive to people's needs. In a less just class society, the lesser interests of the corn-dealer will be protected by the State against the greater interests of the starving. It is then up to the people to secure justice for themselves by whatever means are necessary, so long as those means do not cause greater hardship than any reasonably certain benefit to be gained from their action. You can have a Millian people without necessarily having a Millian State.

The same arguments as the above apply in the case of sedition. The Millian criterion would show it to be sometimes justified and sometimes not to attempt the overthrow of the Government.[3] That the *Government* itself fails to apply the Millian criterion or fails to apply it consistently is of no relevance to the evaluation of the criterion as a criterion. There is nothing in Mill's criterion to indicate that governments are always to be supported against those attempting to overthrow them, any more than to indicate that the corn-dealer is always deserving of protection. (He may be deserving of *personal* protection, but not of protection *as a corn-hoarder*). Mill himself does make statements which have no basis in his theory, such as the following one:

Though society is not founded on a contract, and though no good purpose is answered by inventing a contract in order to deduce social obligations from it, everyone who receives the protection of society owes a return for the benefit, and the fact of living in society renders it indispensible that each should be bound to observe a certain line of conduct towards the rest. This conduct consists, first, in not injuring the interests of one another, or rather certain interests, which, whether by express legal provision or by tacit understanding ought to be considered as rights. [91, p. 203]

But suppose legal provision and tacit understanding disagree? And how can an interest become a right by being recognised by law or understanding? Isn't Mill committed to the view that the interests of humankind in happiness, freedom and self-development are at least relatively independent of whatever the law or 'tacit understanding' happen to think is the realisation of those interests? In which case, there is not an inbuilt conservatism to his argument.

The Millian criterion is essentially an outsider's criterion: the mob at the corn-dealer's door is there because it is hungry, not because it has decided that Mill's criterion permits their action; and the corn-dealer is loading his shot-gun to protect his person and property, not the claims of tolerance. But we are often in the position of outsiders, who are nonetheless compelled to make a judgement, and perhaps use that judgement as a basis for deciding on which side to enter the fray. Thus, some of those who initiated the action against Professor Samuel Huntington at Sussex surely did so because they are at war with the US Government and all its representatives, official or self-chosen. This is a consistent position which dissolves many problems. But someone not at war might nonetheless decide to join or oppose the protestors on a Millian basis. I shall discuss this further below (Section 5).

To return to the question of tolerance in Britain, consider some of the ways in which state agencies or private organisations are intolerant by Mill's standards. In schools, for instance, pupils (and teachers) are rarely free to express their opinions about their school or school in general; Headmasters act as censors of school magazines, and it is accepted that teachers'

names should not be named in any criticism which is permitted
—or rather, teachers enforce the rule that their names should
not be named. Isn't this sometimes intolerance by Mill's
criterion? For it cannot be ruled out that such norms rule out
the expression of grievances and the chances of remedy. Again,
private employers sometimes confront their employees with a
choice between their job and some private activity. It is not
only cases of political victimisation which come in here, but
such instances as those where female employees are sacked or
threatened with the sack for working part-time as strippers,
go-go dancers, etc. These activities do not cause harm to
others and do not interfere with the employee's discharge of the
tasks for which she is employed. Whilst it would, I think, be
legitimate for an employer as an individual to use influence or
authority to persuade an employee to abandon such activities,
there is no question but that it is intolerance to use power or
force to stop such activities or punish someone for them.[4] That
would be intolerance not only in terms of Mill's criterion, but
also in terms of the current ideal of Tolerance as it is used, for
example, to point to differences between the 'Free' and 'Communist' worlds. Things look much worse in 'Communist'
countries in part because intolerance is centralised, not dis-
persed through various public and private organisations. In
Russia, the State deprives someone of their livelihood; in
Britain, the State or private enterprise, [a distinction which
makes an important difference, however].

Importantly, not all of the intolerance of a society shows up
in visible sanctions against behaviours which ought (by the
criterion of Tolerance used) to be protected against such sanctions. For there is also the possibility that individuals may not
even attempt to say things or engage in a way of life, estimating
in advance that such attempts are doomed to sanction and
failure, because they would not be tolerated by those with the
power not to tolerate. Such an area of self-suppression—with
which Mill is much concerned—would be comparable to the
area of non-decisions in political life, the existence of which has
been claimed by Bachrach and Baratz as 'the other face' of
political power. Non-decisions sustain what Schattschneider
(112) called the 'mobilisation of bias' of a political system; they
sustain an apparently formal and contentless system in a par-

ticular substantive way. Bachrach and Baratz define non-decisions in the following way as:

> . . . a decision that results in the suppression or thwarting of a latent or manifest challenge to the values or interests of the decision maker. To be more nearly explicit, non-decision making is a means by which demands for change in the existing allocation of benefits and privileges in the community can be suffocated before they are even voiced; or kept covert; or killed before they gain access to the relevant decision-making arena; or, failing all these things, maimed or destroyed in the decision-implementing stage of the policy process. [7, p. 44]

When someone estimates reasonably that a course of action, which ought to be tolerated, is a sure way to get the sack and therefore refrains from so acting, they are almost as much a victim of intolerance as the person who takes the course of action and does get the sack.

Further, though Mill does not pay much attention to such questions, it is now conventionally accepted that the existence of a purely negative liberty (compare 20, Berlin) is not a sufficient condition for it to be said that a society is a tolerant one. It is agreed that individuals must actually have access to the means of expressing themselves, whether by word or deed, and further that they must not be debarred from being able to have something to express—for example, they must have access to the information and education (e.g. in literacy) necessary to form opinions. In these areas it is fairly clear that society does not realise its *own* ideal. Not only is access to the mass media virtually closed to everyone except professional journalists and broadcasters or the pundits of ruling groups (M.P.s, managing directors, experts, trades union leaders), but if there is any truth in the theories advanced in Chapter V, then large numbers of people are to a greater or lesser degree inhibited by their experience and education (or lack of it) from rationally forming, assessing and expressing certain sorts of opinion about certain topics. Finally, note how the arguments of Chapter II bear on the question of the availability of information, without which reasonable opinions cannot be formed. As Hannah Arendt notes:

... freedom of opinion is a farce unless factual information is guaranteed and the facts themselves are not in dispute. [5, p. 112]

In summary, in this section I have tried to indicate some of the ways in which contemporary British society is intolerant, either by its own standards or by those of Mill. There have been considered, first, overt suppressions; second, covert suppressions—the other face of intolerance; third, the question of access to, and ability to contribute to, debate or join in ways of life.[4a]

3. The Ends of Tolerance

For Mill, tolerance is not only or even at all an end in itself. Freedom also has an instrumental value, both with respect to words and to deeds. For to permit the free expression of opinions and free experimentation in ways of life is a means to knowledge (including scientific knowledge proper), and hence also to rational decision making about the ordering of society. Thus, for example, in a famous passage, Mill summarises his instrumental reasons for favouring freedom of thought and speech:

> First, if any opinion is compelled to silence, that opinion . . . may be true. To deny this is to assume our own infallibility.[5] Secondly, though the silenced opinion be an error, it may, and very commonly does, contain a proportion of the truth. Thirdly, even if the received opinion be not only true, but the whole truth, unless it is vigorously and earnestly contested, it will . . . be held in the manner of a prejudice; Fourthly, the meaning of the doctrine itself will be in danger of being lost. [91, pp. 180–1][6]

The questions arise whether tolerance is (1) a necessary or (2) a sufficient condition for attainment of knowledge.

(1) That it is not always *necessary*, can be indicated by considering the case of *mendacity*, which Mill does not discuss. Thus, an advertiser is interested in selling a product, not in telling the truth about it. If a government passes a Trade Descriptions Act which forbids and penalises demonstrably false advertising, I do not think it can be regarded as interfering with Free Speech. Nor is it even that the 'harm to others' argument is invoked to show that the harm to consumers out-weighs the loss of freedom

which the advertiser must suffer to prevent that harm. It is simply that no one thinks that T/truth has anything to gain from mendacious advertising. Consider the following example.

Example deleted as libellous of a manufacturer of jams and marmalades—T.P.[6a]

The point of this example is to try to show how Mill's instrumental argument fails to apply when in question are deliberate falsehoods. (Equally, the argument would apply to falsehoods which are demonstrably so in terms of the criteria of those propounding the falsehoods). If the example and argument are convincing, then it follows that tolerance is not always a necessary condition for the pursuit of knowledge.[7]

(2) That as a means to knowledge, tolerance alone is not a sufficient condition is indicated by the consideration that if people are not interested in knowledge or rational decision-making, then the practice of tolerance alone cannot bring it about that they become knowledgeable and rational. Specifically, consider the following statement of possibility.

The free expression of thought and opinion is established; tolerance prevails. But this does not alone suffice for the formulation, expression and attention to opinions in terms of their possible truth value: the existence of lying suffices to establish this point. Now, the context of tolerance might be such as to produce powerful pressures against the pursuit of knowledge without there being overt 'interference' with tolerance itself. Thus, the context of capitalism is a context in which surplus value is extracted from labour (exploitation), and this exploitation founds inequalities in wealth and power, which are not rationally and democratically decided upon and to which consent is not freely given. Capitalism establishes differences in power and force, not influence and authority. In such circumstances people cannot attend 'as people' to the arguments of others in terms of the cognitive status af those arguments. They must frequently attend, first of all, to the *power* of the arguer, and this for prudential reasons: there are some people with whom I cannot afford to argue, and with whom I cannot engage in rational discussion whatever the institution of tolerance says I should do. All such oppressive relationships, not founded on influence or authority, constitute obstacles to knowledge as far as I can see.[7a]

Tolerance alone is not sufficient as the means to knowledge. T/truth can only be pursued and be accepted in a context where people enjoy more than a legal (negative) equality. They must be economic and social equals as well. Rousseau comes to a similar conclusion in the *Social Contract* where it is argued that the General Will (which is knowledge) can only prevail in the absence of large differences in wealth and income. [110a, Rousseau; for expansion of this point see my 99c, Ch. 2].

4. Unilateral Tolerance

The instrumental goal of tolerance—the pursuit of truth—is in itself subversive, and has subversive implications as indicated in the previous section. But, in both theory and practice, the instrumental goal of tolerance is increasingly denied or re-interpreted.

At the most general level, the instrumental goal of tolerance is dropped from theory and practice and tolerance is taken to be an end in itself, and no more. This tendency is captured in the popular legitimating expression 'Everyone is entitled to their opinion'. This idea of entitlement—which turns opinions into private property—has no place in classical liberal theory, which does not assert entitlement to opinions, regardless of their rationality (or, for some, their humaneness). One could well claim that the fundamental right in classical liberal theory, specifically in Mill, is the right to attempt to *dispossess* people of their irrational ideas. This, after all, is the role Mill assigns to the intellectual.[7b] It is the right of *response*, not the right to *speak* which needs re-assertion in current circumstances.

In classical theory, to express an opinion is not just to express an opinion—as a sort of *credo*—but to contribute to a debate, and not a debate deliberately without end but a debate aiming at a positive outcome, in terms of the acceptance and applica-tion of one opinion rather than another. Let it be noted in this context that Mill actually looks forward to the day in which there is only one political party:

> In politics, again, it is almost a commonplace, that a party
> of order or stability, and a party of progress or reform are

L

both necessary elements of a healthy state of political life; *until* the one or the other shall have so enlarged its mental grasp as to be a party equally or order and of progress, knowing and distinguishing what is fit to be preserved from what ought to be swept away. [91, p. 175; my italic]

The goal for Mill is not to *have* an opinion, but to *do* something with it. In the modern entitlement conception, the object is to have an opinion (there is a premium on having opinions on every subject); not to be dispossessed of it by rational argument or any other means; and to leave the world as it is. I think that this modern conception functions, quite simply, to preserve the *status quo*. Nowhere has this been clearer (thought perhaps the practice is altering) than in the theory and practice of television debates and increasingly in education. TV organisations are obsessed with ideas of 'impartiality', of giving each 'side' its 'share' of TV time, regardless of the rationality or humaneness of the views expressed. Of course, this ideology often covers up grotesque bias—bias not of the unavoidable sort, but perfectly avoidable. On the other hand, it does sometimes seem to be true that if the BBC cannot find reputable scientists to deny (for example) that there is an environmental crisis, this causes panic not satisfaction among programme producers. For, to put out a programme presenting only one 'side' of a 'case' is bias. It is not considered possible that in some cases there might be a fairly well established 'side' of T/truth. Compare these remarks with those of Marcuse:

> Within the affluent democracy, the affluent discussion prevails, and . . . it is tolerant to a large extent. All points of view can be heard . . . in endlessly dragging debates over the media. The stupid opinion is treated with the same respect as the intelligent one, the misinformed may talk as long as the informed, and propaganda rides along with education, truth with falsehood. This pure tolerance is justified by the democratic argument that nobody, neither group nor individual, is in possession of the truth and capable of defining what is right and wrong, good and bad. Therefore, all contesting opinions must be submitted to 'the people' for its deliberation and choice. But I have already suggested that the democratic argument implies a necessary condition, namely, that the

people must be capable of deliberating and choosing on the basis of knowledge, that they must have access to authentic information, and that, on this basis, their evaluation must be the result of autonomous thought . . . But with the concentration of economic and political power and the integration of opposites . . . effective dissent is blocked where it could freely emerge: in the formation of opinion, in information and communication, in speech and assembly. Under the rule of the monopolistic media . . . a mentality is created for which right and wrong, true and false, are predefined, wherever they affect the vital interests of the society . . . The meaning of words is rigidly stabilised. Rational persuasion to the opposite is all but precluded. [84, pp. 94–6][7c]

I shall return to this quotation from Marcuse. For the moment I want to consider some further aspects of the situation in which the having of opinions is treated as an end in itself.

In order to secure oneself against dispossession, claims to *knowledge* have to be treated as expressions of *opinion* (5, Arendt), and in this sense, such claims are invalidated. For an essential characteristic of a claim to knowledge is that it must be accepted by the hearer too, unless they can produce reasons for not accepting it, or for accepting it but only with a different status (as when they accept that something is probable rather than certain). Their reasons for accepting or rejecting a claim must be good ones; not any reasons will do. Interpretation of claims to knowledge as expressions of opinion is a way of escaping the compulsiveness of such claims and the necessity for rational argument, which any desire to reject the claim entails. The positivist tradition in philosophy provides legitimation for such a practice. By way of crude example of what can and does happen, compare B1, B2 and B3 as possible responses to the assertion of A:

A: The US Government refused to allow elections to be held in Vietnam after the Geneva agreements.
B1: Have you got any evidence for claiming that?
B2: Ah, well, everyone has their opinion.
B3: Well, I respect your opinion.

In sequence A–B1 a claim to knowledge is *challenged*[8] in terms appropriate to the status asserted by the speaker. In sequence A–B2 in contrast, a claim to knowledge is *invalidated*[8] by being treated as the expression of an opinion, whereas formally speaking there is no invalidation in sequence A–B1, though it is possible that it should have the intent or function of invalidating A's claim. A–B2 functions neither as a question, rejection or refutation but instead—one might say—as an *evasion*. In sequence A–B3 the invalidation of the claim to knowledge appears in mystified (repressive) form. For in A–B3, B engages in evident cognitive disrespect at the same time claiming to respect the product of his own disrespect: here there are some essential ingredients of a Double Bind (see Chapter IV).

In terms of its implications for tolerance, the interpretation of knowledge claims as expressions of opinion is a way of halting an interchange which might oblige the hearer to change his beliefs. It is a clear example of a practice which is inconsistent with the classical instrumental aims of tolerance, *yet it is carried out and legitimated by means (such as the expression 'I respect your opinion') which may themselves be taken as paradigmatic ways of expressing or connoting one's own tolerant attitude*. Clearly, a different criterion of tolerance has established itself here: one which displaces the pursuit of T/truth in favour of the protection of illusion. Even where it is genuinely opinions rather than claims to knowledge which are involved in an interchange, it is no part of the classical dialectical theory that differences in opinion should be simply acknowledged ('That is your opinion') and argument abandoned ('Agreeing to differ'): dialectic is the art of reaching agreement on disputable matters.

Now I think that there are other phenomena which indicate the existence of a theory and practice different from and inconsistent with the classical instrumental one. Perhaps I can best get at them by giving a general characterisation of what I think the differences are. I would like to say that the classical ideal is a *reciprocal* one, and existing practice (and an emerging new ideal) increasingly a *unilateral* one. Reciprocal tolerance involves recognition of the right to *reply*, even decisive reply, whereas unilateral tolerance stops practice and analysis at the point of the *initial* utterance. Unilateral theory and practice accords no rights to *hearers*, who perform their duties with respect to tolerance simply in not interfering in the speaker's expression of an opinion, not only by not attempting to suppress that expression, but also by not replying.

What this means in practice is that behaviour not proscribed by the classical theory of tolerance, indeed, even called for by the instrumental goals of that theory, is now stigmatised in the new theory and practice as intolerant, as a transgression rather than an application of the tolerance criterion. For example, the pursuit of T/truth requires that the hearer be free to challenge the speaker's relation to his statement: to say, for example, that he is lying or deceiving himself. These are critical tools in the pursuit of knowledge, including self-knowledge. Of course, they can be abused. But what I suggest is that increasingly they are seen as intolerant in themselves and indicative of intolerant attitudes. They are intolerant by the criterion that 'anything goes', including mendacity. It is not only rational challenge to arguments and arguers that is stigmatised, but challenge to ways of life too. If people feel intolerant when they request someone not to smoke in a 'No Smoking' compartment, how much more intolerant would they feel if they carried out the following demand of Wilhelm Reich: 'Any mother hitting her child in the street should be publicly challenged; if such a measure were systematically carried out, the public would soon be drawn into the conflict over the child as a member of society and against its being subject to the will of its parents' (107, Reich, p. 42).

In summary, I am suggesting that a situation now exists in which kinds of practice which block the achievement of the instrumental goals of tolerance are taken as being tolerant ones, whereas practices which are central to the instrumental exercise are criticised as intolerant. Marcuse would say: Tolerance has turned into its opposite and become repressive; repressive of truth and rationally informed action.

5. What is to be Done?

The contemporary situation has the following important characteristics: that in addition to intolerance by Mill's standard, there are constraints on the effectiveness of tolerance arising from the social context in which it operates, and there is a devaluation of the instrumental goal of tolerance in favour of a unilateral conception and practice which is an obstacle to the pursuit of T/truth. What can be done about such phenomena? I think they are bad things, both because I largely accept the Millian criterion and because I think that conditions in which T/truth is and can be pursued are instrumental to the wider social change which I should like to promote.

In the long term, only a change in context can establish the necessary conditions for a perfect practice of tolerance. Only in a society of legal, political, economic and social equals does Mill's project stand any chance of success. But, in the short term, what can be done: both to make tolerance as successful as possible and to promote its instrumental aspect?

At the simplest level, it is always possible to campaign, and often successfully, against specific instances of intolerance: it seems that laws about blasphemy, obscenity or drugs can be changed, even fairly radically so, without calling into question the basic structure of society. Anyone can make a contribution to tolerance in Britain by joining the National Council for Civil Liberties.

But what of the more complex issues, relating to existing tolerance of things which ought not to be tolerated, and to the practice of tolerance in everyday life?

Let me begin with the most difficult question: In what circumstances, if any, are private individuals justified in withdrawing tolerance from activities currently tolerated? (Where I assume that private individuals have the power to withdraw tolerance.) Specifically, the question has arisen in Universities and colleges with groups of faculty or students wishing to rescind invitations to visiting speakers, or, failing that, physically preventing such people from speaking.[9]

For Mill, it would always be legitimate for one group of people to try to persuade another group, whether belonging to the same institution or not, to rescind an invitation they had issued. The grounds need not be the prospect of harm to others. The right to engage in persuasion would be even stronger where the two groups belong to the same institution, such as a University, and especially where the name of the University is involved: a visiting lecturer visits the University, not Messrs. X, Y and Z. This is not to deny the right of a group to issue an invitation, only to assert the equal right of another group to oppose it. This second right is often overlooked.

But if the inviting group is adamant, in what circumstances could an opposing group legitimately use threats or force? According to Mill, only if the activities of the inviting group would, if implemented, cause fairly certain harm to others greater than the harm caused by obstructing them. It is implausible to suppose that Mill would have ever accepted that the connection between a talk given in a University and harm to others could be direct enough to justify suppression: he only allows that opinions lose their immunity from interference 'when the circumstances in which they are expressed are such as to constitute their expression a positive instigation to some mischievous act' (91, p. 184). And this is not the case with the talks which, for example, Professor Eysenck wished to give at the L.S.E. and Professor Huntington at the University of Sussex.[10] (In 1973, both were physically prevented from doing so). But is Mill right in demanding that there should be positive instigation before interference is justified?

Consider an argument developed in Millian terms to justify the forcible prevention of Professor Samuel Huntington's lecture at Sussex. It could be argued that he was and continues to be active in the promotion of political policies (such as 'forced draft' urbanisation in Vietnam) which cause unjustifiable harm to others, namely, Vietnamese peasants. If Huntington lectures at Sussex, this is not an *instigation* to such harmful acts (the *audience* is hardly likely to collaborate with or participate in them) but does fractionally increase the likelihood of such policies being pursued. For, in being invited and permitted to lecture at Sussex, Huntington's prestige as an actual or potential government advisor is increased, as is the prestige of his government. (If all arguments relating to Huntington were in the past tense, they then are grounds for a 'trial'. But then, of course, Huntington would have the right to defend himself). Multiply this increase of prestige for the many universities where Huntington might speak and for the many Huntington-type Professors in existence and it can be seen how the universities can make a substantial indirect[11] (even unwitting) contribution to the strength and success of the policies of the US Government. (Similar arguments could be made out for the cases of playing with *apartheid* sports teams, and accepting visits from the tame academics of the 'Communist' World).

But there is a crucial Millian objection to this Millian line of argument, namely, that to suppress Huntington's lecture is to beg the question as to the harmfulness of US Government policies. It is to assume infallibility. The US Government has assumed the truth of Huntington's views for the purposes of action, but the US Government does not suppress its opponents' views. No more, Mill would say, should his opponents suppress Huntington's views. Mill might say: his opponents' own interest lies in permitting the expression of Huntington's views in order to refute them, and contribute indirectly to bringing to an end the US government's harmful policies.[12] This (it seems to me) is basically the argument of those who disagree with Huntington but accept his right to lecture; it is the view that allowing Huntington to lecture at Sussex gives one the opportunity to discredit his arguments. Huntington's arguments can be refuted by the assembled faculty and students (provided only that they are given the chance to argue and not subjected to a monologue) and truth will derive all those benefits from its conflict with error which Mill says it will derive. Assuming for a moment that the infallibility point is sound (I don't think it is—see n. 5) is the associated argument just given sound?

Huntington's *curriculum vitae* might well have included statements such as 'Visiting Lecturer, University of Sussex'. Such statements would add to his respectability and liberal image. His *c.v.* would never include a statement of the sort 'Visiting Lecturer, University of Sussex, where my arguments were torn to shreds.' In other words, what matters for professional advancement is not that your arguments are good ones, but that you get invited to utter them in prestigious places. This is consistent with the practice of unilateral tolerance, which makes the end of tolerance the mere uttering of opinions, whether good or bad. Any replies which people at Sussex produce simply have no effect where it matters, namely, in the US, whereas Huntington's presence at Sussex does affect his standing back home. In the last analysis, what is revealed is a radical inequality between speaker and hearer.[13]

[Arguments about whether to allow *x* or *y* to speak here or there are unlikely to be settled abstractly, and it is more fruitful to look at more positive practices which can be supported.] First of all, efforts can be made to reduce the inequalities of access to the means of expression, either by bringing about changes in the organisation of existing media or by creating new media, especially ones with built-in reciprocity features. The danger with the first alternative (inroads on the un-democratic nature of existing media) is that of recuperation. Thus, does the BBC's 'Open Door' series represent a genuine redistribution of access or a recuperation of dissent?

Marcuse, at least in *One Dimensional Man*, regards the prob-lem differently, not as being one of access to the media but one of saturation by the media. Thus, the notorious suggestion that 'The non-functioning of television and allied media might . . . begin to achieve what the inherent contradictions of capitalism did not achieve—the disintegration of the system' (83, p. 246) for 'the mere absence of all advertising and of all indoctrinating media would plunge the individual into a traumatic void where he would have the chance to wonder and to think, to know himself (or rather the negative of himself) and his society. De-prived of his false fathers, leaders and friends, and representa-tives, he would have to learn his ABC's again. But the words and sentences which he would form might come out very differently, and so might his aspirations and fears [pp. 245–6].' Marcuse adds: 'To be sure, such a situation would be an un-bearable nightmare [p. 246].'[13a]

Marcuse also suggests, in *Repressive Tolerance* (84), as also in the *Essay on Liberation* (85), that rational persuasion to the opposite being precluded, non-rational persuasion must take its place; to indoctrination must be opposed counter-indoc-trination:

> The people are indoctrinated by the conditions under which they live and which they do not transcend. To enable them to become autonomous, to find by themselves what is true and what is false for man in the existing society, they would have to be freed from the prevailing indoctrination. . . . But this means that the trend would have to be reversed: they would have to get information slanted in the opposite direc-tion. [84, pp. 98–9; cf. also his specific proposals for ex-clusions from discourse, p. 100]

I think there is some truth in Marcuse's position. For example, I think that teachers have an obligation to be self-consciously biased—biased in favour of telling truths and expressing ideas and opinions not widely disseminated through the press, TV or pop music. If they are not self-consciously biased in this way, teachers will (and do) simply represent the same implicit ideological themes as do the mass media, and thus cement rather than disrupt (as classical theory of tolerance demands that someone should) the existing ideological hegemony. They are then effectively mobilised against the emergence of alternatives, for all that they take pride in their professional neutrality. What they take to be their liberalism in fact cements an illiberalism. If they attempt not to commit themselves to any values, leaving moral decisions to their pupils, their pupils, often having no explicit moral criteria or awareness of moral alternatives, will simply fall into the one-dimensionality of believing that what is defines what is right. The obligation to be biased falls on teachers, I think, because their work situation gives them greater freedom to do and say what they want. They are also in a (technological) position (unlike TV producers) where they could be challenged immediately and effectively. If things were other than they are, the attempt to be neutral and unbiased in the classroom, whether doomed to failure or not, might well be justified. As it is, the attempt is not only bound to fail but to turn into its opposite, discouraging rather than promoting independent thought. At least teachers who come out and say what they believe give the pupils something to argue with; the sort of moral self-annihilation teachers practice upon themselves also takes its toll on their pupils, for they are put in a position where they are told that all opinions are equal, yet where they suspect, even if they cannot formulate, that some opinions are more equal than others. Mystification again takes the form of a Double Bind.[13b]

On the other hand, to think of counter-indoctrination as consisting in the forceful presentation of substantive alternatives to the prevailing ideology is to do some injustice both to the legitimacy of such forceful presentation (what is most pernicious about existing indoctrination is that so much of it is achieved by omission or covertly) and to the complexity of Marcuse's notion of indoctrination. For Marcuse's concept of indoctrination includes those ways in which people are deprived of the formal equipment required for rational thinking (some of the ways in which this might happen were discussed in Chapter V above). The third element in Marcuse's strategy involves promotion of such formal skills:

> Repulsed by the concreteness of the administered society, the effort of emancipation becomes abstract, it is reduced to facilitating the recognition of what is going on, to freeing language from the tyranny of the Orwellian syntax and logic, to developing the concepts that comprehend reality ... where the mind has been made into a subject-object of politics, intellectual autonomy, the realm of pure thought, has become a matter of political education (or rather: counter education. [84, p. 112]

Part of the practice which such a conception requires was described in Chapter I and called philosophy. It is inseparable also from a practice of reciprocal tolerance such as was described in Section 4 of this chapter. It is the conception in this last quotation from Marcuse which has been one of the guiding themes of this book.

NOTES TO CHAPTER VI

0_a. Cf. Georges Balandier, 'The supreme ruse of power is to allow itself to be contested *ritually* in order to consolidate itself more effectively' (8b, Balandier, p. 41).

1_a. Compare James Mill's principle in 'Liberty of the Press' that 'Exhortations to obstruct the operations of Government in detail should, Exhortations to resist all powers of Government at once should not be considered offences' (90a, Mill, p. 13), which he justifies as follows, 'Obstructions, it is evident, may be offered to the operations in detail of a government which possesses and deserves the fullest confidence of the community at large; and the press may be employed in directly and efficiently exciting to these obstructions. A hand-bill, for example, distributed at a critical moment, and operating upon an inflamed state of mind, in a narrow district, may excite a mob to disturb the proceedings of a court of justice. . . . These are clearly hurtful acts; they may be very accurately defined; and penalties, of moderate severity, would be sufficient to deter from the performance of them.' (p. 15)—none of which is true of general exhortations to general rebellion.

2. The argument here overlaps with that being conducted by Philosophers on *rule* and *act* utilitarianism. See, for example, the essays by Urmson, Mabbott, Rawls and Smart in 38, Foot. (The position adopted in my discussion is basically act-utilitarian.)

3. Cf. Locke's criterion for justifiable rebellion: 'The end of Government is the good of Mankind, and which is *best for Mankind*, that the People should be always exposed to the boundless will of Tyranny, or that the Rulers should be sometimes liable to be opposed, when they grow exorbitant in the use of their Power, and imploy it for the destruction, and not the preservation of the Properties of their People?' (76, Locke, p. 466, para. 229.)

4. The distinctions used here between 'influence', 'authority', 'power' and 'force' are those drawn in 7, Bachrach and Baratz. Power involves the threat of the use of material sanctions to secure compliance, and force is the actual use of such sanctions. A person has influence or authority, on the other hand, when they can use the respect they can command or the strength of their argument to secure compliance. (77a, Lukes, pp. 17–18 and p. 32 criticises and revises these distinctions, making 'power' the generic name for force, coercion, authority, influence and manipulation.)

4ₐ. Since the above paragraphs were written, many of the facts of British life on which they touch have become live or livelier arenas of political dispute. Even the blasphemy laws have been resurrected against *Gay News*. I only wish to point out the fatuousness of one argument which I have heard supposedly intelligent people seriously advance or seriously criticise, namely the 'argument' that it is a reason for prohibiting the expression of an opinion or a way of life that it incites its *opponents* to criminal acts: homosexuals should be debarred from public displays of affection, punks from wearing punk gear, and the NF or SWP from marching about because those hostile to them are likely to launch acts of aggression against them. On the contrary, such facts would establish that these groups require and ought to receive police protection. In the case of NF or SWP marches, it is a reason for banning them that they cause reasonable fear among citizens going about their lawful business, which NF marches through areas where black people live clearly do. (There is a good discussion of Toleration of the Intolerant in 105a, Rawls, section 35 and of civil disobedience in Chapter VI. There is also an interesting passage in 92c, Nozick, pp. 264–5.)

5. Is this so? It is possible to recognise that one *may* be wrong, though one's evidence assures one that one is right. Roy

Edgley writes 'the argument that to compel an opinion to silence is to assume infallibility, is simply false' Compare Chapter II.

6. Roy Edgley comments: 'The question also arises of whether knowledge is always a good thing. Mill assumes in each of the points quoted the value of truth, and possibly the *overriding* value of truth. This ignores the fact that some truths are trivial and not worth knowing (especially since we can't just 'be still and know' but need actively to acquire knowledge, something that may absorb scarce resources), and also the fact that some truths and knowledge may be positively harmful or inhumane. This latter possibility is the crucial one in a kind of society Mill didn't envisage, a technological society, i.e. one in which scientific knowledge has an application to practical problems as technology, and where there's division of labour between the scientists who discover knowledge and formulate theories, and government or business who apply them. (Technological) knowledge is power. Increase of such knowledge is thus increase of power. Increase of power, especially to some agents, is far from being always good. See the Huntington case.'

6a. The paragraph missing here has aroused more interest than most of the paragraphs actually printed. I wanted to indicate to the reader that books do run into local difficulties with the law (or lawyers). When my *Television and the February 1974 General Election* (99b, Pateman) was read for libel, even a passage in an article by John Dearlove which had twice before appeared in print (in *The Observer* and *Index*) had to be deleted to satisfy the libel lawyer's objections, it being a libel to repeat a libel. (See the dots at p. 40 which no one would guess represent the discourse of the law.)

7. Mill expresses doubts as to whether certain practices, thought undesirable but not occasioning harm, should be allowed where their proponents are seeking or receiving pecuniary gain from their activities (91, pp. 231–2). One of Mill's statements, however, might seem to preclude banning an advertisement: 'There is the greatest difference between presuming an opinion true, because, with every opportunity for contesting it, it has not been refuted, and assuming its truth for the purpose of not permitting its refutation. Complete liberty of contradicting and disproving our opinion is the very condition which justifies us in assuming its truth for the purposes of action' p. (145). This quotation does not, however, tell us what can be done legitimately when an opinion *has been* refuted. And in the case of the advertising

claim, to suppress it is not to suppress the right of the manufacturer to try to convince the public analyst that he is wrong.

7a. But how one proceeds politically having discovered all this depends upon how one evaluates the role of knowledge. It is
surely strange in criticising a social system to rely *just* on the
argument that it is an obstacle to knowledge.

7b. This comes out clearly in 91c, Mill, and in certain passages in
91a, Mill, who quotes Grote saying dialectics 'is useful for our
intercourse with the multitude; for the procedure directs us to
note and remember the opinions of the multitude, and such
knowledge will facilitate our intercourse with them: we shall
converse with them out of their own opinions, which we may
thus be able beneficially to modify.' (p. 508).

Mill's adherence to a dialectical theory of knowledge allows
him to justify a political position (that of *On Liberty*) by epistemological arguments: freedom is a condition of the possibility
of knowledge. (See my 99c).

7c. Lukes singles out this passage as being incompatible with the
relativism espoused in Chapter I (77b, Lukes).

8. I define the difference between *invalidation* and *challenge* as follows: *Invalidation* is a process or result of communication which
involves denial of the status of a person's utterance, or equally
the imputation of a different statement from the one actually
made. It affects the speaker in ways which may become of
clinical significance (cf. treatment of the Double Bind hypothesis in Chapter IV, Section 3). It may occur in situations
where speaker and hearer are either of equal or unequal power.
To escape invalidation involves being able to understand and
state what is going on, which requires relevant cognitive skills
and freedom to criticise, neither of which are necessarily available. *Challenge* is always explicit, whereas invalidation may be
implicit, and challenge involves the making of a meta-statement
about an utterance or about the speaker's relation to the utterance. (Compare *122*, Watzlawick *et al.*, pp. 83–90).

9. An obvious comparison, though one not frequently made, is
with the activities of hunt saboteurs.

10. In contrast, the circumstances of Enoch Powell's speeches on
race have constituted them a positive instigation to mischievous
acts, namely, physical assaults on black people. Hence the demand that he be prosecuted under the Race Relations Act.

11. Their direct involvement has been amply documented. See, for
example, 29, Chomsky.

12. The way in which one may legitimately assume the truth of

one's own views for the purposes of action is to lend whatever material support one can to the NLF of Vietnam.

13. Roy Edgley comments: 'The trouble with this argument about Huntington is this. The lecture he was scheduled to give wasn't necessarily on the Vietnam war and his published views on it. So if his arguments had been torn to shreds and the fact had been well enough publicised to have reduced his reputation, this might have had little bearing on the forced-draft urbanisation theory. More specifically, that theory was not attacked on the ground of its falsity. The objection was rather to the role of Huntington and other scientists, intellectuals, experts, academics in helping to promote inhumane American policies by providing, under the protection of the academic freedom doctrine, 'value-free' knowledge that had an obvious strategic value to their employers, the US Government. In your terms, it was an intervention at the meta-level. In a technological society heavily dependent on expertise the structural relations involved in the production of knowledge powerfully encourage politically reactionary tendencies both in research and in the use and application of research findings, i.e. in a society with a military-industrial-political-academic complex. Mill failed to foresee this possibility, seeing the intellectual as an independent critic rather than an academic whose institution had 'joined the monolith' (Fulbright). In this contemporary context, Mill's liberalism, with its case for freedom of speech and thought adapted into the doctrine of academic freedom, seems to me, however progressive in his own time, to be a potent part of the technocratic ideology. One reason for this is that it puts two strong barriers between thought and speech on the one hand and the raising of utilitarian considerations on the other. First, Mill's general doctrine of liberalism is utilitarianism of a very indirect sort, ruling out for action in general a whole range of utilitarian considerations as inapplicable. Second, thought and speech specifically are further protected from utilitarian questions about the harm they may do by such assumptions as this, that truth and knowledge in general are good, useful, and necessary, and that their effects are in any case very indirect. The effect of this is to make freedom of speech and thought practically universal, distinguishing speech and thought from (other) action by practically ruling out as illegitimate the question of their utility and possible harm and so protecting the assumption that they're always good: indeed, in the famous passage you quote on p. 159 Mill himself seems to treat truth and knowledge as uncondi-

tionally valuable, since his whole argument simply aims to show that freedom is essential not to happiness but to truth and knowledge. When we approach knowledge not as the philosophers have done, but see that it too is a commodity with its own mode of production, a part of the economy with its productive and social relations, and in particular that on a large scale the production of this commodity is now under the economic control of government and business, questions about the social value, and especially the political effects and utility, of this or that sort of knowledge, must be raised and must not be submerged, as Mill's liberalism tends to submerge them.'

13$_a$. Marcuse's suggestion is traditional to the Frankfurt School: writing in 1944, Adorno and Horkheimer took the view that 'If most of the radio stations and movie theatres were closed down the consumers would probably not lose so very much' (1b, Adorno and Horkheimer, p. 139). The obvious objection to all such suggestions is that they envisage administrative solutions to cultural and political questions, and so put the authors in the same league as Zhdanov. Mayakovsky had more political and cultural sense in proclaiming that one answers a poem with a poem, not an administrative ban (see 88b, Mayakovsky).

13$_b$. What is needed here is a proper analysis of the concept of 'bias'. For its historical origins in empiricist epistemology, see 76a, Locke.

CHAPTER VII

Concluding Remarks [1]

To conclude, there is nothing in this whole Discourse . . . as far as I can perceive, contrary either to the word of God, or to good Manners; or to the disturbance of Publique Tranquillity. Therefore I think it may be profitably printed, and more profitably taught in the Universities, in case they also think so, to whom the judgement of the same belongeth. For seeing the Universities are the Fountains of Civill and Morall Doctrine, from whence the Preachers, and the Gentry, drawing such water as they find, use to sprinkle the same (both from the Pulpit, and in their conversation) upon the People, there ought certainly to be great care taken to have it pure, both from the Venime of Heathen Politicians, and from the Incantation of Deceiving Spirits. And by that means the most men, knowing their Duties, will be the less subject to serve the Ambition of a few discontented persons, in their purposes against the State; and be the less grieved with the Contributions necessary for their Peace, and Defence.

Hobbes *Leviathan*

1. Self Criticism

The greatest weakness of this book is the absence of conclusive or even substantial evidence for many of its claims. As an individual, I have not had the time or inclination to comb the academic journals of a number of disciplines looking for confirming or disconfirming evidence for my ideas.

On the other hand, much of the material of this book is suitable for less formal discussion, indeed, it is intended for a discussion very different from that of the academic. If political activists will argue about the ideas of this book over a drink in a pub, then I shall be happy.

A second weakness of this book is its failure to link its treatment of communication to the work situation of various groups in society. Whilst I have read some of the relevant literature, I have not found enough material in it to establish the kind of connections which I am sure exist. Had I some solid industrial experience, I could perhaps have made more suggestions than I have done. The most fruitful line of research would seem to be that which attempts to connect assembly line technologies, which isolate workers from each other in individual, meaning-

M

less routines, with domestic privatisation and from that with the sort of 'linguistic privatisation' which is one of the themes of this book. Of course any such developments cannot be separated from the effects of TV. Nor are they likely to be illuminated by a narrowly empirical study. A great deal of theoretical reflection is required to which workers are likely to contribute as much, if not more, than academics. The two brought together by shared political concerns would be an unbeatable intellectual combination.

A third weakness of this book is its political vacillation. In such phrases as 'radical and revolutionary', I have tried to make the discourse of this book open to a wider public than its presuppositions possibly allow. For, though far from explicit in what I have written, I think I owe my greatest debts to Marxism and the revolutionary left despite the fact that I am sure this book will be rejected by many Marxists and revolutionaries, among whom I cannot count myself. I am a solitary intellectual belonging to no party.

2. Self Defence

How then do I defend this book if it has three major areas of weakness apparent to its own author—and how many other weaknesses apparent to others?!

I would defend it by suggesting that it be compared with recent Marxist contributions to the theory of ideology and false consciousness. Compare it for example, to relevant contributions in *New Left Review*. I have been subscribing to *NLR* since 1967, and whilst it is always of interest, few of its articles in the relevant area seem to bear on problems in a way which could lead to a union of theory and practice. The articles, with exceptions such as Enzensberger's study of the mass media in *NLR 64* (34) remain academic. I have tried to write a contribution to a theory *for* a practice, and want the book to be judged by whether it is possible for its ideas to be used *in* a practice.

The journal *International Socialism* can be criticised in terms similar to those I have applied to *NLR*, though the journal has made less of an attempt to contribute to the theory of ideology, a weakness reflected in the cultural pages of the weekly *Socialist Worker*.

Again, recent contributions within Marxism to the theory of ideology have, with few exceptions, relied heavily on the approach adopted in the Marxist classics, to which little reference has been made in this book. I don't think the classics can cope with contemporary reality, and I have tried to show how within academic literature there may be found approaches which yield a political 'application': as it were, I have treated academic literature as a curate's egg.

On the other hand, most of what I have written does not seem inconsistent with a Marxist problematic. Lukacs, for example, draws a crucial distinction between *actual* (psychological) and *possible* class consciousness, defining the latter as

> ... the thoughts and feelings which men would have in a particular situation if they were able to assess both it and the interests arising from it in their impact on immediate action and on the whole structure of society. [77, p. 51]

I think I could claim that part of this book is an attempt to explain why and how 'men' are not *able* to perform this assessment, in other words, why and how actual and possible class consciousness diverge. And I have done so from the point of view of theorising a practice which would attempt to close the gap.

But it will be said that I offer no systematic prescriptions for practice in this book, only hints. Here I would offer a theoretical defence. No one who has studied recent developments in the philosophy of science, or equally pedagogy, can doubt that the days of a single canon of rules for thought, experiment or learning are finished (see especially the writings of Feyerabend and of the de-schoolers: 60, Illich; 108, Reimer; 100, Paton; 103, Postman and Weingartner). No more, I think, can one produce a primer for philosophical or political-educational practice or ideological struggle. I have criticised rationally erroneous, idle and repressive discourse and tried to show how discourse might be made impossible. But apart from the minimal conception sketched in Chapter I and suggestions throughout the book, I have not presented a model of Ideal Discourse.[2] For whilst at one moment, rational, serious and scientific discourse may be what is required, at another, it may be the anarchic, joyful and outrageous which is needed. The only common denominator will be the concern for truth, freedom and happiness: and the pursuit of these cannot be reduced to a set of rules. Barthes (14) defines Utopian discourse as that which offers rules for the achievement of some good: communion with God in the case of Loyola; happiness in the case of Fourier; pleasure in the case of Sade. The fact that there are few rules in this book hopefully means that I have produced a dialectical, not Utopian, discourse, displaying some of the virtues of negative thinking. But that is a positive claim to be left to the judgement of my readers.

April–September 1973
Revised 1979

NOTES TO CHAPTER VII

1. Apart from correcting a misprint, deleting two words, and adding this note and the next I have left these *Concluding Remarks* unaltered.
2. A 'model of Ideal Discourse' is surely implied throughout the whole of this book, as also a model of ideal communicative competence. My mistake in this final paragraph of the book is to conflate *ideal* with *context independent* discourse or competence. But to say that context always modifies what is appropriate is not to deny that there is something to be modified, and indeed I refer to a 'common denominator' in the shape of 'the concern for truth, freedom and happiness'. Habermas has done a great deal in the tradition of Kant and Peirce to articulate what is always—already presupposed in human communication (see 48a, 48f, Habermas), and so have Searle and Grice (114b, Searle, 47a, Grice).

APPENDICES

APPENDIX 1

The Experience of Politics [1]

Rightly or wrongly, everyone reading this sentence will be held responsible—legally and morally—for their actions, until such time as a court or a doctor decides otherwise. Even aside from this accountability, most of us will have to consider from time to time what is the morally right course of action and—hopefully—behave accordingly. In these two ways, people are—as a matter of fact—*moral agents*.

But how are they *political agents*? Professor Oakeshott, a reactionary thinker, describes politics as 'the activity of attending to the general arrangements of a set of people' (92d, Oakeshott, p. 2). Unless we are professional politicians in power, then it would seem that we take part in this activity only *indirectly*: when we vote and when we speak our mind about the government and political issues.

Voting in an election both is and seems to be an act which simultaneously excludes and absolves us from further political acts for four or five years. How else could it come to be regarded as *the* political part of our lives? Once 'they' have been elected, 'we' are inclined to let them get on with it—not that we have much choice. Furthermore, people do not, by and large, believe that their votes have appreciable effect, in the sense that they do not seem to tie (and how could they?) the Government elected to any specific policy; that is, in fact, the case. For it is notorious that though in voting we may think we are giving a party a mandate to carry through the programme announced in its manifesto, we also know that the Government is not bound by whatever it is that we think we are doing (though the Government *may* have to take into account what we think we are doing if it wishes to be re-elected). The extent to which these and similar assertions about relations between electorate and Government are true is a matter for the political *scientist* to investigate. Of course, no party may come forward even in its manifesto with policies which a body of electors want to be implemented.

On the other hand, as far as most political *philosophers* are concerned the *act* of voting is a way of consenting both to the form of government under which we live and to the actual Ministry which emerges from the election. Specifically, it is seen as a way of consenting which is implicitly binding, like a promise. If you ask, 'Why ought I to obey the Government?' the philosopher is likely, among other things, to say: 'Because by voting you promised to.' Of course, he will say much else besides, for he wants to say that even people who have not voted at all ought to obey the government (which means, in effect, obeying the law). Thus, John Locke, the eighteenth-century English philosopher, introduces a notion of *tacit consent* that would effectively oblige everybody:

> Every man, that hath any Possession, or Enjoyment, of any part of the Dominions of the Government, doth thereby give his *tacit consent*, and is as far forth obliged to Obedience to the Laws of that Government, during such Enjoyment ... whether it be barely travelling freely on the Highway.
> [Second Treatise on Government (76 Locke, para 119)]

Some writers do not agree. They think it is paradoxical *both* to say that, as a matter of fact, people have little or no control over what the Government *does*, but that nevertheless (and for other reasons) Governments ought to be obeyed: the right of putting in and turning out Governments seems to them insufficient to oblige people to obey, for this right does not, alone, confer effective control. And if it is said that if one does not approve of what the Government does, then one can emigrate, and if one does not one is tacitly consenting and ought therefore to obey—then it can be objected that emigration has to be feasible.

It is useful to reflect on the act of voting. This is political participation, but participation which *excludes* us from further participation and absolves us from so doing; we have done our bit, as it were, and can rest content (though, as a matter of fact, people express considerable discontent). Consider this notion I have developed which involves the suggestion that we do not control the decisions the decision-makers make. (We may control *who* they are, but not *what* they do; and as far as I am concerned, it is irrelevant *who* plunges me into a nuclear war—it is the decision which is important). If this is the case, then it is an objective fact. It is a fact about what people feel, subjectively, that they take some solace in having the right to assign the levers of power among two or more competing groups (in the way that one can, by contract, alienate a piece of land, so one can alienate power—though it may be an illusion that one has it to sign over in the first place: one may lawfully elect a government and see it disappear in a military coup. Power and right do not necessarily coincide.) 'Democracy' means that power resides in the people, even if they choose to transfer its exercise to a few of their number. If one thinks that the vote is *for* the assigning of power, then in voting, one fulfils one's obligations as a voter: that is how things are.

This is certainly how things are, but one goes wrong if one thinks this is how they have to be. For, though it is true in British political life that we give up power (ideally but perhaps illusorily) in voting, this is not true in the way that it is necessarily true that I shall, one day, give up the ghost. That is to say, it is not a fact of nature, which though it may be modified by human action, exists independently of it. Human facts, unlike things and events in the world of nature, depend for their existence on what human beings *do*. The point can be illustrated in the following simple manner: if everyone in the world simultaneously committed suicide, there would still be trees in Parliament Square, the buildings now called Parliament, and so on; but there would be no general elections, no Prime Minister, etc.

Sociologists have used the word 'reification', meaning literally 'thing-ification', to describe those situations where human beings treat human activities and the institutions, like general elections, maintained by those activities *as if* they were like things in the natural world. They also call reified those activities and institutions which are dehumanised as a matter of fact, and treat the former fallacious attitude as expressive of the latter state of affairs. Many idiomatic expressions like, 'It's human nature', 'That's life', frequently occur in utterances which commit the fallacy of reification (the fallacy comes in where one regards human facts as *unalterably* like natural facts, not where one accurately describes dehumanised states of affairs). For example, economists tend to view economic life in terms of an interaction between *commodities* in the market, and see the fate of man as hingeing on price fluctuations—they speak of men being thrown out of work *by* a fall on the gold market. Yet as Marx long ago pointed out:

> It is plain that commodities cannot go to market and make exchanges of their own account. We must, therefore, have recourse to their guardians, who are also their owners. Commodities are things, and therefore without power of resistance against man. . . . In order that these objects may enter into relation with each other as commodities, their guardians must place themselves in relation to one another. [88a, Marx, p. 84]

These are philosophical points—of course, in the *last analysis* the existence of a realm called 'economics' or 'politics' depends on human activities; but we tend to 'forget' this and imagine otherwise, because in a different, but equally important sense, these realms do not depend on our activities in the sense that we do not *control* the decision-makers' decisions in the way I control my own activities (except when I am coerced, asleep, mad or under the influence). Yet there is nothing which makes this *inevitably* so. Of course, we may be prepared to let things go and say, 'Let them get on with it' (rather as the hymn says 'Trust and obey/There's no other way'). The only problems this attitude raises, however, are (a) how they get on with 'it' has very deep effects on how we get on with anything at all, since the 'it' they get on with is identical with ordering our lives in particular ways; hence (b) they cannot get on with 'it', or anything at all, unless we carry on in a certain way.

Confining ourselves to politics, consider first point (a). If we think of government in terms of its impact on us individually, we do not have to look far for it; through laws we have to obey, taxes we should pay, through governmental provision for education (including religious instruction), health, etc. The extreme case is presumably where the Government calls on us to fight in consequence of a war it has declared. Now consider point (b). No government can function without some minimum of externally uncoerced compliance from those subject to it: it simply could not make us obey all its decrees out of fear of other-inflicted punishment, for it could not have the resources to detect and punish every misdemeanor unless we spied either on ourselves or were spied on electronically, as in George Orwell's *1984*. Of course, in relation to a *single* individual's relationship to the state, we can loosely speak of the two as opposed; when we think of all individuals, we can only speak of some individuals as opposed to others or themselves in the relations they have with each other or themselves. Political society considered objectively (although we must not forget we are ourselves *in* one) is no more than an ensemble of social relationships which may, of course, be very unequal.

From these points, we can derive two others. By analogy with the alienation of property by contract, we can say that when what the state does is not controlled by us and is experienced by us as nothing to do with us, then we can say that it appears alien to us. Yet—drawing on our earlier reflections—we can say that it is in the last analysis (which, if you think about it, is also the *first*), sustained by our activities. From this it follows that to the extent that the State is and appears alien, the activities which sustain it are and appear alien. That is to say, what we do has (and seems to have) only a coincidental relationship with what we want to do, indeed, with our *selves*. If we are prepared to let 'them' get on with 'it', we must also be prepared ourselves to knuckle down and get on with 'it', as defined by them—and then, of course, we are letting our activity be an 'it'. Of course, what the government requires of me may coincide with what I want to do. But even if I *want* to fight in Vietnam, I can only do so if I am permitted or ordered to; it is no good volunteering to do battle if peace has broken out. Hence, even if my private wish coincides with the State's demands of me, I am dependent on the objective demand for the possibility of fulfilling my wish. In this case, we can say the initiation of the activity is alien to me; it is also true that I have to bring an activity to an end when required by someone else. Further, the activity can be *sustained* only so long as the other demands it. What price my wishes?—heads you win, tails I lose. Of course, I do not want to suggest that this could ever be entirely otherwise—I do not want to confuse alienation with the very existence of society, as some ultraindividualists would do.

Now in such circumstances it is highly likely that we shall commit the fallacy of reification. For, it is precisely in such circumstances that it will appear that human institutions (government and so on), sustained by human activity are in the same class as those natural phenomena which are, in principle, not dependent on us for their existence: we shall treat a call to fight in Vietnam as if it were an act of God or as if it were a thunderbolt, rather than a demand backed up by the threat of force, made by some men of other men. And if we commit this mistake, then we are no longer in a position to see the human nature of human institutions. Only, if we do *not* live in a reified fantasy world can we see the sense of John and Yoko's 1969 Christmas message, 'War is Over!—if you want it'.

But their Christmas message, while it recognises that war is a human institution, wrongly suggests that it is a human institution over which we have individual control. It is not true that war can end if I want it to in the way that it is true that I can stop writing if I want to; I am not, personally, fighting. The confusion which frequently emerges here is between individual and general. Though the existence of war depends on what millions of individuals do simultaneously, it does not depend on what I do individually and separately. If I thought it did, I should be in a mental hospital. But even more strongly, from what I said earlier it does not depend on what *many* individuals do separately but simultaneously or even together and simultaneously: a majority of people in the world wanting America out of Vietnam (or a majority of Americans or Vietnamese— and who should it be?) does not mean that the Americans will leave. Far from it. But then to whom does the sphere of political decision-making belong? It can only belong to persons other than myself (barring the extreme cases discussed below). Who are these persons? In the first instance, the Government. What, then, is the Government? Why does it pursue certain policies and not others? In whose interests are the policies which it does pursue?

In the logically possible extreme case, alienation could be so great that the war in Vietnam could carry on even if *every* single US soldier in Veitnam and every person in America was opposed to it. This is not going to happen, as a matter of fact, but the nature of such a situation is worth investigating. In the case in question, the motive for acting against belief might be fear. But of whom? The court martial composed of other soldiers equally opposed to the war and the firing squad composed of. . . . In which case, we can legitimately say that the activity of fighting is *coerced*. But, then, who coerces the coercers? Answer: themselves. This could occur in two ways. First, they may reify what they are doing, that is their roles. This is equivalent to saying that they treat an utterance like 'I'm only doing my job' *as if* it were an utterance like 'I will die'. Dying is not something I can stop; but I can down tools. Or, second, downing tools would produce such a burden of guilt that they carry on with their job as the lesser evil. But, on reflection, the second way would probably involve reification too, for what sorts of considerations could make me feel guilty: it would be absurd to feel I ought to fight for 'my country', forgetting that countries are composed of individuals, and what countries are like depends on what individuals do, and hence a country does right only if people do. Now if everyone believes that the war is wrong, I cannot, by failing to fight, be failing to do right by my country. But, in the example, everyone believes the war is wrong. Of course, there are again problems of particular and general, but in the possible situation where everyone, including the civilians, is against the war, yet continues to fight it, there is a straightforward contradiction—a contradiction which consists in doing X to serve my country when no one in my country, including myself, believes X to be right. If I feel guilty because I believe 'my country right or wrong', then —in the last analysis—I could not be concerned to do right rather than wrong, and hence my problem and possible guilt feelings could not arise. If this seems incredible, then consider the following analogous case: when a family is 'struck' by a scandal, then the actions of every single member may not only be conditioned by what they feel they *ought* to do, but even more by what they think they need to do in the light of what they think the other thinks or is saying (gossip). And everyone may act on the basis of what they think the other thinks and at no stage need any other person think what the first person thinks they think. If this fantasy world is possible, then it is possible that every American should act in the way he does because of what he thinks other Americans think. It is not necessary that any other American thinks what the first person assumes he thinks; nor need the first person share the thoughts imputed to the others. Or one might fight the Communists on the grounds of their supposed motives or intentions, and they might fight you on the basis of the motives or intentions you supposedly have and *neither* of you may think what the other thinks you think. For more examples, see R. D. Laing's *The Politics of Experience* (72, Laing).

One detects the scent of bad faith, of self-deception. We should be inclined to think, in some of the above cases, and do think in the case of concentration camp commanders, that the man who claims (say) that he was only doing his job is deceiving us, or himself, or both: you cannot honestly say that you become a camp commandant in the way you become bald; it is just not the sort of thing that *happens* to you—it is something you do. And for things you do, you are responsible.

But this is an extreme case. Is it plausible to speak of insincerity or self-deception when *anyone* says, 'I am only doing my job': the policeman who will not let you park *here*, or the nurse who asks you to leave at the end of visiting time? We can understand the question better if we consider the utterance 'I have no *choice*—I'm only doing my job', for it seems that whether or not we want to speak of bad faith or deception depends on the extent to which we can speak of choice. If I have no choice, I am not responsible: I am just alienated from what I am doing and even should my wishes coincide with what I am doing, that avails little, as we saw.

Consider further the meaning of this last remark. I am alienated from what I am doing when what I do is someone else's decision, though someone else's deciding for me does not replace the necessity of my putting myself to do whatever they have decided I should do. It is only possible to speak of an alienated situation if we can implicitly contrast it with a disalienated one, one where I both decide to do X rather than Y, and do X rather than Y—which is simple enough and would only be impossible if we reified everything (an awful prospect!). The problem is, what is the *scope* of the class of actions (which class I shall call 'practice') of which we can plausibly speak of the *possibility* of acting in such a way that we decide what to do, *and* do it. (Later on, I shall discuss whether the definition of 'practice' makes it necessarily morally right to extend the scope of practice as far as possible and wrong to restrict it.) This is also Rousseau's problem:

> How to find a form of association ... under which each individual, while uniting himself with the others, obeys no one but himself, and remains as free as before. [*Social Contract* (110a, Rousseau, Book 1, Ch. 6)]

Now we can ask why practice occurs—for example, why do I choose to go for a walk through the park? We could say three things, where there is no further end involved: 'Because I wanted to'; 'because it satisfied a need'; or 'I just did'—meaning 'I wanted to—no further reason'. That is to say, the walk was *an end in itself*. What characterizes nonpractice? I am asked 'Why did you shoot him?' and reply 'I was ordered to'; or 'Why are you doing this?'—'I am a woman'. Only coincidentally would this be what I wanted to do (though still I am dependent on the other for the opportunity to do what I wanted); or satisfy a need; and I certainly did not 'just' shoot him—for it was not my decision; I just obeyed the order. But why? Well, if I didn't I should have been court-martialled (fear of coercion) *or* I would not keep my husband for very long (means-end argument).

Compare Marx on labour under capitalism:

> Labour is something external to the worker, i.e. it does not belong to his essential being, that in his work, therefore, he does not affirm himself, but denies himself ... The worker, therefore, only feels himself outside his work, and in his work feels outside himself. He is at home when he is not working, and when he is working he is not at home. His labour is therefore not voluntary, but coerced: it is forced labour. It is therefore not the satisfaction of a need, it is merely a means to satisfy needs external to it. Its alien character emerges clearly in the fact that as soon as no physical or other compulsion exists, labour is shunned like the plague. [*Economic and Philosophic Manuscripts of 1844* (86, Marx, pp. 110–11)]

But what grounds have we for believing that, in general, practice, in my sense, is a need—as opposed to, say, something people capriciously *want*. What we need to do is observe those situations where practice is impossible to the utmost extent, that is situations where people are confined to doing X, the decision what is to be done (X), residing elsewhere, or where recognition of my practice is simply denied so that it might just as well not have existed. For as Hegel long ago pointed out in his portrayal of the Master-Slave dialectic (*Phenomenology of Mind*, Ch. 4, Sec. A; 54a, Hegel) recognition is essential to the reality of interpersonal relationships.

In their studies of the families of schizophrenics, R. D. Laing and A. Esterson (*Sanity, Madness and the Family*, 71, Laing and Esterson) have discovered that the parents of schizophrenic adolescents deny both practice (autonomy) and the recognition of a distinctive personality to their children, to the extent of refusing to pay any attention to the child's own definition of itself and imposing in place of that definition their own fantasy of the child's nature. For Laing and Esterson, schizophrenia can be understood as a fugitive practice: that is to say, as an attempt to negate the parents' denial of autonomy and recognition through the development of behaviour unamenable to parental control and definition, notably catatonic (withdrawal) behaviour. It would seem to follow that in the limiting case of a 'person' who totally acquiesces in the denial of autonomy and recognition, he never emerges as fully human, for being human involves the notion of being *directly* conscious of oneself (self-conscious) and the world for oneself and not mediately (indirectly) conscious through another's (mother's or father's) perceptions. But it does not follow that the more practice the better, for something else, if not schizophrenia, might follow from the greatest possible extension of practice (the sociologist Durkheim suggests suicide): this would be the consequence of something like Fromm's *Fear of Freedom* (40b, Fromm), though here again there is a danger of confusing particular and general. For, from the *fact* that individuals in existing society who arrogate to themselves or find themselves in situations of the most extensive freedom of choice and action tend to commit suicide, it does not follow that everyone would commit suicide if all were free agents in this sense. Indeed, it is no contradiction to suggest that the bonds of community might be even stronger where they are personally forged, not 'impersonally' imposed. But whereas the child denied practice often has no choice other than that between schizophrenia or submission, we are in the position of being able to extend practice step by step, and we can thus feel our way—learning by doing.

But we might ask at this point whether there is any analogy to schizophrenia in the larger social nexus. We saw that schizophrenia can be understood as a fugitive practice in the family situation. We have seen both that we have a social relationship to the state and that we do not choose what sorts of social relationship we participate in, in the way Marx claims to be true of the relations of production: 'In the social production which men carry on, they enter into definite relations that are indispensable and independent of their will.' (Marx—*Preface to the Critique of Political Economy* (88 Marx, p. 182))—though they may enter *at a point* which is dependent on their will.

But whereas it is impossible that I should be born into a world of my choosing, is it impossible *in just the same way* that my social relationships remain necessarily beyond my control—or would this be a reification? Political society is the ensemble of political social relations: are *these* relations necessarily or only contingently alien? From what has gone before, it is clearly the case that this is only contingently so. Now, if we can find an analogy to schizophrenic practice, then we are in a position to see if we can establish a moral presumption in favour of dis-alienation, for—as is well known—it only makes sense to say we ought to do something if we can do it.

I want to treat the phenomenon of privatisation as parallel to that of schizophrenia. What is privatisation? We can begin by saying it consists in an attempt to withdraw totally in experience and action actually and possibly from the political world—despite the fact, shown above, that this is logically impossible. Someone trying to do this might say, 'Let them get on with it. I just want to be a housewife.' Now a rationalisation for this fugitive practice could be and frequently is the argument that 'they' know best; that if only enough well-meaning experts could get together 'the' problems could be resolved. But, again, even the experts can only solve 'the' problems with co-operation; solving a problem consists essentially in rearranging the structure of social relationships; if the chessmen are glued to the board, there is nothing the experts can do, except look solemn and 'deliberate'. Less metaphorically speaking, individuals or

N

groups with economic power in our society are in a position not to co-operate; a pressure group can—within limits—dictate to the politicians or experts. Such groups clearly do trust their perceptions of reality. They think they know where their interests lie—that is to say, the ways of satisfying needs and wants. On the other hand, we who put our trust in the experts, refuse to trust our own perceptions in the political world, and this is precisely analogous to the behaviour of the schizophrenic:

> The vagueness and contradictoriness described clinically seemed the expression of conflict between a desire to think things out for herself and her uncertainty over the validity of her perceptions and evaluations. [71, Laing and Esterson, p. 225]

And if we do not trust our perceptions, then the attempt to exercise them could only be disturbing and anxiety-making: 'I don't know, perhaps they are right after all.' Add to this the fact that we all feel our ability to comment inhibited by our lack of information (the inadequacies of the mass media)— *then* we have a situation where we either submit and swallow whole others' descriptions of our situation, or try to establish some fugitive practice; in the present case, *apathy*, a practice which not only the triviality of the press but also the attitudes of the bureaucracy reinforce. Fifty years ago, Alexandra Kollontai commented graphically on this process as it was then developing in the Soviet Union:

> Every comrade can easily recall scores of instances when workers themselves attempted to organise dining-rooms, day nurseries for children, transportation of wood, etc. Each time a lively, immediate interest in the undertaking died from the red tape, interminable negotiations with the various institutions that brought no results, or resulted in refusals, new requisitions, etc. Wherever there was an opportunity under the impetus of the masses themselves—of the masses using their own efforts—to equip a dining-room, to store a supply of wood, or to organise a nursery, refusal always followed refusal from the central institutions. . . . How much bitterness is generated among working men and women when they see and know that if they had been given the right, and an opportunity, to act, they could themselves have seen

the project through. . . . Their initiative is therefore slackening and the desire to act is dying out. 'If that is the case,' people say, 'let officials themselves take care of us.' As a result, there is generated a most harmful division: *we* are the toiling people, *they* are the Soviet officials, on whom everything depends. This is the whole trouble. [Alexandra Kollontai, *The Workers' Opposition* (67a, Kollontai, pp. 36–7)]

Clearly, from what has been said, 'apathy' is not *synonymous* with lack of confidence in ourselves: it is not just an individual psychological state. It is something other, though it can also be such a state. And the something other we have already recognised as the origin of the lack of confidence. That is, we have recognized that it is objectively the case that the kind of information relevant to an informed decision is extremely inaccessible, for it is not provided—this has been widely claimed —by the newspapers or radio or TV. Additionally, we have recognised that even possessing enough information would not entail we gained a significant share in decision-making and implementation. The practice of apathy is then intelligible even without psychological assertions; it can be comprehended simply in terms of a response by default to the objective nature of the social system, or that part of it we are considering. Voting is then a tentative and transitory expedition out of apathy, but its pointlessness only serves to reinforce our attempt to confine everyday life to private life and to experience everyday life as essentially private—but such a consciousness of our situation would be false to the extent that we failed to recognise our objective political-social role—even paying my taxes ensures a system works and is participation in it. This analysis of apathy is radically different from that proposed by bourgeois professors of political science who interpret political apathy, as indicated by low voting figures, etc., as a sign of popular contentment and political health. Nothing could be further from the truth.

Now we are ready to tackle the question of choice. To what extent can we honestly say that we are not obliged to concern ourselves with the ends which our activities—for example, our work—serve? In the first place, in private life we are entitled to ignore the consequences of an act which is beyond our control;

conversely, if something is beyond our control, we cannot be held responsible for it. If in doing X (picking up the sugar) I accidentally do Y (knock over the milk), I am not responsible —making allowance for any lack of due care. Hence, if in doing my job, I contribute to the murder of innocent people, then I am not responsible to the extent that my job is beyond my control—to the extent that doing my job is an alien activity. But have I taken due care in letting it be so? Only historically is this state of affairs so; to think otherwise is to commit the fallacy of reification. But from this fact it does not follow that, individually, I must decide to take every consequence into account and act accordingly. The situation that exists can be changed, but only *collectively*. This point can be illustrated by analogy to the situation of asking for a pay rise. Unless there is an acute labour shortage, to insist individually on a pay rise and to carry through a threat of strike action would, likely as not, lead to my dismissal; to insist together and strike collectively does not guarantee success, but makes dismissal less likely to a high degree: hence the Trade Union motto: 'Unity is Strength'. Analogously, in other areas certain changes can only be brought about by simultaneous activity. In any particular case, the scope of possible practice (a definition of 'freedom'?) will lead us to a specific evaluation of whether a man is individually responsible for what he does. If I think hanging people is wrong, I will have difficulty justifying my being the public hangman—this is unlikely to be the only job I can get. If I think capitalism is wrong, then there are few jobs I can do which do not in some way help keep it going, and though I will be unhappy at what I do, I can scarcely be accused of hypocrisy. But if *everyone* thinks capitalism is wrong?

In addition, some changes, though possible, are only possible if a certain stage of historical development has already been reached: it is not just a case of getting enough people to want something; that something must be available.

I have formulated what are the problems on the agenda in philosophical terms; the precise extent to which they are soluble is a subject for more technical discussion, as is the question of means—though with regard to the latter it has been implicitly suggested that the 'usual channels', are not those through which these problems will be solved, for they are the very

channels which embody what we now recognise as problems:
Parliamentarism is not enough.

But there remains a philosophical question: how do we create
a moral *presumption* in favour of solving these 'problems'? We
have discovered that within as yet undefined limits man is a
being who needs practice: further it does not seem if we
examine the concept of a practice-less being that it could be
other than the concept of someone either totally insane or
a robot:

> Even on the assembly line, production is based upon man as
> an active conscious being. The transformation of the worker
> into a mere cog . . . would mean the immediate breakdown
> of the productive process itself. From the capitalist point of
> view, this contradiction expresses itself as the simultaneous
> attempt on the one hand to reduce work into the mere
> execution of strictly defined tasks (or rather *gestures*), on the
> other hand constantly to appeal to and rely on the conscious
> and willing *participation* of the worker, on his capacity to
> understand and do much more than he is supposed to. [Paul
> Cardan, *The Meaning of Socialism* (25b, Cardan, p. 8)]

Cardan argues here what was said earlier: that even the
denial of practice leaves to the individual the act of 'getting on
with the job'. And the latter act cannot be eliminated without
eliminating men as we know them (it is in fact *possible* that
production could continue with 'mere cogs': they would just
not be men). This is only a point in a chain of argument which
stretches backwards, as well as forwards—backwards, notably,
to the impossibility of conceiving human beings or their experience of the world as described in language without the
characteristic of being purposive agents:

> To be a conscious human being, and therefore a thinking
> being, is to have intentions or plans, to be trying to bring
> about a certain effect. We are therefore always actively follow-
> ing what is happening now as leading into what is to happen
> next . . . intentional action is eliminable from our notion
> of experience. [Stuart Hampshire, *Thought and Action* (51d,
> Hampshire, p. 119)]

Forwards, we are trying to establish the moral claim which

the enlargement in width of the realm of free action has. It can also be enlarged in depth: that is, in control over our own nature, and the two processes are not independent. The question is, then, is it possible to deny that its capacity to fulfil a need is always a ground for an action? Is it rational to deny of an action that satisfies a need, that its need-satisfying character is always a *reason* (not necessarily conclusive) for doing it? Here I am reduced, like Mrs. Foot, to expostulation:

> It is surely clear that moral virtues must be connected with human good and harm, and that it is quite impossible to call anything you like good or harm. Consider, for instance, the suggestion that a man might say he has been harmed because a bucket of water had been taken out of the sea . . . it would be just as odd if someone were supposed to say that harm had been done to him because the hairs of his head had been reduced to an even number. [Philippa Foot, 'Moral Beliefs' (38a, Foot, p. 92)]

This is as far as one can go *at present*. At least in the language philosophers use, with some exceptions like Mrs. Foot, it is now generally held that there is no *contradiction* in denying the necessary relevance of a need to questions of good and evil, right and wrong. The locus classicus for this argument is Professor Ayer's *Language, Truth and Logic* (5c, Ayer). Yet the possibility of holding Ayer's position depends on certain contingent facts about the development of concepts. But this development is historical, as Professor MacIntyre is tireless in pointing out (see his *Short History of Ethics*, 78 f, MacIntyre). In so far as the development of language allows the possibility of denying the relevance of human needs to questions of good and bad without contradiction, this 'linguistic stop' (122a, Weldon, p. 32) shows that to that extent language is dehumanized. This is only the final result of the development of moral codes denying or ignoring human fulfilment in societies based on unnecessary denial of human satisfaction. Hence, we shall only be able to go beyond expostulation when people change the societies in which they live so as to abolish the denials which an ossified social structure and its defenders inflict upon them. In this sense, it is up to people to prove the truth.

The argument of this text has been implicitly that in politics the truth is that the path of greater democratisation is the path we must tread. The obstacles in the way of that lead us naturally into the critique of economics, before returning to politics to answer the question of method.[2]

NOTES TO APPENDIX 1

1. Written 1969 for an evening class held at the City Literary Institute, London, discussions in which provided many of the examples employed in the text. First published in *Philosophy and Phenomenological Research*, XXXIII, 1973, pp. 547–60, and reprinted by kind permission. For much more sophisticated and detailed treatment of issues treated in this essay, see the work of my namesake 95a, 95b, Pateman, C. Ch. 5 of the latter is especially relevant.

2. In checking the typescript of this Appendix before sending it to the printer, I began making stylistic changes to eliminate use of generic 'he', 'man', and so on. But then I realised that in some cases to make this change would lead to misleading anachronisms: it would make it appear that in 1969 I was a lot more sensitive to linguistic sexism than I was. And not only this: when in 1969 I was writing, like other Marxists and neo-Marxists, phrases like 'Man is a being who needs practice', I am sure that if any image accompanied this thought, it was a masculine, not an androgynous, sexless or feminine one. So in the end, I have compromised: eliminating masculine generics where even in 1969 I used or might have used sexless generics (e.g. 'people' instead of 'men'), but leaving them in where to alter them would have been obviously anachronistic.

APPENDIX 2

Claus Mueller's
The Politics of Communication [1]

In this short book (91f, Mueller) Professor Mueller attempts 'an empirically grounded analysis of advanced industrial society and of those problems that appear insurmountable within the established institutional context' (p. vii), and especially an analysis of what Marxists call the superstructure. However, Mueller emphasises such elements as 'language codes', 'socialisation strategies' and 'legitimating rationales', rather than 'the usual factors like education, occupation and religion' (p. vii), and this is undoubtedly new and fruitful.

In his opening chapter, 'Distorted Communication', Mueller advances a central thesis that 'the absence of sufficient conceptual development and of certain value predispositions, which is related to both socialisation patterns and language codes, can prevent the individual from understanding the political code of society at large' (p. 17). This absence is to be accounted for by *distortion* of communication and Mueller identifies and defines three types of distorted communication:

  (i) in *directed* communication, the government intervenes directly in the mass media and educational system in an attempt to influence the use of language and interpretational schemes (p. 21);
 (ii) in *arrested* communication, their linguistic environment limits the capacity of individuals to engage in political communication independently of any apparent political intervention (p. 19);
(iii) in *constrained* communication, private and government groups successfully intervene 'to structure and limit public communication in order that their interests prevail' (p. 19).

(Clearly, these distortions of communication are defined in opposition to an implicit communicative Utopia, the features of which it would be an interesting exercise to articulate.) [2]

Mueller elaborates the concept of directed communication by reference to the government-decreed 'Newspeaks' of Nazi Germany and East Germany. The treatment of the latter, at least, is tendentious. Mueller contrasts unfavourably the definitions of terms given in the East German *Duden* with those given in the West German equivalent. For example *militarism* is defined in the East as 'subordination in imperialist States of all societal and governmental areas under military command and concomitant repression of the mass of the population and aggressive foreign policy' (p. 39); and in the West as 'dominance of military convictions' (p. 39). Mueller concludes on the basis of such examples that 'the semantic space is abundantly structured by predefinitions, the individual is barred from evolving his own interpretations' (p. 40).

But one might equally conclude that the West German definition is vacuous and that it is unrealisable Utopianism to believe that individuals can or will fill with their own interpretations whatever empty semantic space the government or anybody else allows them. It seems to me more likely that the 'fuller' the space, that is, the more elaborate the conceptual scheme, the more chance there is that the individual can and will transform it creatively.

In any case, Mueller is not at all clear about the difference between full and empty semantic space, since he also quotes as applicable to East German usage the sentiment that 'Linguistic clichés, which often have a minimum of content only, constitute communication to a large extent' (p. 41)—a clear contrary criticism from that previously advanced. Thus Mueller succeeds only in conveying his dislike of linguistic developments in East Germany, nothing more.

In Ch. 2, the author develops the idea of arrested political communication within the theoretical paradigm of Basil Bernstein's theories of *restricted* and *elaborated* codes, and of class specific socialisation strategies (21, Bernstein). I have done this myself, but the powerful arguments that are being developed against the Bernstein type of theory (e.g. 69, Labov; 109, Rosen, none of which arguments Mueller cites or confronts) have led me to attempt an approach in a forthcoming book (*Language, Truth and Politics*) less dependent on these contentious theories than the argument developed by Mueller.

If the Bernsteinian theory is correct, however, the political implications are clear and Mueller summarises them:

> Seen politically, this language reinforces the cohesion of a group which shares a specific code, but it can prevent the group from relating to the society at large and its political institutions. The individual experiences his deprivation subjectively; cognitively speaking, however, he lacks the reference points necessary to perceive the objective reasons for his condition and to relate to the structure of the society in which he is living. The individual's language thus becomes his internal plausibility structure. In narrowing his ability to discriminate, to conceptualise, and to analyse, it renders his condition more acceptable to him. He is immune from perceiving alternatives. [p. 55]

But one really needs to be much more sceptical than Mueller of some of the claims of the theorist. For instance, Mueller quotes Pierre Guiraud as noting the use by the French working class of 'exaggerations, redundant terms, tautologies, repetitions, and illogical derivations', and it is implied that these are all Bad Things. But wait a moment. Let's look at 'exaggerations'. If working-class speakers use exaggerations, do they know that they do so? If they do, it seems unlikely that any harm is done. And if they don't, what *sort* of harm is done? Is there any connection between spontaneous exaggeration and inability to conceive global features of the social system, such as exploitation? I think not.

Again, consider 'tautology'. I have always been taught that there are two sorts of tautology: the interesting sort and the trivial sort. Before we knock the workers for using tautologies, we need to know what sort they use, when, how and why. Professor Mueller, by the way, is rather given to using the uninteresting sort of tautology: 'If the linguistic and cognitive capacities of an individual are sufficiently developed, he is able to engage in effective political communication' (p. 19). Better to say: 'We shall take ability to engage in effective political communication as a *criterion* of sufficient development.' This at least facilitates discussion of the criterion and permits the question to be raised as to why we desire that people should be able to engage in effective political communication.

In Ch. 3, Mueller discusses constrained communication under the chapter heading 'The Maintenance of the Status Quo'. The theoretical distinction between directed and constrained communication is obviously rather difficult to draw, and Mueller does not devote much attention to the issue, but rather uses the concept for an illuminating discussion of the United States and Western Europe. He discusses ways in which governments structure communication, defining the issues of public debate, and he analyses the decline of old-style ideologies, a decline not based on any real attenuation of social conflict, but one for which new para-ideologies have been substituted. These consist of 'collective imagery rooted in material and social compensations and slogans' (p. 108). Habermas has analysed para-ideology in his essay 'Technology and Science as "Ideology" ' (48, Habermas). Para-ideology 'makes the exercise of governmental power acceptable by seemingly depoliticising politics' (p. 111).

Further the absence of a counter-ideology assures the acceptance of the *status quo* (p. 118) and higher wages, more leisure and the promise of affluence can be used as a means of controlling and administering society (p. 125).

However, Mueller believes that these means of system maintenance are ultimately rather fragile. Unlike old-style ideology, they cannot command strong allegiances, or rather 'the normative compliance of groups other than the working class' (p. 126). And so Mueller entitles Ch. 4 of his book 'A Crisis of Governmental Authority'. But why the qualification 'other than the working class'? This rather surprising exclusion from the ranks of those who might challenge the existing order of things seems to me the perfectly logical consequence of a resolutely superstructural analysis which is not related to the economic base, and which is informed by idealist beliefs. If Knowledge is a necessary condition for revolutionary action, then if the working working class lacks this Knowledge, it cannot engage in such action. Conversely, those with Knowledge (the upper middle class, p. 170) are in a cognitive position to engage in revolutionary action, even if they don't *actually* do so. And what of their real *ability* to do so? What of their position in relation to the means of production, their real power to *enforce* change? And what of the contradictions and conflicts between economic position and actual consciousness, which constantly pull the working class in opposite directions?

Such questions, which are at the centre of the work of dialectical thinkers such as Gramsci, are absent from Mueller's book. In this crucial respect he has not gone beyond the idealist position of his earlier essay, where he implied a rather naïve, two-stage model of political change: consciousness first; action second:

> Not being able to become conscious of one's situation beyond the emotive stage precludes the articulation of experienced conflicts and contradictions, especially if they are located in dimensions exceeding material needs. The lack of articulation precludes political action, or, to paraphrase A. Martinelli, the lack of class-consciousness in periods of consensus (as opposed to periods of coercion) makes any change impossible. [91g, Mueller, pp. 107–8]

This kind of approach cannot cope with the ways in which people are *forced* into action and learn *in the course of* action. Mueller's thesis is this: the masses can be bought off with bread and circuses, for they can conceive nothing better. The intellectuals demand something more, a normative justification that the system cannot provide and that they themselves feel unable to supply. In consequence, they will demand (even if they cannot enforce) real social change and not mere ideological manipulation. If this is a correct diagnosis, it is very depressing. But I think it is more likely that we are really dealing here with *la vanité des clercs*.

NOTES TO APPENDIX 2

1. Written 1974. First published in *The Human Context*, v. 7, 1975, pp. 621–3.
2. Note added. Such an articulation is to be found in Habermas' work (see especially his 48a, 48b, 48d, 48f, 48h, 48j). In my 99c I try to set out the distinctive features of the structure of an ideal public sphere as envisaged by Rousseau, Condorcet and nineteenth-century English utilitarians.

APPENDIX 3

Liberals, fanatics and moral philosophers: Aspects of R. M. Hare's Freedom and Reason [1]

I have recently re-started work on a study of Tolerance and rummaging through my books for any which I might usefully read or re-read as background or foreground picked out R. M. Hare's *Freedom and Reason*, Ch. 9 of which has the title 'Toleration and Fanaticism' (52a, Hare). I have now read the book through, which is something I did not do in my time as a Philosophy student: marginal annotations to my copy (purchased for seven shillings and sixpence) show that in the past I had read only chapters one, two, three, and five.

I was impressed in my reading by the presence in Hare's book of explicit, substantive moral argument conducted from the point of view of a liberal, protestant morality and directed, principally, against positions attributed to Nazi and racist 'moralities' and to a lesser extent against those who would make crimes of sins. Whilst Hare does make the common distinction between the activities of moral philosophy, on the one hand, and moralising and the moral life on the other, his book does not, either in intention or execution, include only the former to the exclusion of the latter. The image I had of Hare's work as typical of an academic philosophy which eschewed substantive moral discussion or action was false. I think part of the explanation for this is that teachers of philosophy, working in exam-oriented systems which attach immense importance to objectivity neutrality, etc., exclude from their curricula the substantive (first order) moral discussion contained in books like Hare's. I doubt if I was the only student to read only the analytical (second order) bits of *Freedom and Reason*. I think that my image of Hare was probably a creation of the system which first mediated his work to me.

Whatever mediators might do, Hare has and states a clear conception of his readership and what he wants from it, and the kind of reading which he thinks it ought to give him. The most important feature of this conception is a negative one, for Hare does not imagine himself as addressing either students or teachers of Philosophy (or any other subject), but rather as writing for and being read by liberal members of the professional classes: judges, stockbrokers, army officers and leaders of Himalayan expeditions are the characters (not traditionally liberal!) who figure both in his hypothetical arguments and as the audience for his discourse. Explicitly, Hare sees himself in an intellectual relation to such people founded upon an intellectual division of labour which creates moral philosophy as one profession among many.[2]

The moral philosopher's most important direct relationship is with these liberal professionals; he relates directly to 'ordinary members of the public' (p. 180) only in so far as he himself is a liberal. One of the major, if not the major, tasks of the moral philosopher is to assist liberals in their war of attrition against fanaticism (here in its Nazi and racist forms) and its confused but basically non-fanatical adherents:

> ... on the whole (though there are set-backs) liberalism advances against fanaticism, provided that there is freedom of communication, and that the influential part of the public thinks seriously about moral questions, understands their nature, and respects the truth. The liberal should therefore above all struggle to preserve these conditions; and that is why it is important to the liberal that the moral philosopher, who is professionally concerned in preserving them (especially the second), should do his job properly. Fanatics will always be with us. ... The strategy of the liberal must be to separate from the true fanatics, whose ideals really are proof against the ordeal by imagination and facts, those who support them merely because they are thoughtless and insensitive. [p. 184]

Though Hare obviously makes a large number of unargued assumptions about the structure of fanatical movements, the relation between leaders and led, the quantitative relation between true fanatics and the simply confused, what is undeniable is that he has a coherent, liberal conception of philosophical practice and its relation to other practices, notably the political-educational practice of influential liberals. The conception may be wrong; I think it is. But it is a fuller, much more practical, certainly less academic conception than that usually attributed to people like Hare by radical critics. It is rather sad that Hare's actual readership is probably so very different from that which he intends. He deserves a better class of liberal reader than he gets.

The work of a radical moral philosopher would presumably differ from that of Hare at least in its range of practical concerns; its substantive arguments; and its intended audience (say: jury people rather than judges). I think it would be less optimistic about the power of Reason than is Hare[3] (but then why write books?) and probably it would be more sceptical of the viability of the analytical distinction between moral philosophy and morals—it would be likely to answer the essay question 'Is the principle of universalisability a purely formal principle?' in the negative, though I don't think it would have to in order to count as a radical work.

The way in which Hare relates the (formal) principle of universalisability to the (substantive) principle of toleration is something I should like to comment on, both as illustrative of remarks in the preceding section and as relevant to my own concerns.

Consider the following passage:

Suppose that somebody argues as follows: according to the universalist, when a man makes a moral judgement he is committed to saying that anybody who says something different about a similar case is wrong; therefore, according to the universalist, toleration in moral matters is impossible. In order to understand this matter clearly, it is necessary to distinguish between thinking that somebody else is wrong, and taking up an intolerant attitude towards him. The universalist is committed to a denial of relativism ... he holds that if anybody disagrees with me about a moral question, then I am committed to disagreeing with him, unless I change my mind. This appears a harmless enough tautology, and need hardly trouble the universalist. But the universalist is not committed to persecuting (physically or in any other way) people who disagree with him morally. If he is the sort of universalist that I am, he will realise that our moral opinions are liable to change in the light of our experience and our discussion of moral questions with other people; therefore, if another person disagrees with us, what is called for is not the suppression of his opinions but the discussion of them, in the hope that, when he has told us the reasons for his, and we for ours, we may reach agreement. Universalism is an ethical theory which makes moral argument both possible and fruitful; and it enables us to understand what toleration is, as we shall later see. [pp. 49–50]

I don't think this passage is a model of clarity; I think it can be read as saying or suggesting that the principle of toleration can in some way be derived from the principle of universalisability, perhaps in a way which would flout 'Hume's Law' and perhaps in a way which would cast doubt on the claimed formal status of the universalisability principle, or which would lead to an ideological claim for formal status for the substantive toleration principle.[4] It need not be so read, but then it has to be said that Hare is wrong at one point. He writes: 'Universalism is an ethical theory which makes moral argument both possible and fruitful . . .'. Now, whilst it is true that universalism makes moral argument possible (we are not obliged to agree to differ, as emotivism would require if it were correct), it is false that it makes argument fruitful, except in a most trivial, tautologous way which Hare does not have in mind, for he also writes 'If he is the sort of universalist I am, he will realise that our moral opinions are liable to change in the light of our experience and our discussion of moral questions with other people'. But this realisation can only be based on evidence, or it is a matter of (liberal/Enlightenment) faith. It does not follow from the thesis of universalisability, though that thesis explains the logical possibility of what Hare asserts is empirically liable to happen.

That Hare does or tends to jump from proving a logical possibility to asserting it as an empirical fact is evident from the text of Ch. 9, in which he sets out to show the liberal how to deal in argument with the Nazi. He suggests that but for a hard-core of 'really intractable Nazis' (p. 171) the rest will be motivated not by moral ideals but by self-interest and for such a person 'If his conduct is interpreted in this way, he is open to arguments' (p. 171). Here 'open' can only mean 'logically open' which is not the same as 'empirically open'. It cannot and does not solve the practical problem of the liberal faced by the Nazi. For people logically open to argument in virtue of the structure of their beliefs may nonetheless refuse to argue, fail to accept the outcome of an argument, fail to act on such an outcome etc. Hare recognises this (see, e.g., Ch. 5 on 'Backsliding') but does not consider the empirical consequences of such empirical facts. For example, Clear Thinkers in the 1930s, in whose steps Hare follows, were not (I imagine) notably successful in stopping the spread of Nazism and Fascism by separating the confused from the fanatics whose logic was impeccable. What has to be asked and found out is how successful they actually were, which means looking at how they worked and with whom.[5] Contrasts should be made with the work of those who had different strategies for halting the Nazis and Fascists and their relative successes and failures. At a minimum, if he were writing today, Hare would need to read and comment on Reich's *Mass Psychology of Fascism* and *What is Class Consciousness?* (106, 107, Reich). I think he could accept this, for there is no doubting the seriousness of his intent (try pp. 177–85 of the book if you doubt this). On the other hand, the astounding failure in a book so preoccupied with Nazism, racism and even world war to discuss the relation of moral and political philosophy, morals and politics, must be attributed to a structural weakness of Hare's liberal-individualist morality rather than to any personal failing on Hare's part.[6]

Whilst Hare's moral philosophy either proves that rational moral argument is possible over a much wider area than had previously been thought, or (to put it relativistically) sets out to create the conceptual conditions in which such argument is possible, it does leave open the possibility of rational disagreement. There are those who disagree with 'us' whose logic is impeccable, and whom Hare christens 'fanatics' when they allow their ideals 'to override all considerations of people's interests, even the holder's own in actual or hypothetical cases' (p. 176). These people cannot believe in the liberal ideal of toleration, 'that is to say a readiness to respect other people's ideals [or interests—TP] as if they were his own' (p. 177).

Hare defines the limits of this tolerance in classically Millian

o

terms (p. 178). The liberal ' . . . tolerates other people's pursuit of their ideals provided that, where the pursuit of one ideal hinders the pursuit of another, there shall be, as in the cases of conflicting interests discussed above, a just distribution of advantages and disadvantages. It is only the last proviso which prevents the liberal from allowing even the fanatic to pursue his ideals without impediment; but the liberal is not required by his own ideal to tolerate intolerance' (p. 180).

This, in the context of a discussion of Nazism, would seem to put Hare on the side of the International Socialists and other groups intolerant of the National Front and wishing to smash it by their own action if it isn't banned by the State. Interestingly, in the recent *Socialist Worker* pamphlet *Organise against the National Front, the new Nazis* (92 f), distinctions analogous to Hare's are drawn between National Front sympathisers and new members with some of whom 'discussion is worthwhile', and the 'hard core fascist members of the National Front' for whom 'only one argument is successful: physical force' (p. 9). The pamphlet is only less 'philosophical' than Hare's book in it greater concreteness—the National Front rather than Hare's sometimes indeterminate 'Nazis' and its sensitivity to the actual empirical possibilities of argument—whereas Hare tends to relate toleration of the bare logical possibility of argument. (I am intrigued to know if the author(s) of this pamphlet have read Hare, and whether Hare has read this pamphlet.)[7]

To recapitulate. I suggest to anyone reading or re-reading *Freedom and Reason* that he or she focus not just on the narrowly philosophical theses for which Hare is famous (universalisability, prescriptivity), but on the detailed conception and exemplification of a moral practice which he advances. I think Hare is wrong in substance and form, but I do think his book could only have come from the pen of an educator who had himself been educated; and Hare tells us whereabouts in the last sentence on page 183.

NOTES TO APPENDIX 3

1. Written 1974. First published in *Radical Philosophy*, 10, Spring 1975, pp. 25-6. I am grateful to Professor Hare and Hillel Steiner for permission to use their comments on the article in the notes now added to the text.

2. R. M. Hare comments, 'These professions figure in the examples (because they provide good ones); why do you think the work is *addressed* to them? Certainly the academic profession is one among many, and philosophy one of its disciplines, but my works are *addressed* to anybody who I think will understand what I am trying to say, and I should doubt if this includes many stockbrokers or army officers.'

3. R. M. Hare: 'I am in fact profoundly pessimistic about the prospect of people actually doing the right sort of philosophical thinking; I am optimistic only in the sense that I think that *if they did*, it would make the future of the world a great deal more rosy.'

4. Hillel Steiner says that Hare cannot mean to derive the principle of toleration from the universalisability requirement, since: 'Hare is quite insistent that really intractable fanatics (i.e. really intractable non-affirmers of the principle of toleration) are nevertheless capable of using moral terms intelligibly in defence of their commitments.'

5. R. M. Hare: 'Since the great majority of those who are politically active greatly prefer excitement to clarity, the 'clear thinker' you mention is at some disadvantage. As typified by Hume and Mill he did have some successes in this country, and could claim some of the credit for the absence of any large violent fascist or communist movement in England, and the peacefulness (on the whole) of our progress towards equality of distribution of goods. . . . Not that I am a very extreme egalitarian; I think that moderate inequalities have more good results than bad.'

6. R. M. Hare: 'This, I am afraid, is claptrap. The reason is that I do things in the logical order; I got interested in moral philosophy because of its implications for practical issues, including political ones; but I saw that if it was going to do any good one had to get the theory straight first.'

   Hillel Steiner says I am ' . . . quite wrong to suggest that the failure of *Freedom and Reason* to discuss the relation between moral and political philosophy must be attributed to a structural weakness of Hare's liberal-individualist morality. Indeed, he himself cites Hare's remark that the liberal tolerates other people's pursuit of their ideals provided that, where the pursuit of one ideal hinders the pursuit of another, there shall be, as in the cases of conflicting interests discussed above, a *just distribution* of advantages and disadvantages (emphasis added). There are, it seems to me, quite good grounds for believing that Justice just is Toleration writ large. A brief perusal of Kant's *Metaphysical Elements of Justice* is sufficient to indicate that there is an identity between not persecuting those with whom we morally disagree (toleration) and allowing to others the same amount of personal liberty as one exercises oneself (justice). It would be an exceedingly novel position to claim that the subject of distributive justice—and the institutional framework it requires—do not come under the heading of 'political philosophy'. That Hare does not discuss these matters is undeniable. That he ought to have done so, given the widely accepted conventions of academic division of labour, is questionable. That his liberal-individualist morality precludes such a discussion is just false.'

Hare has written extensively about political questions and about the relation between 'morals and politics' (see for instance his *Applications of Moral Philosophy* (52aa)), and I do not see now that the claim made in my article can be substantiated.

7. R. M. Hare: 'I haven't read the pamphlet.'

APPENDIX 4

Remarks *on* L'Empire des Signes
of Roland Barthes [1]

In his *Mythologies* (11 Barthes) Roland Barthes advanced three important theses: first, that there are very few non-signifying fields in everyday life (p. 112, note 2); second, that the fields of signification habitually signify at the two levels of denotation and connotation; third, that the connotations are properly called 'myths', for they are the representations which a social class, the bourgeoisie, 'has and makes us have of the relations between man and the world' (p. 140). The short mythologies, which comprise the first half of the book, are a 'revelation' and critique of the myths of everyday life; the second half of the book ('Myth Today') develops the two-level theory of signification.

Though it is not written as a development or commentary upon the three theses of *Mythologies* specified above, Barthes' later book *L'Empire des Signes* (14c, Barthes) clearly bears upon them, and I wish to examine this later work in relation to the three theses. This is to take some liberties with Barthes' text, but surely fewer than Barthes himself takes in constituting a textual system, 'Japan', which does not claim to represent or analyse the reality of Japan. For in *L'Empire des Signes* Barthes claims simply to have selected from somewhere in the world 'a certain number of traits' (p. 9)—where 'trait' is used as in graphics and linguistics—out of which the system 'Japan' is deliberately formed.

The thesis that there are very few non-signifying fields in everyday life is sustained in *L'Empire des Signes* by an ingenious maneouvre. What is the privileged field of signification? It is language, written or spoken. How might one best demonstrate the uniquity of signification? Why, place oneself in a country where not only does one not speak the language, but where the clues which a common alphabet or way of speaking provide are absent. And proceed to write about that country's sign system.

This is the manoeuvre Barthes makes, explicitly as a refutation of the 'ideological assertion' that 'there is no communication other than in language' (p. 18). Indeed, it may be the very
opacity of language which allows one to appreciate the vastness
and richness of the 'empire of signifiers' (pp. 19–20).

Though perhaps unintended, this strategy has, I think the
virtue of bringing to prominence the doubts about the possibility of a semiology worthy of the name of *knowledge* which the
earlier *Mythologies* raised, but failed to settle.

In *Mythologies* the theory of knowledge at work in the short
mythologies, which permits the definiteness of the interpretations given there, is an empiricist one. Myths are seen and
heard; the senses provide the knowledge which Barthes trans-
cribes in the mythologies themselves. Knowledge of myths is
acquired without the mediation of language, and language is
required only to convey what is already known. Thus, of a
photograph of a Negro soldier saluting the French flag, Barthes
writes, 'whether naïvely or not, I see very well what it signifies
to me; that France is a great Empire' (11, Barthes, p. 116).

Now in *L'Empire des Signes* this epistemology, which is simultaneously a method of work and means of validation, is more
obvious and even more necessary. As a foreigner in a land
where he does not speak the language, Barthes is 'reduced' to
observing what passes before him. He cannot translate, interro-
gate, or compare the meanings he imputes to what he observes
with those of native speakers. His method of work becomes that
of walking about—the method of the *flaneur*. If what he sees is
to be worthy of record in a public text, then observation alone
must yield all that is necessary in the way of evidence and proof
for his conclusions, which become a mirror of the world.

But Barthes describes himself as being a 'reader', not a
'visitor' in Japan (p. 107). He seems to deny belief in the
primacy of perception which I have been imputing to him, and
assert the primacy of codes. Yet how can these codes be known
to him, if the possibility of explanation in language is excluded?
The answer must be that the codes are knowable without the
mediation of language; the culture of the world is therefore an
open book, which offers itself to be read (rather than mirrored)
without other context than the system ('Japan'), supposedly to
be constituted, but in fact already constituted at the beginning.

I conclude that we must take him literally when he designates
as a 'haiku' 'every discontinuous trait, every event in Japanese
life, such as it offers itself to my reading (*tel qu'il s'offre à ma
lecture*)' (p. 113).

The theory of reading imputed to Barthes in the previous
paragraphs may well appear most implausible. It becomes explicable in relation to a thesis developed in *L'Empire des Signes*
which is antithetical to the second thesis I attributed to Barthes
in *Mythologies*. For whilst the culture of the Occident is full of
connotation and myth, that of Japan is devoid of either.
L'Empire des Signes constitutes a system where a second level of
meaning does not exist, a blissful world which offers no excuse
for paranoia. A picture of a cucumber and two aubergines has
no other meaning, open or concealed; it is a picture of a
cucumber and two aubergines, *à la lettre* (p. 95).[2]

The empire of signs is free of the possibility of symbolic substitution, with us an obsession (p. 100); it renders commentary
impossible, for 'commentary' could only be repetition (p. 96)—
the sort of commentary known to that age which also knew the
open book of the world. Signs are unequivocal and univocal. In
the theatre, for example, there are only bodies, not souls; eyes,
not a look. The signs of the actor neither reveal, express or
represent (p. 121). 'Empire of signs?', concludes Barthes, 'Yes,
if one appreciates that these signs are empty (*vides*) and that the
ritual [of exchanging signs, as in kow tow—TP] is godless'
(p. 145).

This grand theme gives unity to Barthes' text, which while
structured like a series of short mythologies, insistently denies
the relevance of the theory of myth developed in the earlier
work. Whether in relation to *Pachinko*, a Japanese 'equivalent'
of pin ball; or of the haiku; or *Bunraku*, the puppet theatre; or
Zen, Barthes is insistent, 'there is nothing to grasp (*il n'y a rien à
saisir*)' (p. 150). So much for the mysteries of the East! There
are none. Everything lies flat, expressionless, significant—on the
surface.

'Empty' signs mean by their opposition and combination;
the empire of signs is a structuralist field. In the terminology of
Roman Jakobson, the Japanese sign is dominated by the poetic
function (the haiku is written just for the sake of writing—p.
112), where the sign itself is foregrounded and becomes the

centre of attention, and where the combination of signs is the object of study, though the combination is itself constituted in the structuralist activity.

In *Mythologies*, myth is the work of a social class, the bourgeoisie. In *L'Empire des Signes* there is no myth, and no bourgeoisie. The dimension of political critique has disappeared, unless as an indirect critique of the full, ideological signs of the Occident. Even the *Zengakuren* are introduced not as contestants of the Empire, but as confirmation of the correctness of the grand theme, which is applied to them. Thus, the violence of the *Zengakuren* is not expressive of hate, or indignation, or morals; it is not expressive at all. It is immediately a sign (*'elle est immediatement signe'*—p. 139) having its origins and sufficiency in itself. Conformably, the rhythmic slogans of the *Zengakuren* do not announce the Cause or Object of the action— that for or against which one is fighting—but simply *double* or repeat the action in announcing it: 'The *Zengakuren* are going to fight' (p. 143). It is an action outside time; therefore outside politics. It is inside the void of signs.

These signs might be characterised as performative, for they perform their function in being announced. 'Japan', like music, is a system of deeds.

NOTES TO APPENDIX 4

1. Written 1976. Not previously published. Translations from *L'Empire des Signes* are my own.
2. This idea is anticipated in Barthes' 1964 essay, 'Rhetoric of the Image': 'Since it is both evictive and sufficient, it will be understood that from an aesthetic point of view the denoted image can appear as a kind of Edenic state of the image; cleared utopianically of its connotations, the image would become radically objective, or, in the last analysis, innocent' (14b, Barthes, p. 42).

APPENDIX 5

How to do things with Images:
An Essay on the Pragmatics of Advertising [1]

1. Introduction

The object of this essay is to show how concepts and theories
which have been developed within contemporary Anglo-
American philosophy of language can be applied, more or less
directly, to the study of what are usually called 'images'.
Though I shall confine myself to the case of the sort of advertising images which can be found in the pages of almost any
magazine, I think my analysis is generalisable to other varieties
of image. My purpose in undertaking the wholesale transfer of
concepts and theories from philosophy of language is that I
think these permit an analysis of images which is at least as
interesting and could be more precise or intersubjectively veri-
fiable than the image analysis which has come out of recent
Franco-Italian semiology and semiotics—from which I shall
take Roland Barthes' essay, 'Rhetoric of the Image' as a point
of contrast for what I am going to say. That essay is an outstanding specimen of its kind, and has been very influential. It is
a sustained meditation on a single advertisement for *Panzani*
products (see 14b, Barthes, facing p. 97), and to facilitate comparison it is to this same advertisement that I shall mainly refer
in the course of this study.

As for Anglo-American philosophy of language, I mean by
that principally the work of the late L. Wittgenstein and J. L.
Austin, and of J. R. Searle and H. P. Grice. This brand of
philosophy of language is being very actively developed in
America, in close connection with Chomskyan and neo-
Chomskyan linguistics and likewise in Europe, especially in
Germany. Though originating in Cambridge and Oxford
(Wittgenstein was a Professor in Cambridge until his death in
1953, and Austin in Oxford until his death in 1961), British
philosophers no longer shape the developing form of this
philosophy of language, though some are contributing importantly to it, or to its criticism.

Outside of philosophy, the work of the authors I have just mentioned is having a growing impact. Their concepts have been employed by literary critics (or, rather, literary theorists) and, interestingly, Austin's most important work, the posthumous, *How to do things with words* (5b), has been received in its French translation very much from a literary point of view. In America, the work of M. L. Pratt *Towards a Speech Act Theory of Literary Discourse* (104a) is a recent example of literary theory influenced by the philosophy of language. Other kinds of discourse analysts have also taken a close interest in the work of the philosophers I have cited, including socio-linguists interested in family and classroom interaction: see, for instance, the place given to the philosophy of language in M. Coulthard's recent book, *An Introduction to Discourse Analysis* (30a) and in A. Wootton's *Dilemmas of Discourse* (127a).

The name 'philosophy of language' is, indeed, misleading for what at least some of these philosophers I have mentioned have been doing. Though they take their examples predominantly from everyday, conversational exchanges, at least some of them have thought of their work as generalisable to other kinds of communication (see, for instance, 47c, Grice) and have from time to time used non-linguistic examples. The enormous intellectual and cultural impact of Chomsky's revolution in linguistic theory, launched by his *Syntactic Structures* (29a) has, perhaps, helped to focus the philosophers' attention on exclusively linguistic communication: there are so many exciting things to be discovered in that area. But in my view the work of the philosophers provides the basis for a general theory of human communication, in the sense of a theory about how it is possible for human beings to communicate (successfully) with one another by means of signs. And it is in that belief that I have attempted to use their concepts in this essay.

I hope that by now the reader will be impatient to know what are these concepts and theories which the philosophers have been developing. My procedure in the rest of the essay will be to outline some of the key concepts and theories one by one, illustrating them first with linguistic examples, and then showing how they can be used in the analysis of images, taking the *Panzani* advertisement already studied by Barthes as a recurrent example, though not entirely to the exclusion of others.

Though I shall find it necessary to use expressions like 'the philosophers', the reader is warned not to assume that because some concept or theory is attributed to them in general it can therefore be attributed to each individual philosopher in particular. (If there is an odd man out in the list I gave earlier, it is Wittgenstein, to whose work I shall make no explicit reference, and who is not directly responsible for the concepts and theories I shall introduce in this essay. But, indirectly, he is responsible for a great deal).

2. Speech Acts

Speech Acts is the title of an important book by J. R. Searle (114b, Searle) who closely follows Austin in the analysis he develops. According to Searle, 'speaking a language is performing acts according to rules' (pp. 36–7). These acts, called *speech acts*, are identified in ordinary language by such expressions as 'assertions', 'orders', 'promises', 'wishes', 'verdicts'. Austin believed that in English there are between 1,000 and 10,000 terms which identify different kinds of speech acts and, partly because the analysis of such a large number of different kinds of act would be unmanageable, both Austin and Searle attempt to group them into families. Thus, for example, Searle (114e, Searle; but see now 51e, Hancher) classifies speech acts into (1) *Representatives*, or acts which commit the speaker to something's being the case—as do 'assertions'; (2) *Directives*, by which the speaker attempts to get the hearer to do something—as with 'orders'; (3) *Commissives*, which commit the speaker to a future course of action—for example, 'promises'; (4) *Expressives*, which express a psychological state of the speaker—for instance, 'wishes'; and (5) *Declaratives*, successful performance of which brings the world into conformity with the 'propositional content' (about which more below). Declaratives include such things as 'verdicts', and also christenings, marriage vows, the naming of ships, umpires' decisions, etc.—examples with which Austin was much concerned.

Searle's most important contention is that the kinds of acts of which I have just given examples are 'characteristically performed by uttering expressions in accordance with sets of constitutive rules' (114b, p. 37), and it is his aim to specify the rules which constitute different central kinds of speech act. The rules are *constitutive* rules in the sense that unlike *regulative* rules which impose some kind of order on a pre-existing activity (as table manners bring some order to eating), constitutive rules actually create new kinds of activity, without which that activity could not exist. There would be no game of chess without the rules of chess.

Before I proceed to give an example of the rules governing one particular kind of speech act, it remains to clarify the meaning of the expression *propositional content*, which figured in the account of Declaratives above, and this has to be done in relation to the introduction of one more technical term, namely, *illocutionary force*.

Consider the following utterances, which could all be made 'about' the same youthful individual, John Smith, but, let us assume, by different speakers:

(1) John is going to have his hair cut. (Said by a friend)
(2) Smith, get your hair cut. (Said by Smith's teacher)
(3) I wish you'd get your hair cut, John (Said by John's mother)

Now each of these utterances would typically be used to perform different speech acts: (1) falls within the class of Representatives; (2) within the class of Directives; and (3) would typically count as an Expressive. But these utterances would all have something in common, provided only that the same 'John Smith' was in question in all of them. What they are all *about* is something which we might render as 'John Smith's getting-his-hair-cut', and it is this which is their common *propositional content*. The propositional content of an utterance *refers* to something (here, refers to John Smith) and *predicates* something of what is referred to (here, the action of his 'getting-his-hair-cut'). This statement should suffice to make things clear for our present purposes, but the reader is warned that some of the knottiest and most controversial philosophical problems develop from trying to pin down the nature of propositions, of reference, and of predication.

But the three utterances, though sharing a common propositional content, differ in *illocutionary force*, which is only a way of saying that they are used to do different things, more precisely, perform different speech acts. What is most relevant for our purposes is to have some idea of the very many different ways in which a speaker can indicate the illocutionary force he intends his utterance to have, that is, indicate which speech act he is performing (assuming only that he is clear about this himself, and wishes to be clear to others, which is not always the case). Searle says that 'Illocutionary force indicating devices in English include at least: word order, stress, intonation contour, punctuation [in written English—the speech act analysis is equally applicable to speaking and writing—TP], the mood of the verb, and the so-called performative verbs' (114b, p. 30)— the 'so-called performative verbs' being those which explicitly indicate the character of the speech act being performed, as with 'bet' in the utterance 'I bet you sixpence it will rain to- morrow'. In our examples (1), (2) and (3) above, the nature of the illocutionary force of the speech act is variously indicated: probably by a combination of word order, stress, and intona- tion contour in the case of (1); principally by the use of the imperative in (2), and by the use of the explicit 'I wish' in (3). In addition, a hearer works out the force of an utterance not just from what is said or how it is said (i.e. by using knowledge of semantics, syntax, and phonology), but also and importantly from *who* says it: 'Smith, get your hair cut' would standardly be taken by Smith as an *order* when uttered by his teacher, but as a *joke* when uttered by his friend. So the hearer also makes use of *pragmatic* knowledge, that is knowledge about the relations which standardly exist between 'signs and their users' (91e, Morris, Sec. V), utterances and their utterers. This point is important, and has a part to play in what follows.

It is now possible to give some rules for performance of one kind of speech act. I shall use *orders* from the class of directives, since later on I shall argue that *advertisements* can fruitfully be regarded as, indeed are, another kind of directive.

The rules for successfully and non-defectively performing the speech act of giving an order are outlined by Searle (114b) as follows. First, it is a *preparatory condition* of a speaker, S, giving a hearer, H, an order that S 'must be in a position of authority over H'. It is a second preparatory condition that H is able to perform the action, A, which he is ordered to perform. (H's doing of this action is the propositional content of the order: 'Smith's getting-his-hair-cut', for instance). Third, it is a preparatory condition of S giving H an order to do A that it 'is not obvious to both S and H that H will do A in the normal course of events of his own accord'. Fourth, it is a *sincerity condition* of S's utterance counting as an order that 'S wants H to do A'. Fifth, it is an *essential condition* of S successfully giving an order that in virtue of certain conventions S's utterance standardly or typically counts 'as an attempt to get H to do A', and this 'counting as' depends partly on the rules of English usage (or whatever other language is being used), and partly on the existence of the authority relationship. It is, indeed, very tricky to work out what part the conventions of *language* play, and what part the knowledge of *circumstances* or *context* plays: in the Army, for example, a sergeant might perfectly well succeed in giving an order to a private to get his hair cut by exclaiming, 'Who do you think you are—Mozart?' (the example is Roy Edgley's: see above, p. 115).

Now this analysis in terms of preparatory, sincerity, and essential conditions seem to me pretty directly transferable to advertising, where advertising is to be thought of as a class of speech act performed, like ordering, according to rules. The analysis may sound strange at first, but then that does not show it to be wrong. I will proceed in two stages, first taking a hypothetical spoken radio advertisement for *Panzani*; then turning to the *Panzani* advertisement studied by Barthes, attempting to make increasing allowance for the specificity of its visual elements, though this will only be fully achieved in the next section of this essay.

Suppose, then, a really unsophisticated advertisement for *Panzani* broadcast on a local radio station, and consisting of the six words:

(4) Buy *Panzani* pasta, sauces and parmesan.

(The reader can, if she/he wishes, regard all the advertisements as having been translated from French). Now here we have an utterance which contains an expression for a propositional content ('Your-buying *Panzani* pasta, sauces, and parmesan') and an indicator (in the imperative mood of the word 'Buy') of the illocutionary force of the utterance ('Do it!') which identifies the action which the advertisement seeks to get the hearer to perform.[2] Now just as in most speech acts, the explicit verbal indication of the illocutionary force of the utterance is generally absent, since it is unnecessary to the hearer's recognition of the kind of speech act being performed, so in advertisements on radio listeners do not need a word like 'Buy' to allow them correctly to identify an advertisement as an advertisement. The context of utterance, for example, a change in the person speaking or a change from music to the spoken utterance, and the intonation of the utterance will usually over-determine the recognition of the utterance as an advertisement. So a slightly more sophisticated advertiser might drop 'Buy' and simply broadcast:

(5) *Panzani* pasta, sauces and parmesan.
or
(6) *Panzani* Italian de-luxe pasta, sauces and parmesan.

But if 'advertising' is a variety of speech act performed according to rules, what are these rules? (Note that it is entirely irrelevant that the 'advertiser', who takes the place of the 'speaker' of the earlier examples, may not be and usually isn't a uniquely identifiable individual. The only way to understand an utterance *as* an utterance as opposed to mere *noise* is to assume that it is *somebody's* utterance. The force assigned to the utterance may vary crucially according to whose utterance it is taken to be, as we saw in the example of a teacher's order becoming a friend's joke. Advertisers are perfectly well aware of this, and sometimes seek to confuse the reader into thinking that the *source* of the utterance is different from what it is: as when advertisers in magazines present their advertisements in the format of magazine text. More on this below).

What, then, might be the preparatory conditions for an utterance's being an advertisement? First, the speaker (advertiser) must stand in a certain relationship to the manufacturer of the product (provider of the service, etc.) advertised. Either the advertiser and the manufacturer must be the same, or the advertiser must be the *agent* of the manufacturer. If this condition is not fulfilled, then what results is not advertising for a product but something like 'free publicity' for it, and this is a distinguishable (speech) act, as advertisers well know: they hope (perhaps) that the tennis star who wears their sweat shirts will not be perceived as their *agent*, and hence as *advertising* their product, but rather as someone who simply happens to wear that brand of sweat shirt. This is also to say that hearers ('consumers') are assumed to draw the distinction between advertisements and other related kinds of (speech) act. Second, the hearer must be in a position to perform the action (i.e. buy the product) which the speaker seeks to get them to perform. Because we are dealing generally with many hearers rather than a single one, this condition will ultimately have to be formulated in a rather more precise form—for example, we might have to say that it is a preparatory condition for an advertisement's being an advertisement that *at least one* hearer be able to perform the action (buy the product). Third, the product must be available for purchase: confronted by an utterance which in some respects seemed like an advertisement for the Moon, people would almost certainly seek to reclassify it as some other kind of speech act—i.e. an act which had a different point, and possibly a different propositional content. (It is not an advertisement *for* the Moon, but a *cartoon about* space research: though see the discussion of the distinction between *what is said* and *what is implicated* in the next section.) Fourth, it is a preparatory condition of S's utterance being an advertisement that it is not obvious to both S and H that H will do A (buy the product) in the normal course of events. This condition may only amount to saying that it is this which gives the advertisement its *point*: it would be a waste of money to advertise something which was going to be bought in a fixed quantity regardless. But it is important to state the condition, for hearers (consumers) assume that advertisers don't waste money, at least in this particular way.

Fifth, it is the sincerity condition of S's utterance being an advertisement that S wants to sell the product advertised, if only because S is the manufacturer's agent and is bound to do what the manufacturer wants. Put more precisely, the advertisement is unintelligible as an advertisement unless the hearer can assume that *someone* wants to sell the product, that is, wants them to buy it. Only if hearers think that the speaker wants them to buy the product can they be expected to consider the advertisement from the point of view of whether it contains any 'reasons' (in the loosest sense—they can be appeals to prejudice, unconvincing reasons, etc.) for them to buy the product. In other words, it would be pointless for advertisers to seek to persuade the consumer by reasoning of any kind if they could not be sure that the reader would assume that they were trying to sell the product. It is partly because of this that I am inclined to think that advertisers who seek to disguise their advertisements as, say, magazine text are misguided. For they then make it possible for the reader who has read their advertisement with rapt attention to conclude a reading, quite appropriately, with the thought 'How interesting'—for by making their 'advertisement' apparently a *declarative* rather than a *directive*, they make inaction (as opposed to a decision or failure to act) an appropriate response. Hidden persuasion is usually no persuasion.

Sixth, the utterance must standardly or typically count as an attempt to get H to do A—buy the product—even though, of course, it may through incompetence fail miserably in achieving this: 'Buy *Panzani*' would certainly count as an attempt to sell Panzani, but the agency responsible for it would soon go bankrupt. (Actually, much advertising *is* as unsubtle as this. At my railway station right now there is a poster telling me to 'Visit Battle'.) But under no circumstances could the utterance of:

(7) Don't buy *Panzani*

count as an advertisement for Panzani, unless it had a sting in its tail—that is, was in fact a quite different utterance, such as:

(8) Don't buy *Panzani*, unless you want to be thought a gourmet.

The reader may be impatient with these silly examples. So let me give one a little more plausible, where the interpretation which consumers would give to it could only be understood by using the idea of 'counting as' which I have introduced in the sixth condition. Suppose then a full-page colour advertisement in a magazine for a well-known brand of cigarettes. In it, a slatternly, pregnant woman is offering a cigarette from the well-known pack to a red-eyed, hollow-cheeked man, bent double, one hand over his mouth as if seized by a fit of coughing. In the background, ill-clothed children are playing on the floor of a dirty kitchen, where dishes are piled high. Would anyone 'read' this advertisement as an advertisement *for* the

P

brand of cigarette, remarking as they did so that it was remarkably ill-judged for persuasiveness (despite its 'realism')? Or would they rather seek to interpret it as an advertisement for something else, and specifically as an anti-smoking advertisement? Even though this hypothetical advertisement is almost entirely visual, it seems to me that just as in language, so in images, there are quite clear standards for 'counting as' and that these standards are to a large extent mutual knowledge between advertisers and consumers.

This last example brings me to the actual *Panzani* advertisement studied by Barthes. The first question to consider in relation to it is this: How is it recognizable as an advertisement (that is, count as performing the speech act of advertising) despite the fact that it does not, apparently, bear any indicator of illocutionary force, either in the shape of words which would conventionally count as an advertising slogan ('Buy *Panzani*') or an identifying label (the printed word 'Advertisement')? I think this question is crucial to understanding how images like that studied by Barthes are actually read, and that the neglect of it gives rise to misreadings or under-theorised readings of images. For I do not think that it is possible to describe the content of the image (state its propositional content), or its connotations (its implications—see next section), without identifying it as the kind of utterance it is, and knowing how this identification is made, and realising the consequences of this identification.

If the *Panzani* spread was the typical full-page colour magazine advertisement which I imagine it was (and Barthes more or less indicates that it was), then for all but a very few readers of the magazine, identification of the advertisement was no doubt heavily over-determined, and it is, I suspect, rather difficult to break down the factors involved into a statement of necessary and sufficient conditions. I would point to at least the following as usually involved in determining the identification of this sort of advertisement as an advertisement, though it is impossible to know in the absence of having a copy of the original magazine which of them apply to the *Panzani* advertisement. First, the positioning of the image (I shall call it 'image' for convenience) at the beginning or end of the magazine, a very common convention of magazine layout. Second, the use of full colour rather than black and white, not so common but a discriminator in some magazines. Third, and more importantly I think, the quantitative spatial predominance of image over text. Though very important, this is quite clearly neither a necessary nor sufficient condition, rather it is a probabilistic discriminator. Fourth, the presence of a 'caption' inside rather than outside the frame of the image. This seems to me to be fairly well conventionalised—look, for instance at the *Sunday Times* colour magazine. Fifth, the size of type-face used for the caption (larger than those used for captioning text-related images in the non-advertising content of the magazine). Sixth, the style of the caption: it is asyndetic (lacking conjunctions). Seventh, the presence of a caption. Again, this is not necessary, and one can well imagine this particular *Panzani* advertisement giving rise to no problems of identification even without its caption. However, in an art magazine lacking its caption the image could conceivably be mistaken for a still life painting. Again, a particularly unknowledgeable reader might conceivably interpret the image minus its caption as an advertisement, but as an advertisement for fresh vegetables or string bags. However, to do this they would also have to be ignorant of the role of brand names in most advertising. For, eighth, the correct identification of the advertisement as an advertisement is determined by the prominence of the labelled *Panzani* products.

In the final sentence of the previous paragraph I use 'correct identification' deliberately. For it is important to realise that one would be mistaken not to identify this speech act or utterance *as* an advertisement. Images may be polysemic (that is, have multiple meanings—see next section), but they are not in general polysemic at the level of what one might call the 'primary' speech act which they perform, about which one can be both correct and mistaken. There are correct and incorrect readings of the *Panzani* image. An incorrect reading is to make a primary identification of it as a still life composition.

In the eight factors I have listed which determine the identification of the speech act as counting as an advertisement (and the list is no doubt not exhaustive), some factors are strictly *contextual*, that is, relate to information available to the reader from outside the image itself and applied on the basis of cultural knowledge. In other words, the reader interprets the context in order to identify the message (speech act), for advertising images just as much as for spoken messages. Some factors are internal to the image, such as the presence of the caption. So merely in order to identify the advertisement as an advertisement, readers have to relate three kinds of factor: (1) factors having to do with their assumptions about who has uttered the image and why; (2) factors having to do with the placing of the image in a context, though here 'context' means the context of the other utterances which 'surround' the utterance in question, not the extracodic context which is covered under (1); and (3) factors having to do with the 'syntax' and 'semantics' of the image itself. My main point against certain kinds of structuralism would be to say that there are no 'syntaxes' and 'semantics' which can be used to determine the meaning of either spoken utterances or images without reference to the first and second range of factors. All syntaxes and semantics are pragmatically modified, or, have a pragmatic component.

The identification of the speech act as an advertisement tells the reader what the illocutionary force of the utterance is; it is to do something, namely, *buy*. But buy what? Well, *Panzani* products of course. This is the referential content of the utterance, spelt out in images—the photographs of the pasta, sauce tin and parmesan packet—and that part of the caption which reads 'Pates Sauces Parmesan'. Usually, of course, readers will come to this image assuming it will be an advertisement and so proceed directly to the identification of referential content: the product they are being urged to buy. But as I have, I hope, sufficiently indicated, mistakes are possible, and it is worth spelling out the 'pragmatics of the advertisement' in order to appreciate all the dimensions involved.

We can now see why the correct identification of the primary speech act performed is so important. For it determines the identification of the referential content, *Panzani* pasta, sauces and parmesan. *If the image was interpreted in the pages of an art magazine as a still life composition, then the referential content would be different.* The still life would be identified as a still life *of* some tomatoes, peppers, mushrooms, packaged products, spilling out of a string bag. The referential content would be *all* that follows 'of' in the previous sentence.

But this, of course, does imply that the reader rules out the tomatoes and peppers, etc., as part of the referential content 'belonging' to the illocutionary force indicated by the imperative mood of 'Buy'. How is this achieved, and what are its necessary consequences? First, it is achieved, as Barthes observed, by the role of the caption element 'Pates Sauces Parmesan', which 'anchors' the message and 'dispatches' the reader towards a correct identification of the product. (See 14b, Barthes, pp. 38–41). Second, it is achieved in virtue of the reader's knowledge that advertisements are usually advertisements for *branded* products, and the only branded products in the photograph are *Panzani* products. It seems to me that these two operations are perfectly analogous to processes which occur in the identification of the referential content of linguistic utterances. But they do leave the problem, what are readers then to make of the presence of the remaining part of the caption ('à l'Italienne de luxe'), and of all those peppers, tomatoes, mushrooms and string bag? My answer is that they are to make of them (are meant to make of them; will make of them by means of a perfectly intelligible process) exactly what they would make of analogous elements in a purely verbal utterance, that is, that they will make of them *reasons* advanced by the advertiser *for* buying the product. How and why they do this and must do this is the subject of the next section.

3. What is Said and What is Implicated

As in the previous section, I shall again outline some concepts and theories of philosophy of language, illustrated with linguistic examples, and then show their application to the *Panzani* advertisement, the analysis of which will then be, at least in outline, complete.

This time it is from the work of H. P. Grice (especially 47a) that the relevant ideas are taken. They can be approached directly by means of an example, though not itself one used by Grice. Suppose, then, in an everyday context, the following conversational exchange occurs between A and B:

(9) A: Is Smith at work today?

(10) B: No, he's got a cold (or: No. He's got a cold, or: He's got a cold).

Now the utterance by B of 'No' would alone constitute a full answer to A's question. To use an expression favoured by logicians, the utterance of 'No' by B constitutes a *direct answer* to A's question, that is an answer which 'counts as completely, but just completely, answering the question' (18b, Belnap and Steel, p. 13). From a logical point of view, B's speech act constitutes an answer, though it lacks any indicator of illocutionary force ('I answer you that . . .') and its propositional content, which might be given in expanded form as 'Smith's-not-being-at-work-today', is contracted to the single word 'No', though this causes no problems for A, the context of utterance of 'No' by B being adequate to identify it as a direct answer to A's question. However, B does more than provide a direct answer to A's question, for he also says 'He's got a cold'. Now whether this should be regarded as the performance of a new, distinct speech act by B (a speech act of *assertion*), or whether it should be regarded as part of his *answer*, and either way, *what* the connexion between the two elements or acts is, is an extremely knotty problem which I am simply going to evade here. For our purposes, what needs to be explained is *why* the standard consequence of B's adding to his direct answer the words 'He's got a cold' are what they are.

For the standard consequence of B's complete utterance will be for A to think that Smith is away from work *because* he has got a cold, for A to think that B *intends* him to think this, and for A to be *entitled* to think this. Though not part of *what is said*, Smith's being absent from work *because* he has a cold is part of, if not the whole of, *what is implicated* by what B says, and Grice's object is to explain how what is said can give rise to implications, that is consequences which haven't been said but only implicated. We can all recognise that A is entitled to think Smith is absent *because* he has a cold, and the strength of this entitlement can be realised by means of a counterfactual example.

Suppose then that the conversational exchange given in (9) and (10) above does occur. Suppose that a little later A discovers independently of B that Smith is actually absent because he is attending his daughter's wedding. He goes up to B and tells him that Smith is absent because he is attending his daughter's wedding. If B replies by saying:

(11) I know. I didn't say he wasn't, and he does have a cold,

could A's response be other than one of complete mystification? Wouldn't A be quite justified in feeling misled? And isn't this to say that we cannot imagine a sane, adult person so communicatively incompetent that they do not realise that saying certain things in certain contexts standardly and typically implicates certain other things, which one's hearer is entitled to infer? The answer to all these questions must surely be yes. It is possible to achieve the effect of a lie by telling the truth, but not the whole truth.

What Grice wants to understand is the rules of conversation which *entitle* A to make the inference he does, and which *explain* how B's utterance can carry the implications which it does. He argues that conversation is standardly a co-operative activity, or is assumed by the participants to be so. He says that conversation is governed by a 'Co-operative Principle', which he states, informally, as a principle that you should 'Make your conversational contribution such as is required, at the stage at which it occurs, by the accepted purpose or direction of the talk exchange in which you are engaged' (47a, Grice, p. 45), and he says that this principle is generally realised by adhering to various conversational maxims, which he classifies into four kinds: (1) Maxims of *Quantity*—such as 'Be informative'; (2) Maxims of *Quality*—such as 'Do not say what you believe to be false'; (3) Maxims of *Relation*—that is, 'Be relevant'; (4) Maxims of *Manner*—such as 'Avoid obscurity'.

Now, in the case of our exchange (9) and (10) between A and B, A must either assume that B is adhering to the co-operative principle, or that he is not, or that partly he is and partly not. If A assumes B will not adhere to the co-operative principle, e.g., that he will lie in response to A's question, then there is no point in asking B the question (this can be shown by a speech act analysis of the rules for asking questions). If A assumes that B will only partly co-operate, then he must have a decision-procedure for deciding which parts of B's reply to discount (this is just like the problem faced by readers of newspapers in which they have less than perfect confidence). If A assumes that B is adhering to the co-operative principle, then he must find a way of reconciling the fact that B does more than directly answer his question with his adherence to the principle. This it is not exactly difficult for him to do, though to unpack it fully would require going into more detail than is really necessary for our present purposes. Suffice to say that *if* A assumes that B is being *informative* by saying 'He's got a cold', and furthermore is being informative *relevant* to A's interest in Smith's absence (as expressed by A's asking the question in the first place), *then* he will look for a way of relating what B says in addition to directly answering his question about Smith's absence, and the 'obvious' relationship is that there is a causal connexion between Smith's cold and his absence. So A infers that B intends to implicate a causal connexion between Smith's cold and his absence. Furthermore, B's actual utterance can carry such an implication because of the existence of certain conventions of English usage, whereby to juxtapose (temporally) utterances or utterance elements is standardly to imply a connexion between what it is that the different utterances or utterance elements are about. (Again, there are tricky problems about the relation of *intention* and *convention* in all this, as well as about the relationship between the cohesion of texts and the coherence of discourses).

In short, to account for the difference between what is said in an utterance and what is implicated in its saying, Grice invokes the existence of 'conversational conventions', to which others (e.g. David Lewis and Jürgen Habermas) would want to attribute a more than merely empirical existence and importance, arguing that they are constitutive conditions of the possibility of any use of language whatsoever. For our present purposes, it is enough to say that Grice's theory is one which argues that we standardly assume that all utterances are *motivated*, and can be given a *point*, a point which may lie in what they implicate, rather than what they say (or in addition to what they say).

This is directly relevant to the *Panzani* advertisement. For there in addition to a 'direct advertisement' (cf 'direct answer') for the product we have (1) images of selected vegetables and a string bag; (2) the caption element 'à lItalienne de luxe'; and (3) a choice of colours for the advertisement, not entirely explicable by the natural colours of the objects depicted. My suggestion is that the presence of these elements in 'what is said' gives rise to 'implications' just as do linguistic utterances, and they can do so and actually do so because the reader seeks to or does *account* for them (not necessarily in a fully conscious way) in a way consistent with the assumption that the co-operative principle is fulfilled. (If it sounds odd to speak of advertisers making their utterances according to a co-operative principle, I should perhaps point out that I argue below that it is necessary to first assume that the co-operative principle is being fulfilled in order to reach the conclusion that actually it isn't being fulfilled). In other words, my argument is that the advertisement can only carry what Barthes calls 'connotations' because the reader assumes that the advertiser has a purpose (motivation) in using all of the elements of the advertisement, that, in other words, none of the elements are accidental. (This is not to say that accidental features do not exist; they do, and they cause headaches for consumers as well as making for poor advertising copy. In modernist literature, 'accidental' elements are deliberately exploited to set up such problems. Some years ago, I agonised (99a) over finding an explanation for the leaves on the tree in Act 2 of Samuel Beckett's *Waiting for Godot*, before deciding that they were 'deliberate accidental features'.) This is not to say that none of the features are 'redundant', in the sense of information theory. No doubt some are, but the point of redundancy is to beat 'noise' and ensure that the message received is pretty close to the message intended to be received.

We are now in a position to ask: what point can be assigned to the so-far unaccounted for elements in the advertisement, consistent with the co-operative principle (and that means, consistent with the identification of the advertisement as an advertisement for *Panzani*)? Now, just as in (9) and (10) the obvious solution to the problem of explaining the element 'He's got a cold' was the implication of a causal relationship, so in the *Panzani* advertisement, the 'obvious' solution to the problem of explaining those additional elements is the implication that they are *reasons for buying Panzani*. As far as I am concerned, reasons don't have to be spelt out in words; they can be implicated by words—and they can be implicated by images. I shall now try to reconstruct the process whereby this comes about.

First of all note one way in which representation by means of images necessarily differs from representation in speech. In the latter, numerous devices (conjunctions) exist for indicating what relation exists between two parts of an utterance: devices which include 'and', 'but', 'despite', 'because' and so on. As we have seen in example (10) above the explicit employment of such devices is often not necessary in an utterance which can easily carry the meaning which such devices would carry, if employed, by means of implications arising from application of the co-operative principle. Most speech is elliptical. In contrast, images are necessarily elliptical, for they have at most a few means of representing the different kinds of conjuction which I partly listed above. It may be that they have a single means of representing all the different conjunctions, namely *spatial juxtaposition*. If this is so, then we are entitled to say that there is a visual 'syntax', but an impoverished one, relative to that of language. However, just as verbal ellipsis is often perfectly compatible with the correct identification of intended meaning, temporal juxtaposition providing the necessary clue that *some* relationship exists, so spatial juxtaposition is perfectly compatible with the correct identification of the meaning intended, or correct identification of the range of meanings possibly intended.

In this connection, consider the vegetables in the *Panzani* advert. Quite clearly, they are not part of what I have called the 'direct advertisement'. But the reader will assume that their *presence* is motivated, and that the *choice* of vegetables present is motivated. Further, the reader will assume that the juxtaposition of the vegetables and the *Panzani* products represents some kind of connection. In short, she/he generates (no doubt in a fraction of a second) an implication which *accounts* for the presence and choice of vegetables in terms of their connection with the propositional content of the direct advertisement, *Panzani* products.

It seems to me that there are at least two clear implications of what is said in this advertisement, which can be specified and which account for what is said. These map on to connotations suggested by Barthes. First, there is the implication that the vegetables are included because they are *compatible with* Panzani products. This implication is specified in terms of a weak relationship (compatibility) and could perhaps be strengthened: the vegetables are *necessary* to the completeness of a meal otherwise made up entirely from *Panzani* products. On the other hand, there is no way in which the vegetables could be accounted for in terms of an *incompatibility* relationship ('fresh and canned are incompatible') or as making an ironic commentary. For this would be *inconsistent* with the identification of the advertisement as a directive speech act attempting to sell *Panzani*, given the mutual knowledge of advertiser and consumer that fresh vegetables are evaluated positively from a culinary point of view. This is an interesting result, for it shows how *the identification of the speech act performed guides the working out of the implications generated*. But this analysis does not prevent a consumer from working out an intended implication as a means of accounting for what the advertiser says, but then going on to *reject* the implication as false or unconvincing. It is quite open to a consumer to say: they are suggesting that there is nothing incompatible in combining fresh vegetables with a tinned sauce —How ridiculous! But to reject an implication, which is what the advertiser offers as an implicit *reason* for buying his product, you have first of all to identify it. (See further my remarks on cigarette advertising below).

The string bag, I suggest, facilitates the working out of the compatibility implication. It strengthens the weak syntax of visual juxtaposition, by inserting the 'phrase', '*Panzani* produce and fresh vegetables', within an implied *narrative*. The string bag implies a 'before' and 'after' of what is represented here as an instant, and this 'before' and 'after', which the reader is able to work out from elementary knowledge of shopping and food preparation, furnishes further implied reasons for buying *Panzani* products (as well as explicating a preparatory condition of advertisements, that the product is *buyable*). As Barthes remarks (14b, p. 34) the narrative implied is that of personal shopping in the market (this is the 'before'). But there is also the 'after', which he also remarks upon: the (personal) preparation of food freshly bought. (Why personal preparation? Because string bags are not used to buy food which will be institutionally prepared: the inclusion of the string bag rules out (on the basis of mutual knowledge) that *Panzani* products are for institutional purchase and preparation).

Some 'implications' may seem more tenuous than others, and unnecessary to the correct reading of the advertisement. This is indeed so. A correct reading does not have to be a complete reading, just as a convincing argument is not always a complete argument. The rhetoric of the advertisement aims only to marshall a persuasive argument for a product. And it fails if the *cogito* is exhausted before it has been persuaded! But note that this 'incompleteness' of the actual reading which the advertisement will receive from any one consumer does not arise from some supposed peculiar 'polysemy' of the image (cf. 14b, Barthes, p. 39). Most messages, whatever their medium, are polysemous—which is to say that messages are interpreted by creative receivers! But in most instances, the context of utterance and reception controls the meanings actually imputed to any one message (perhaps in a probabilistic way, since we do not usually have all day to ponder over each message we receive, and so operate the most probable interpretation as a rational maximising strategy for message 'decoding'). Grice points out that verbal messages are 'polysemous' in that they frequently give rise to open disjunctions of implications which will equally account for them, writing that:

> Since, to calculate a conversational implicature is to calculate what has to be supposed in order to preserve the supposition that the Co-operative Principle is being observed, and since there may be various possible specific explanations, a list of which may be open, the conversational implicatum in such cases will be a disjunction of such specific explanations; and if the list of these is open, the implicatum will have just the kind of indeterminacy that many implicata do in fact seem to possess. [47a, Grice, p. 58]

Turning now to the choice of vegetables, it seems to me that it is easy enough to work out the implications. First, that these vegetables are chosen because they are required to (or can be used to) make a complete meal together with the *Panzani* products advertised. Second, that they are chosen because they are Italian, like the *Panzani* product. But how does the consumer know *Panzani* is Italian? First, it is said explicitly (the phrase 'à l'Italienne'). Second, it is mutual knowledge between advertiser and consumer that the average French consumer is able to recognise stereotypical foreign names and assign them to the correct country of origin. Now whilst the use of an Italian-sounding name in an advertisement for *Panzani* products is unavoidable (unless the product name is changed), the explicit remarking of the Italian character of the products, and the need to include reference to Italy in accounting for the choice of vegetables (not to mention to account for the colour scheme of the advertisement) is only explicable if it is mutual knowledge that *things Italian are positively valued,* that is to say, if 'Italianicity' might be able to serve as a reason for buying the products. If it was mutual knowledge that Italian products were rated as inferior, then it would be rational to play down the Italian connection (just as goods used to be 'Empire Made' rather than 'Made in Hong Kong'). But in this advertisement 'Italianicity' is so massively present (call it 'redundancy', 'doubling' or what you will) that this cannot be regarded as other than a selling point. And it is present both in what is said and in what is implicated. To speak here of a 'connotation' of Italianicity would seem to me to be misleading.

This leaves the expression 'de-luxe' unaccounted for. Does it need such accounting for? What it says is that the advertised products are de luxe products. Why is this said? The implication, for which there are no prizes, is plainly that this is a reason for buying those products. Of course, it is an ad man's cliché which is employed here, and a reason which is hardly persuasive. But this is only to say that it is the weak link in the chain of argument which constitutes this advertisement, a weak link which could have been spotted and modified. And the possibility of passing this kind of judgement seems to me one advantage of my method of analysis. For this method allows one to consider besides everything else the success and failure of advertisements, which is inseparable from consumer evaluation of them just as much as from advertisers' evaluation of their own work. In contrast, the denotation/connotation analysis, at least as offered by Barthes, stops short of this kind of evaluation and, fixing an image in a gaze, loses sight of the utterance in action. Any analysis of advertising images which wants to keep a line open to the actual consumption of such images in society must realise that though the most tenuous implications of an advertisement, which take hours to work out, are the most interesting, it is the implications worked out by the consumer in the first half second which are the most important. It is in that half second that one either persuades or not.

This last remark may help us to account for certain trends in contemporary cigarette advertising, in which an enlarged cigarette packet is presented on a flat, coloured background. No doubt that this style has implications if one looks hard enough. But I suspect that from the advertiser's point of view it's advantage is that nothing is implicated beyond what is said (where what is said amounts to no more than 'Buy *x*' where *x* is the brand name). For with shifts in cultural knowledge, not to mention health warnings which the advertiser is compelled to print at the bottom of advertisements, it is increasingly the case that anything which the advertiser might like to implicate is patently false, and to boot immediately contradicted by the Health Warning. At one time you could have people smoking cigarettes by babbling brooks and crashing waterfalls, carrying the implication that enjoying cigarettes and enjoying the healthy, open-air life were compatible. Now, this 'obvious' implication is obviously false. Unable to think of any good reasons why you should buy cigarettes, advertisers retreat to a message in which no reasons are given, saying only 'Buy *x*'. And this puts cigarette advertising in a class of its own. For it has to remove itself from the sphere of rational argument, where it can only bring ridicule upon itself. In contrast, almost all of the rest of advertising belongs entirely to the domain of rational argument. The reasons used may be bad, no matter. What is important is that one can only produce connotations, or, as I have called them, implications, in an audience which assumes that your message has the characteristics of rational persuasion, that is, that you are engaging in a conversation with them in which the co-operative principle is fulfilled. To imply, as advertisers do, that some lousy beer increases your potency is to advance an argument for drinking that beer. Whether this reflects something rather interesting about advertisers or about beer drinkers or both is not my present concern. I only wish to point out that advertiser and consumer are locked together in a dialectical argument, possessing its own rhetorical style, and governed by the co-operative principle of conversation. There are right and wrong ways of doing things with advertising images, and the criterion for that is to be found not only in the rhetoric of the image, but in what we might now decide to call *the pragmatics of advertising*.[3]

NOTES TO APPENDIX 5

1. Written 1978, and accepted for publication in *Theory and Society*. I have now discovered that two other authors have used speech act theory in discussing the use of pictures: see 66a, 66b, Kjørup, and 92a, 92b, Novitz. Neither author seeks to extend Gricean conversation theory to pictorial pragmatics. Pratt's book (104a) is also similar in its approach to that adopted here.

2. I am grateful to Roy Edgley for pointing out a mistake in my original formulation of this relationship.

3. Note added. To say, as I do, that 'advertising is to be thought of as a class of speech act' (p. 220 above) is pretty implausible. For Searle, speech acts are the *minimal* units of linguistic communication (114b, Searle, p. 16), whereas an advertisement is plainly not a minimal unit—it may be made up of speech acts, but is not itself one. In a paper to a conference on 'Discourse Processes and Practical Reasoning' (Oxford, July 1979), Stephen Levinson argued that Gricean-type pragmatic inferences operate, not directly on individual speech acts, but *via* our understanding of the activity-type (or language-game) in which such speech acts (utterances) are embedded, and that for each such activity type there will be a set of inferential schemata. Now while I do not want completely to particularise inferential schemata to activity types (and hence multiply entities on a large scale), it is clear that in the present essay, my implicit argument in Section 3 is that inferences from the 'utterance' content of an advertisement are made on the basis of an understanding of the activity-type 'advertising' (misleadingly called 'speech-act' in Section 2) in which that content occurs. The idea of general principles of inference (as opposed to wholly particularised ones) is, however, also present in Section 3 in the notion that advertisements *like all activity-types* have a *point*. In this connexion, I discover that in recent work, Dan Sperber and Deirdre Wilson (see, e.g., Wilson and Sperber, 'L'interprétation des énoncés', in *Communications 30*, Paris 1979, pp. 80–94) have sought to reduce Grice's four conversational maxims to a single principle of *pértinence* (translating Grice's *relevance*). I hope to develop a revised version of the present paper, taking into account such ideas as those of Levinson and Sperber and Wilson, in an article commissioned for H. Davis and P. Walton, Eds., *Language and Media* (Basil Blackwell, forthcoming) and provisionally entitled, 'How is understanding an advertisement possible?'.

APPENDIX 6

Is there Power in Words? [1]

This paper has the limited objective of showing how an utterance can make an independent contribution to sustaining a particular kind of social relationship. Specifically, I shall seek to show how use of an ill-formed speech act can make an independent contribution to sustaining (reproducing) the power, authority, or control exercised by one person over another in a social situation. I think this analysis is worthwhile for the following reason: We speak fairly freely about the 'power of words', but on close inspection most cases in which words are supposed to have power turn out to be situations in which people have power. If I can show *one* instance in which words have power, then it might be considered reasonable to look for others and to seek to develop a general account. My argument will rely to a considerable degree on establishing a concordance of intuitions between the reader and myself, but I have put things in a way which suggests how the argument might be made more rigorous. For my argument makes use of computational metaphors, and I use this metaphor because I think that one possible way of testing my argument would be through computer simulations of human conversation. In a Postscript I also suggest how game theory might be used to develop the analysis. A second Postscript sets out criticism of the paper, and offers a reformulation of the analysis.

A teacher walks into a noisy class and loudly commands, 'Be quiet!' Silence follows. This episode tells us nothing about the power of words; and something about the power of teachers. (I shall use 'power' as a catch-all for power, authority and control relations.)

Seating himself behind his desk, the teacher asks the boy immediately in front of him, 'What's your name?' The boy answers, 'Smith, sir.' This episode tells us nothing about the power of questions; but again tells us something about the power of teachers. (Smith's alacrity in answering the question may depend partly on what he infers from the pitch, stress and intonation of the question to the 'state' of the teacher who asks it; in this sense pitch, stress and intonation offer 'intention free' —'indexical' in Peirce's sense—evidence for something's being the case. On this basis, and following J. Bennett's argument in *Linguistic Behaviour* (18e, Bennett) I exclude such factors from the scope of this paper.) The teacher indicates to the class that he is going to talk about Advertising for this lesson, and proceeds to talk about it, interspersing his talk with questions directed to the class in general and to individuals in particular. There arrives a point at which the teacher perceives that Smith looks inattentive; acting on what by analogy with H. P. Grice's Co-operative Principle (47a, Grice) we might call the *Strategic Principle of Conversation*, the teacher selects an utterance adapted to his overall purpose or purposes in the situation he is in, and asks Smith, 'Smith, is advertising important?' Now, first suppose Smith does not realise he has been inattentive (indeed, allow that he was actually paying attention), and suppose that he does not hear the question as directed at his inattention. He looks slightly baffled, but after a pause may say 'Yes'. The teacher then proceeds (perhaps commenting on Smith's reply, 'Yes, of course it is. I don't know why it took you so long to answer'). But now suppose that Smith was being inattentive, knows it, and hears the question as directed at his inattentiveness. Nonetheless, he still has to attempt to answer it (in virtue of the social relation obtaining between teacher and pupil), and after a pause he may also say 'Yes'.

I believe that an episode such as I have characterised in the previous paragraph can help us locate the power of a speech act (an action performed in words) distinct from the power present in the social situation in which it is uttered (and which, for example, explains the fact that Smith must try to answer the question: questions in the classroom generally have the force of imperatives or requests, rather than that of invitations to what D. Harrah calls 'information matching' (52b, Harrah).[2] My argument is that the power of at least some utterances is located in the features of those utterances which allow us to characterise them as ill-formed tokens of the speech act types to which they are *correctly* assigned by hearers on the basis of computations made *from* the linguistic form of the utterance plus its context of utterance *to* its speech act type, where by 'context of utterance' I mean such variables as speaker, addressee, place (social place—e.g. school), time (social time—e.g. lesson time), and so on, to which values are assigned by the hearer in performing the computation.

Very importantly, the way I have put things in the previous paragraph allows me to distinguish the class of ill-formed speech acts from the class of indirect speech acts (on which see 114d, Searle). The teacher's utterance addressed to Smith is not to be classified as a speech act of *request*, performed by indirection (by means of an interrogative form). For though its mediate aim may well be to make Smith more attentive (and this is not essential to my argument), Smith cannot satisfy the teacher by 'matching' the teacher's utterance with a show of attentive behaviour, in the case where he hears the question as directed at his inattentiveness. For suppose Smith did react in this way. The teacher might appropriately comment: 'That's right, Smith, pay attention. Now, Is Advertising important?' In other words, the immediate aim of the teacher is to receive an answer to his utterance, which is therefore correctly classified as a question.

In real time conversational processing, I imagine that the assignment to speech-act types is done on the basis of a partial computation which is halted as soon as an assignment can be made with a high enough degree of probability. This idea has a part to play in what follows.

Grant, then, that Smith has assigned the teacher's utterance to the speech act classification, *Question*. Part of Smith's communicative competence consists in his knowledge of what a question is; this includes the knowledge that it is usual to answer questions (which is partly if not wholly distinct from his knowledge that there are good reasons for usually doing what teachers tell you to do—here, answer a question). But before he can answer the teacher's question, Smith has to work out *what* is the question to which he has to find an answer. I am not sure how to label the process by which this is done. Perhaps the most open is to say that Smith must assign a 'semantic interpretation' to the question. This will have at least three parts. First, interpreting what the question is about (what might be called its propositional content).[3] Second, interpreting the range of answers which the question indicates as permissible. It might be argued that this stage or routine is performed as part of the speech act classification of the utterance, so that in the assignment process, the utterance would be classified as *Genus* (*Question*), *Species* (*Yes-No*). I am not sure about this. Allow for purposes of argument that the *Yes-No* interpretation belongs in what I'm calling the semantic interpretation and follows the assignment of propositional content. At this point we can say that Smith has computed two things:

(a) Advertising's importance (propositional content);
(b) The possibility of his either assenting to or dissenting from this (indicated range of acceptable answers).

The third stage Smith comes to must be the decision as to what his answer will be—that is, the third stage is the making of a judgement, which will involve him in evaluating 'advertising' by criteria of 'importance'. Now, it is at this stage that I suggest Smith is going to get into difficulties and that the teacher's utterance exercises its real time power. For making very minimal assumptions about Smith's attention, intellectual capabilities, and general worldly knowledge, we can almost certainly say that the answer will be *obvious* to him. It is obvious because the teacher is devoting a lesson to the subject about whose importance he is asking. Of course, the answer is 'Yes'. And if it is obvious to him, it must be obvious to the teacher. (Pupils do, of course, put down the intellectual powers of their teachers, but ambivalently; by the end of this paper I hope to have offered some insight into such ambivalence.) Furthermore, it ought (Smith reasons) to be obvious to the teacher that it is obvious to Smith that Smith knows the answer to the question (only allowing that the teacher does not treat Smith as *particularly* stupid, etc.). In other words, if all this is true, the teacher is apparently asking a question which violates at least one rule on asking questions, even allowing for the contextual modification on that rule which is generally made to allow for exam questions. What rule is this? It is the rule which Searle specifies as follows:

(1) The Speaker does not know the answer to the question, except where the question is an 'exam' question, in which case the speaker wants to know if the hearer knows the answer (see 114b, Searle, pp. 66–7).

Here we have a situation where the hearer supposes not only that the speaker knows the answer to his own question, but knows the pupil knows it. Nor does the case fall under another contextual modification of this rule on question-asking, which we might specify as follows:

(1a) The Speaker does not know the answer to the question, except where the question is an 'exam' question . . . or is a 'starter' question in an end of term quiz, in which case the speaker asks a question to which he knows the hearer will know the answer.

But Smith is not in an exam, still less in a quiz situation. So he is being asked what must appear to him an ill-formed question, ill-formed in the sense of being *trivial* (a term I borrow from 18a, Belnap, though extending its range to include questions where the speaker knows the hearer knows the answer as well as questions where the speaker knows the answer). My suggestion is that in such a situation a general crisis-resolution principle will tell Smith to reprocess his computation, but if he does so, he will do it under growing time pressure, and in a heightened state of tension, with a consequent increased probability of error or breakdown ('Confusion'), *or else* if he stands by his computation, he must generate some explanation for the fact that he has been asked a trivial question.[4] As far as I can see, he can generate one of three explanations. First, that the teacher is stupid. Second, that the teacher thinks Smith is stupid. Third, that the teacher in asking the question is seeking to get in something by way of an implicature, relying on Smith's knowledge of the Strategic Principle of Conversation ('Your behaviour suggests to me that you might not think advertising is important enough for you to try to pay any attention to what I'm saying about it', and so on). Whatever Smith does (and one cannot tell what he will opt for without a fuller specification of the circumstances), it will all take him time, raise what I'll simply call his 'anxiety level', and at the end of the day leave him in the unenviable position of people asked trivial questions not admitted as such:[5] he will have to give a trivial answer. Or rather, he will have to give a trivial answer because the only way of avoiding this which language allows is barred to him in virtue of the social relationship which obtains between teacher and pupil. For Smith cannot reply to the teacher's utterance with a meta-communication, such as 'That's a trivial question'. So even if the specific power of words is to be located, for at least some cases, in the performance of ill-formed speech acts, the effectivity of such means will *usually* depend on the fact that the social relationship is such that meta-communication specifically referring to the ill-formed nature of the speech act is debarred, though it could depend on the inability of the hearer to meta-communicate, or lack of skill in doing so. This latter alternative is crucial in the double bind account of schizogenesis, and may have a part to play in the account of control in the classroom. (I just don't know how and when children develop metacommunicative skills.)

Finally, it is important to observe that in the way I have located the power (or, rather, a power) of words, the power of an ill-formed speech act actually *depends* on the communicative competence of the hearer. For if Smith was incompetent, and did not know a well-formed from an ill-formed question, then the teacher's question could cause him no problems whatsoever. If he knew that advertising was important, knew that the teacher knew, knew that the teacher knew he knew, he could still, and quite cheerfully, answer 'Yes' to the question, without any bothersome recomputations, imputations of stupidity or generations of implicatures. This particular conclusion I can imagine being welcome to those who would follow Habermas in wanting to argue that distorted communication always operates parasitically on a presupposed ideal speech situation with normative force.

I have sought to establish one way in which we can legitimately talk about the power of words. That does not preclude there being other ways. How important ill-formed speech acts are in sustaining relations of power, I do not know. But what I hope to have done is suggest to those interested in these questions at least a precise focus for research into the power of *language* in the classroom, the family, and politics, a focus which can analytically separate this power from that of teachers, parents and politicians.

Postscript

It has been put to me (by Max Clowes) that I could replace the
expression 'computational difficulties' used in this paper with
the concept 'uncertainty' and thereby clarify the kind of power
which I'm claiming the utterance of defective tokens of speech
act types can exercise. For such utterances create uncertainty
in the hearer with respect to the appropriate course of action
for them to pursue in the two-person game in which they are
being engaged (for opening up a talk exchange creates a new
context, and the initial utterance is the first move in that context, creating a further new context in which the addressee may
or must respond). In the present case, the pupil's uncertainty
has to do with whether what looks like the appropriate or
correct answer to the teacher's question will, in fact, satisfy it,
since the apparent correct answer entails the conclusion that the
question is trivial. Further, it is plain that questions cannot be
put and receive answers of their own account; we must have
recourse to those who ask them, who are also responsible for
them: the pupil has to consider whether the answer will satisfy
the teacher, as well as whether it will satisfy the question. In
other words, the range of possible or permissible answers is not
uniquely specified by consideration of the syntactic form and
semantic interpretation of the question; the person asking the
question, his knowledge and expectations must also be taken
into account. (Some teachers ask apparently straightforward
questions and reject answers to them which are appropriate on
the basis of consideration of their form and meaning; one can
say either that the question was carelessly framed, or that the
teacher is capricious.)[6] If the pupil thinks that the teacher, in
general, is not satisfied with trivial answers, then in the example
given above the pupil finds himself in a no-win situation, where
the best he can do is to minimise the losses he will incur through
giving a trivial answer—losses of such things as status with the
teacher or his peers.

　The allusion to game theory in the previous paragraph could
be more systematically developed. First, it may be observed
that defective speech act tokens or undecidable utterances can
be deliberately employed by speakers to achieve a purpose
which is served by creating uncertainty in hearers. This purpose

clearly cannot be a purpose common to, shared by, speaker and hearer. Rather, such a purpose would be characterised in a two person zero-sum game, as a situation in which a speaker plays a language game against a hearer with a view to maximising his share of the fixed sum rewards (e.g. control) available. Use of language in such a situation can appropriately be termed strategic, since one participant in the conversation is pursuing a policy which cannot be mutually beneficial. So we can speak of such conversations as governed by the Strategic Principle.

It should be observed that such zero-sum conversational games do not necessarily involve conflict over the distribution of a fixed sum amount of a pre-existing good. Rather, the game may itself bring into being the good to be divided: one can pick an argument as one can pick a fight.

In contrast to zero-sum games, when conversation is governed by a co-operative principle the reward is non-zero sum, that is, the sum available for distribution can be increased by successful co-operation, paradigmatically by yielding truths known to, or agreed upon, by all participants, who could not have arrived at them singly. Such co-operation will be inefficient to the degree that participants unintentionally make use of uncertainty-creating utterances in the sense defined above for zero-sum games.

In addition, we can imagine various kinds of mixed games and these we may suppose to model actual human conversations most closely. Further development of these game-theoretic metaphors would depend on my getting a closer acquaintance with game theory!

Second Postscript

I am afraid that the account in the preceding paper founders on the objection (made by Dell Hymes, personal communication 1978) that 'Is advertising important?' is not obviously an ill-formed token of a speech act type: Hymes says 'It seems perfectly ordinary, natural, proper, whatever you want and indeed your presentation partly depends upon it seeming all these things'.

In the paper I in fact find a label for the question in question; I call it a 'trivial question'. And though I actually get the term 'trivial' from Belnap, the term is available commonsensically. But why should trivial questions be regarded as defective tokens of the speech-act type, *question*, rather than as tokens of a sub-species of the question type, namely *trivial questions?*

One answer would be to say that the concept 'trivial' belongs to a different universe of discourse from that of 'question'. The latter is a concept from the field of the theory of illocutionary force; the former from the field of logical appraisal (in fact, from erotetic logic, in the development of which Belnap has played a major role). Hence, it could be argued, one cannot justifiably treat 'trivial question' as a speech-act type; one would be mixing domains.

Against this it could be argued that one can give a rule-based account for trivial questions along standard speech-act theoretic lines, and nor would such an account have to be given in terms of 'violation' of one of the rules on question asking. For one would say, 'To ask a trivial question, ask a question to which you know the answer, you know the hearer knows the answer, and to which the hearer knows you know he knows the answer.'

An alternative approach to the analysis of 'Is advertising important?' would be to take the Gricean line, indicated in the text where I say of the pupil that 'he must generate some explanation for the fact that he has been asked a trivial question' (p. 242 above). The point is that the teacher's question in being trivial is incompatible with fulfilment either of the maxim of Quantity or the maxim of Manner or both. What is unclear is whether this incompatibility arises from a *violation* of those maxims, not meant to be detected as such and therefore incompatible with the assumption that the Co-operative Principle is being adhered to or, rather, whether this incompatibility arises from a *flouting* of those maxims, with a view to getting in something by way of an implicature, which relies on the assumption being made that the Co-operative Principle holds good. In the final analysis, it may be the real-time uncertainty created in the pupils mind as to whether he is dealing with violation or flouting which accounts for the specific effects of the utterance I have attempted to analyse.

This much said, I conclude by noting that Professor Hymes had a second objection to my paper, 'It has always seemed to me a grave mistake to omit the considerations that Bennett omits. I can't imagine any ultimate reason for omitting them except to preserve the relevance of the trained incapacity of philosophers, etc., who don't want to have to deal with actuality. Most of the linguistic analysis of speech acts seems to me to be worthless for its neglect of part of the phenomenon to be analysed, namely, the part that doesn't get written down. All this seems to me just a deepseated ethnocentric and disciplinary bias.' I have no brief answer to this objection, and no long one either. For Hymes' own utilisation of data which don't get written down, see Ch. 9 of his *Foundations in Sociolinguistics* (58b, Hymes).

A different line of criticism is developed by Keith Graham who asks, 'Have you really lighted on an instance of the power of language *as distinct* from the power of teachers? It is surely the position of the speech-agent which allows this speech act to function as it does. If, in exactly the same situation, Smith's neighbour Jones had uttered the same words, the unfolding of the story would be quite different (Smith might reason that Jones must be asking the question so as to decide whether it's worth foregoing his daydreaming for the next half hour). In short, I'm not sure you can even get the analytical separation you seem to want.' This seems to me correct: uttered by Jones, the words 'Is advertising important?' will be constituted by Smith into a genuine, full-blown, standard, normal [etc., etc.] question; uttered by the teacher, they will be constituted into the asking of a trivial question. My implicit concern is with the questions, Is the asking of a trivial question an effective way of controlling a pupil? Can it be more effective than a straightforward command ('Pay attention')? If so, how? If we think of the teacher as able to realise a *strategy* by choosing among a number of linguistic *options*; if some of those options are better adapted to the end in view than others; and if their superiority is to be related to factors non-specific to the *particular* individual addressed, like general social and cognitive competence, then I think those options involve 'the power of words', though only as partly constituting a particular Speaker-action (and this is to concede to Graham). So the focus of attention should be on *actions performed in words*, and clearly not on words in abstraction from actions. (The variables which have to be taken into account simultaneously are usefully analysed in 74a, Lewis.)

NOTES TO APPENDIX 6

1. Written 1978. Not previously published. The notes and Second Postscript have been added. I am grateful to Max Clowes, Dell Hymes and Keith Graham for permission to use their comments.

2. This obviously suggests that there is something wrong with the treatment of 'question'. For 'question' is supposed to characterize the illocutionary force of an utterance, as opposed to 'interrogative' which characterises its grammatical form (see for instance, 78a, Lyons, p. 30). But it seems that 'question' can be further analysed using the illocutionary concepts of 'imperative', 'request' (and 'invitation'). I am not sure how to handle this. See also 78b, Lyons, pp. 753–68, and 41c, Gazdar, pp. 8–10. [Stephen Levinson in the paper referred to in App. 5, n. 3 used the example of questions to illustrate drawbacks in the speech-act approach, arguing that what a question is depends on the activity-type within which it occurs].

3. Quine denies that propositions exist (104f, Quine, Ch. 1); Gazdar (41c, p. 26) says that the 'propositional' content of a question is not a proposition.

4. This point is taken up in the Second Postscript.

5. In a class quiz, it is enviable to be asked a trivial question, since its triviality is admitted (i.e. is mutual knowledge of both first and second order: the teacher and pupil both know that the question is trivial, and know that the other knows).

6. Here is an example of what I have in mind:

> Teacher: In a *blast* furnace. Good. What type of temperature do we need, ahm Calder, what type of temperature do we need?
> Pupil: Sir, very high temperature.
> Teacher: Yes that's pretty obvious but what *type* of *range* are we talking about? Three candle power?
> Pupils: (Laughs.)
> Pupil: A thousand degrees.

In this instance, it could be argued that 'very high temperature' directly and appropriately answers the question about 'what type of temperature', and indeed the teacher accepts it. But he also criticises it for failing to fulfil the maxim of Quantity, and amends his question to indicate what he requires, though the cue is pretty obviously provided by the word 'three' and not by the amendment of 'type' to '*type* of *range*'. Note that the teacher could have replied to the answer 'very high temperature' by saying, for example, 'Yes, that's right. How high?' Instead he indicates that to answer this question satisfactorily the pupil must seek to satisfy a 'non-obviousness' condition, not itself indicated by his *question*, but only by its *context*. This involves him in putting down the respondent pupil.

(The example is from a transcript, 'Answering Teachers' Questions' used by Martyn Hammersley in a talk at Wolfson College, Oxford, and also published in 51c, Hammersley. I am grateful for his permission to use it.)

BIBLIOGRAPHY

Bibliography

1. ADELSTEIN, D. ' "The Philosophy of Education" or the Wisdom and Wit of R. S. Peters', in Pateman, T. (Ed.), *Counter Course: A Handbook for Course Criticism*. Penguin Books, Harmondsworth, 1972.

1a. ADORNO, T. *The Jargon of Authenticity*. Routledge & Kegan Paul, London, 1973.

1b. ADORNO, T. & HORKHEIMER, M. *The Dialectic of Enlightenment*. Allen Lane, London 1973.

2. ALTHUSSER, L. *For Marx*. Allen Lane, London 1969.

3. ALTHUSSER, L. *Lenin and Philosophy*. New Left Books, London 1971.

4. ALTHUSSER, L. & BALIBAR, E. *Reading Capital*. New Left Books, London 1970.

4a. APEL, K. O. 'Einfuhrende Bemerkungen zur Idee einer "Transzendentalen Sprachpragmatik" ' in Heidrich, H. Ed., *Semantics and Communication*, pp. 81–108. North Holland, Amsterdam 1974.

4b. APEL, K. O. 'The *A Priori* of Communication and the Foundation of the Humanities', in *Man and World*, Vol. 5, pp. 3–37, 1972.

5. ARENDT, H. 'Truth and Politics', in Laslett, P. & Runciman, W. G. (Eds.), *Philosophy, Politics and Society*, Vol. II. Blackwell, Oxford 1967.

5a. AUSTIN, J. 'A Plea for Excuses' in *Philosophical Papers*. Oxford University Press, 1961.

5b. AUSTIN, J. *How to do Things with Words*. Oxford University Press, Second Edition, 1975.

5c. AYER, A. *Language, Truth and Logic*. Gollancz, London. Second edition, 1946.

6. BACHELARD, G. *La Formation de l'Esprit Scientifique*. Vrin, Paris 1970.

7. BACHRACH, P. & BARATZ, M. *Power and Poverty*. Oxford University Press, New York 1970.

8. BAGEHOT, W. *The English Constitution*, Ed. by Stevas N. St. J. (1959). The Bagehotian epigraph to Chapter V is cited from a paper by Stuart Hall in *Working Papers in Cultural Studies*, Birmingham, n. 3 (1972), p. 74.

8a. BAKER, K. *Condorcet.* University of Chicago Press, 1975.

8b. BALANDIER, G. *Political Anthropology.* Penguin Books, Harmondsworth, 1972.

9. BANNISTER, D. & FRANSELLA, F. *Inquiring Man, the theory of Personal Constructs.* Penguin Books, Harmondsworth, 1971.

9a. BAR-HILLEL, Y. Comments on K-O Apel, 'Einfuhrende Bemerkungen zur Idee einer Transzendentalen Sprachpragmatik', in H. Heidrich (Ed.), *Semantics and Communication.* North Holland, Amsterdam 1974.

9b. BARKER, C. *The Pilkington Strike.* Socialist Worker Pamphlet, London 1970.

10. BARTHES, R. *Writing Degree Zero.* Cape, London 1967.

11. BARTHES, R. *Mythologies.* Cape, London 1972.

12. BARTHES, R. *Elements of Semiology.* Cape, London 1967.

13. BARTHES, R. 'L'Ancienne Rhetorique', in *Communications 16* (Paris) December 1970.

14. BARTHES, R. *Sade, Fourier, Loyola.* Seuil, Paris 1971.

14a. BARTHES, R. *S/Z.* Editions du Seuil, Paris 1970 (English translation, Jonathan Cape, London 1975).

14b. BARTHES, R. 'Rhetoric of the Image', in *Image, Music, Text,* pp. 32–51. Fontana, London 1977.

14c. BARTHES, R. *L'Empire de Signes,* Skira, Geneva 1970.

14d. BARTHES, R. *Leçon.* Editions du Seuil, Paris 1978.

14e. BARTHES, R. 'The Photographic Message', in *Image, Music, Text.* Fontana, London 1977.

15. BATESON, G. *Steps to an Ecology of Mind.* Paladin, London 1972.

16. BAUDRILLARD, J. *Pour une critique de l'economie politique du signe.* Gallimard, Paris 1972.

17. BECKETT, S. *Malone Dies.* Penguin Books, Harmondsworth 1962.

18. BECKETT, S. *Waiting for Godot.* Faber, London 1962.

18a. BELNAP, N. 'Questions: their Presuppositions and How they can fail to arise', in K. Lambert (Ed.), *The Logical Way of Doing Things,* pp. 23–37. Yale University Press, New Haven 1969.

18b. BELNAP, N. & STEEL, T. *The Logic of Questions and Answers.* Yale University Press, New Haven 1976.

18c. BENVENISTE, E. 'La Decouverte Freudienne', in *Prob-*

lèmes de Linguistique Generale, pp. 75–87. Gallimard, Paris 1966.

18d. BENJAMIN, W. 'Karl Kraus' in W. Benjamin, *Reflections*. Harcourt, Brace, Jovanovitch, New York 1978.

18e. BENNETT, J. *Linguistic Behaviour*. Cambridge University Press, 1976.

19. BERGER, P. & LUCKMANN, T. *The Social Construction of Reality*. Allen Lane, London 1967.

20. BERLIN, I. 'Two Concepts of Liberty', in *Four Essays on Liberty*. Oxford University Press, 1969.

21. BERNSTEIN, B. *Class, Codes and Control. Volume 1. Theoretical Studies Towards a Sociology of Language*. RKP, London 1971.

21a. BERNSTEIN, R. J. 'Hannah Arendt: Opinion and Judgement', Unpublished paper for the American Political Science Association Annual Meeting 1976.

21b. BODEN, M. *Artificial Intelligence and Natural Man*. Harvester Press, Hassocks 1977.

22. BOTTOMORE, T. B. & RUBEL, M. (Eds.), *Karl Marx: Selected Writings in Sociology and Social Philosophy*. Penguin Books, Harmondsworth 1963.

22a. BOURDIEU, P. & PASSERON, J.-C. *Reproduction in Education, Society and Culture*. Sage, London 1977.

22b. BOWLES, S. & GINTIS, H. *Schooling in Capitalist America*. Routledge & Kegan Paul, London 1976.

23. BREUER, J. & FREUD, S. *Studies in Hysteria*, trans. by A. A. Brill. Beacon Press, Boston 1964.

23a. BROWN, P. & LEVINSON, S. 'Universals in language usage: Politeness phenomena', in E. Goody (Ed.), *Questions and Politeness*, pp. 56–289. Cambridge University Press, 1978.

23b. BUCHANAN, J. & TULLOCK, G. *The Calculus of Consent: Logical Foundations of Constitutional Democracy*. University of Michigan Press, Ann Arbor 1962.

24. BURNS, J. H. 'J. S. Mill and Democracy 1829–61' in Schneewind, J. B. (Ed.), *Mill*. Macmillan, London 1969.

25. BURNS, T. & BURNS, E. (Eds.), *Sociology of Literature and Drama*. Penguin Books, Harmondsworth 1973.

25a. CALLINICOS, A. 'Review of *Language, Truth and Politics*', in *International Socialism 85*, p. 32. 1976.

R

25b. CARDAN, P. *The Meaning of Socialism.* Solidarity Pamphlet No. 6, Bromley 1966.

26. CASSIRER, E. *An Essay on Man.* Yale University Press, New Haven 1944.

26a. CAVELL, S. 'Must we Mean What we Say?' in *Must We Mean What We Say?*, pp. 1–43. Scribners, New York 1969.

27. CHISHOLM, R. *Perceiving: a Philosophical Study.* Cornell University Press, Ithaca 1957.

28. CHISHOLM, R. *Theory of Knowledge.* Prentice-Hall, New Jersey 1966.

29. CHOMSKY, N. *American Power and the New Mandarins.* Penguin Books, Harmondsworth 1969.

29a. CHOMSKY, N. *Syntactic Structures.* Mouton, The Hague 1957.

29b. CHOMSKY, N. *Reflections on Language.* Fontana, London 1976.

29c. COLE, P. & MORGAN, J. (Eds.), *Syntax and Semantics, Vol. 3, Speech Acts.* Academic Press, New York 1975.

29d. COLLIER, A. *R. D. Laing: The Philosophy and Politics of Psychotherapy.* Harvester Press, Hassocks 1977.

29e. COOPER, B. *Bernstein's Codes: A Classroom Study.* University of Sussex Education Area, Occasional Paper 6. 1976.

30. COULTHARD, M. 'A Discussion of restricted and elaborated codes' in *Educational Review*, Birmingham, Vol. 22, 1969.

30a. COULTHARD, M. *An Introduction to Discourse Analysis.* Longman, London 1977.

30b. CRESSWELL, M. 'Semantic Competence' in F. Guenther and M. Guenther-Ruetter (Eds.), *Meaning and Translation.* Duckworth, London 1978.

30c. DARNTON, R. *Mesmerism and the End of the Enlightenment in France.* Harvard University Press, 1968.

30d. DAVIDSON, D. 'Radical Interpretation', *Dialectica*, Vol. 27, pp. 309–23. 1974.

31. DESCARTES, R. 'Discours de la Méthode' in *Ouevres Philosophiques*, Vol. 1, edn. Alquié, F. Garnier, Paris 1963.

32. DIDEROT, D. *Rameau's Nephew and d'Alembert's Dream.* Trans. by L. W. Tancock. Penguin Books, Harmondsworth 1966.

32a. DITTMAR, N. *Sociolinguistics*. Edward Arnold, London 1976

32b. DOWNS, A. *An Economic Theory of Democracy*. Harper & Row, New York 1957.

33. DUGDALE, R. 'Economic Theory in Class Society', in Pateman, T. (Ed.), *Counter Course*. Penguin Books, Harmondsworth 1972.

33a. DUMMETT, M. *Frege*. Duckworth, London 1973.

33b. EDGLEY, R. *Reason in Theory and Practice*. Hutchinson University Library, London 1969.

33c. EDGLEY, R. 'Practical Reason', in *Mind*, 1965. (Reprinted in J. Raz (Ed.), *Practical Reason*. Oxford University Press, 1978.)

33d. EDGLEY, R. 'Reason and Violence', in *Radical Philosophy 4*, pp. 18–24. London 1973.

34. ENZENSBERGER, H. 'Constituents of a Theory of the Media', in *New Left Review 64*.

35. ESTERSON, A. *The Leaves of Spring. Schizophrenia, Family and Sacrifice*. Penguin Books, Harmondsworth 1972.

35a. EVANS, J. *Aristotle's Concept of Dialectic*. Cambridge University Press, 1977.

35b. FAY, B. *Social Theory and Political Practice*. Allen & Unwin, London 1975.

36. FEYERABEND, P. 'Against Method', in *Minnesota Studies for the Philosophy of Science*, Vol. 4. 1970.

36a. FEYERABEND, P. *Science in a Free Society*. New Left Books, London 1978.

36b. FINDAHL, O. & HOIJER, B. *Fragments of Reality: An Experiment with News and TV Visuals*. Swedish Broadcasting Corporation, Stockholm 1976.

36c. FODOR, J. *The Language of Thought*, Harvester Press, Hassocks 1976.

37. FOOT, Paul. Review of the film *State of Siege*, in *Socialist Worker*, 4 August 1973, p. 11.

38. FOOT, Philippa (Ed.), *Theories of Ethics*. Oxford University Press, 1967.

38a. FOOT, P. 'Moral Beliefs', in 38. Foot, P., pp. 83–100.

39. FOUCAULT, M. *Madness and Civilisation*, trans. by Richard Howard. Tavistock, London 1973.

39a. FOUCAULT, M. *The Order of Things*. Tavistock, London 1970.

39b. FREGE, G. 'The Thought: A logical Inquiry', in P. Strawson (Ed.), *Philosophical Logic*, pp. 17–38. Oxford University Press, 1967.

40. FREUD, S. 'Psycho-analytic Notes on an Autobiographical Account of a Case of Paranoia (Dementia Paranoides), in Vol. XII, *Standard Edition of the Complete Psychological Works of Sigmund Freud*. Hogarth, London 1958.

40a. FROHLICH, N., OPPENHEIMER, J. & YOUNG, O. *Political Leadership and Collective Goods*. Princeton University Press, 1971.

40b. FROMM, E. *The Fear of Freedom*. Routledge & Kegan Paul, London 1942.

41. GABEL, J. *La Fausse Conscience, Essai sur la Réification*. Eds. du Minuit, Paris 1969.

41a. GABEL, J. *False Consciousness*. Basil Blackwell, Oxford 1975.

41b. GALLIE, W. *Pierce and Pragmatism*. Penguin Books, Harmondsworth 1952.

41c. GAZDAR, G. *Pragmatics. Implicature, Presupposition and Logical Form*. Academic Press, New York 1979.

41d. GAZDAR, G. 'Speech Act Assignment', to appear in A. K. Joshi, I. Sag and B. Webber (Eds.), *Proceedings of the Pennsylvania workshop on computational aspects of linguistic structure and discourse setting*. Cambridge University Press, forthcoming.

42. GELLNER, E. *Words and Things*. Penguin, Harmondsworth 1968.

42a. GELLNER, E. 'Concepts and Society', in B. Wilson (Ed.), *Rationality*, pp. 18–49. Basil Blackwell, Oxford 1970.

43. GERAS, N. 'Essence and Appearance: Aspects of Fetishism in Marx's *Capital*', in *New Left Review* 65.

43a. GLASGOW UNIVERSITY MEDIA GROUP. *Bad News*. Routledge & Kegan Paul, London 1976.

43b. GLASGOW UNIVERSITY MEDIA GROUP. *More Bad News*. Routledge & Kegan Paul, London. Forthcoming.

43c. GOLDMANN, L. *Lukacs and Heidegger*. Routledge & Kegan Paul, London 1977.

44. GOLDSTEIN, K. *Human Nature in the Light of Psychopathology*. Schocken, New York 1963.

45. GOLDTHORPE, J. & LOCKWOOD, D. *et al. The Affluent Worker*, 3 vols. Cambridge University Press, 1968.

45a. GRAHAM, K. 'Review of *Language, Truth and Politics*', in *Philosophy of the Social Sciences*, September 1979, pp. 382–90.

45b. GRAHAM, K. *J. L. Austin: A Critique of Ordinary Language Philosophy*. Harvester Press, Hassocks 1977.

46. GRAMSCI, A. *Prison Notebooks*, Ed. by Hoare, Q. and Nowell-Smith, G. Lawrence & Wishart, London 1971.

47. GREEN, R. Contribution in *Rights of Children*, Report of the first national conference on Children's Rights, National Council for Civil Liberties (1972).

47a. GRICE, H. 'Logic and Conversation', in P. Cole and J. Morgan (Eds.), *Syntax and Semantics, Vol. 3, Speech acts*. Academic Press, New York.

47b. GRICE, H. 'Further Notes on Logic and Conversation', in P. Cole (Ed.), *Syntax and Semantics, Vol. 9, Pragmatics*, pp. 113–27. Academic Press, New York 1978.

47c. GRICE, H. 'Meaning', in *Philosophical Review, 1957*. (Much reprinted, for instance, in P. Strawson (Ed.), *Philosophical Logic*, pp. 39–48. Oxford University Press, 1967.)

47d. GROTE, G. *Aristotle*. Third edition. John Murray, London 1883.

47e. GROTE, G. *Plato, and the other Companions of Sokrates*. New edition, Vol. 1. John Murray, London 1888.

48. HABERMAS, J. 'Technology and Science as "Ideology" ', in *Toward a Rational Society*. Heinemann, London 1971.

48a. HABERMAS, J. 'Toward a Theory of Communicative Competence', in H. P. Dreitzel (Ed.), *Recent Sociology, No. 2*, pp. 115–48. Collier-Macmillan, London 1970.

48b. HABERMAS, J. *Strukturwandel der Offentlichkeit*, Luchterhand, Neuwied 1962. (French translation, *L'Espace Publique*. Payot, Paris 1978.)

48c. HABERMAS, J. 'Wahrheitstheorien', in H. Fahrenbach

(Ed.), *Wirklichkeit und Reflexion: Walter Schulz zum 60 Geburstag*, pp. 211–65. Neske, Pfullingen 1973.

48d. HABERMAS, J. 'Some Distinctions in Universal Pragmatics', in *Theory and Society*, Vol. 3, pp. 155–67. 1976.

48e. HABERMAS, J. 'The Scientization of Politics and Public Opinion', in *Toward a Rational Society*, pp. 62–80. Heinemann, London 1971.

48f. HABERMAS, J. 'Was heisst Universalpragmatik?' in K-O Apel (Ed.), *Sprachpragmatik und Philosophie*, pp. 174–272. Suhrkamp, Frankfurt 1976.

48g. HABERMAS, J. *Knowledge and Human Interests*. Heinemann, London 1972.

48h. HABERMAS, J. 'Hannah Arendt's Communications Concept of Power', in *Social Research*, Vol. 44, pp. 3–24. 1977.

48i. HABERMAS, J. *Legitimation Crisis*. Heinemann, London 1976.

48j. HABERMAS, J. 'The Public Sphere', in *New German Critique, 1974*.

48k. HACKING, I. *Why Does Language Matter to Philosophy?* Cambridge University Press, 1975.

48m. HACKING, I. *The Emergence of Probability*. Cambridge University Press, 1975.

49. HADDON, C. 'Quizzical Errors on TV Shows', in *Sunday Times*, London, 24 June 1973, p. 11.

49a. HALL, S. 'The Determinations of News Photographs', in *Working Papers in Cultural Studies*, No. 3, 1972, pp. 53–87.

50. HALLAS, D. 'Building the Leadership', in *International Socialism, 40*.

51. HALLIDAY, M. A. K. 'Relevant Models of Language', in *Educational Review*, Birmingham, Vol. 22, 1969.

51a. HAMBLIN, C. *Fallacies*. Methuen, London 1970.

51b. HAMBLIN, C. 'Mathematical Models of dialogue', in *Theoria*, Vol. 37, 1971, pp. 130–55.

51c. HAMMERSLEY, M. 'The Organisation of Pupil Participation', in *Sociological Review*, Vol. 22, No. 3, 1974.

51d. HAMPSHIRE, S. *Thought and Action*. Chatto & Windus, London 1959.

51e. HANCHER, M. 'The Classification of Co-operative illocutionary acts', in *Language in Society*, Vol. 8, No. 1, pp. 1–14. 1979.

52. HANFMANN, E. & KASANIN, J. *Conceptual Thinking in Schizophrenia*. Nervous and Mental Diseases Monograph series, No. 67. New York 1942.

52a. HARE, R. M. *Freedom and Reason*. Oxford University Press, 1963.

52aa. HARE, R. M. *Applications of Moral Philosophy*. Macmillan, London 1972.

52b. HARRAH, D. *Communication: a Logical Model*. MIT Press, Cambridge, Mass. 1963.

53. HARVEY, M. 'Sociological Theory: The Production of Bourgeois Ideology', in Pateman, T. (Ed.), *Counter Course*. Penguin Books, Harmondsworth 1972.

53a. HEATH, A. *Rational Choice and Social Exchange*. Cambridge University Press, 1976.

54. HEATH, S. *The Nouveau Roman*. Elek, London 1972.

54a. HEGEL, G. *Phenomenology of Mind*, trans. J. Baillie. Allen & Unwin, London 1949.

54b. HEIDEGGER, M. *Being and Time*. Basil Blackwell, Oxford 1967.

55. HINDESS, B. *The Decline of the Working Class Politics*. McGibbon & Kee, London 1971.

55. HINTON, J. Review of *Language, Truth and Politics*, in *Philosophy*, Vol. 51, p. 235, 1976.

56. HOBBES, T. *Leviathan*, Ed. by C. B. Macpherson. Penguin Books, Harmondsworth 1968.

56a. HOLT, J. *Escape from Childhood*. Penguin Books, Harmondsworth 1975.

57. HONDERICH, T. 'Mill on Liberty', in *Inquiry*, Vol. 10, 1967.

57a. HOWELL, W. *Logic and Rhetoric in England, 1500–1700*. Princeton University Press, 1956.

57b. HOWELL, W. *Eighteenth Century British Logic and Rhetoric*. Princeton University Press, 1971.

58. HUDSON, L. *Frames of Mind*. Penguin Books, Harmondsworth 1970.

58a. HUME, D. *Essays Moral, Political and Literary*. World's Classics Edition. Henry Frowde, London 1903.

58b. HYMES, D. *Foundations in Sociolinguistics*. Tavistock, London 1974.

59. IGGERS, W. *Karl Kraus*. Nijhoff, The Hague 1967.

60. ILLICH, I. *Deschooling Society*. Penguin Books, Harmondsworth 1973.

61. INGLEBY, D. 'Ideology and the Human Sciences. Some Comments on the role of reification in psychology and psychiatry', in Pateman, T. (Ed.), *Counter Course*. Penguin Books, Harmondsworth 1972.

62. JAKOBSON, R. 'Two Aspects of Language and two types of aphasic disturbance', in Jakobson, R. and Halle, M. *Fundamentals of Language*. Mouton, The Hague 1956.

63. JAKOBSON, R. 'Linguistics and Poetics', in Seboek, T. (Ed.), *Style in Language*. MIT Press, 1960.

64. JANIK, A. & TOULMIN, S. *Wittgenstein's Vienna*. Weidenfeld & Nicholson, London 1973.

64a. JOHNSON-LAIRD, P. & WASON, P. *Thinking: Readings in Cognitive Science*. Cambridge University Press, 1977.

65. KASANIN, J. (Ed.), *Language and Thought in Schizophrenia*. Norton, New York 1964.

66. KENNER, H. *Samuel Beckett: A Critical Study*. Augmented edn., University of California Press, Berkeley 1968.

66a. KJØRUP, S. 'George Innes and the Battle at Hastings, or Doing Things with Pictures', in *The Monist*, Vol. 58, 1974, pp. 216–35.

66b. KJØRUP, S. 'Pictorial Speech Acts', in *Erkenntnis*, Vol. 12, pp. 55–71, 1978.

66d. KOCHMAN, T. Review of *Language, Truth and Politics* in *Language in Society*, Vol. 7, pp. 111–24, 1978.

67. KOHN, C. *Karl Kraus, le Polemiste et l'Ecrivain, defenseur des Droits de l'Individu*. Didier, Paris 1962.

67a. KOLLONTAI, A. *The Workers' Opposition*. Solidarity pamphlet, No. 7, Bromley 1968(?).

67b. KRAUS, K. *In These Great Times*. Engendra Press, Montreal 1976.

67c. KRAUS, K. *The Last Days of Mankind*. Frederick Ungar, New York 1974.

67d. KRIPKE, S. 'Naming and Necessity', in D. Davidson and G. Harman (Eds.), *Semantics of Natural Language*. Second edn., pp. 253–355. Reidel, Dordrecht 1972.

68. KUHN, T. *The Structure of Scientific Revolutions*. Second edn. Chicago University Press, 1970.

69. LABOV, W. 'The Logic of Non-standard English', in

Giglioli, P. (Ed.), *Language and Social Context*. Penguin Books, Harmondsworth 1972.

69a. LABOV, W. 'Rules for Ritual Insults', in T. Kochman (Ed.), *Rappin' and Stylin' Out*, pp. 265–314. University of Illinois Press, 1972.

70. LACAN, J. 'D'une question préliminaire à tout traitement possible de la psychose', in *Ecrits II*. Seuil, Paris 1971.

71. LAING, R. D. & ESTERSON, A. *Sanity, Madness and the Family*. Penguin Books, Harmondsworth 1970.

72. LAING, R. D. *The Politics of Experience and the Bird of Paradise*. Penguin Books, Harmondsworth 1967.

72a. LAING, R. D. *Intervention in Social Situations*. Association of Family Caseworkers and Philadelphia Association, London 1969.

72b. LAING, R. D. *Self and Others*. Second edn. Penguin Books, Harmondsworth 1971.

73. LAKOFF, G. 'Linguistics and Natural Logic', in *Synthese*, Vol. 22, Nos. 1/2, 1970.

73a. LAKOFF, R. *Language and Woman's Place*. Harper & Row, New York 1975.

73b. LANIGAN, R. *Speech Act Phenomenology*. Nijhoff, The Hague 1977.

74. LEVI-STRAUSS, C. *La Pensée Sauvage*. Plon, Paris 1962. Trans. as *The Savage Mind*. Weidenfeld & Nicholson, London 1966.

74a. LEWIS, D. 'General Semantics', in D. Davidson & G. Harman (Eds.), *Semantics of Natural Language*. Second edn., pp. 169–218. Reidel, Dordrecht 1972.

74aa. LEWIS, D. 'Scorekeeping in a Language Game', in *Journal of Philosophical Logic*, Vol. 8, No. 3, pp. 339–59, 1979.

74b. LEWIS, D. 'Radical Interpretation', in *Synthese*, Vol. 27, pp. 331–44, 1974.

74c. LEWIS, G. C. *An Essay on the Influence of Authority in Matters of Opinion*. John Parker, London 1849.

75. LOCKE, J. *An Essay Concerning Human Understanding*, Ed. by J. W. Yolton, 2 vols., revised edn. Dent, London 1964–5.

76. LOCKE, J. *Two Treatises of Government*, Ed. by Peter Laslett. Mentor, New York 1965.

76a. LOCKE, J. *Of the Conduct of Understanding*. G. Bell, London 1916. (Many other editions.)

77. LUKÁCS, G. *History and Class Consciousness*. Merlin, London 1971.

77a. LUKES, S. *Power*. Revised edn. Macmillan, London 1976.

77b. LUKES, S. 'A discourse on discourse'. (Review of *Language, Truth and Politics*), in *Times Higher Education Supplement*, 3 October 1975.

78. LYONS, J. *An Introduction to Theoretical Linguistics*. Cambridge University Press, 1968.

78a. LYONS, J. *Semantics, Vol. 1*. Cambridge University Press, 1977.

78b. LYONS, J. *Semantics, Vol. 2*. Cambridge University Press, 1977.

78c. LYONS, J. 'Human Communication', in Hinde, R. A. (Ed.), *Non-Verbal Communication*. Cambridge University Press, 1972.

78d. MACINTYRE, A. 'The Idea of a Social Science', in B. R. Wilson (Ed.), *Rationality*, pp. 112–30. Basil Blackwell, Oxford 1970.

78e. MACINTYRE, A. *Against the Self-Images of the Age*. Duckworth, London 1971.

78f. MACINTYRE, A. *A Short History of Ethics*. Routledge & Kegan Paul, London 1967.

78g. McKAY, D. M. 'Formal Analysis of Communicative Processes', in Hinde, R. A. (Ed.), *Non-Verbal Communication*. Cambridge University Press, 1972.

79. McKENZIE, R. & SILVER, A. *Angels in Marble*. Heinemann, London 1969.

80. MALINOWSKI, B. 'Phatic Communion', reprinted in *Communication in Face to Face Interaction*, Eds. J. Laver & S. Hutcheson. Penguin Books, Harmondsworth 1972.

81. McPHERSON, T. *Political Obligation*. RKP, London 1967.

81a. MANN, M. *Consciousness and Action Among the Western Working Class*. Macmillan, London 1973.

82. MARCUSE, H. *Eros and Civilisation*. Sphere, London 1969.

83. MARCUSE, H. *One Dimensional Man*. RKP, London 1964.

84. MARCUSE, H. 'Repressive Tolerance', in *A Critique of Pure Tolerance* by R. P. Wolff, B. Moore Jnr. and H. Marcuse. Beacon Press, Boston 1965.

85. MARCUSE, H. *An Essay on Liberation*. Allen Lane, London 1969.

86. MARX, K. *Economic and Philosophic Manuscripts of 1844*, Ed. by D. J. Struik. Lawrence & Wishart, London 1970.

87. MARX, K. & ENGELS, F. *The German Ideology*. Lawrence & Wishart, London 1965.

88. MARX, K. & ENGELS, F. *Selected Works*. Lawrence & Wishart, London 1965.

88a. MARX, K. *Capital, Vol. 1*. Lawrence & Wishart, London 1967.

88b. MAYAKOVSKY, V. *How are Verses Made?* Jonathan Cape, London 1971.

89. MEPHAM, J. (Ed.), *Social Science, Ideology, Free Speech* forthcoming. (Publication of this book was abandoned for legal reasons.)

89b. MEY, J. *Uber manipulatorische Sprachgebrauch*. Grazer Linguistische Studien, No. 7, Graz 1978.

89c. MEY, J. 'Marxism and Linguistics: Facts and Fancies. A Review of Trevor Pateman, *Language, Truth and Politics*', in *Journal of Pragmatics*, Vol. 2, pp. 81–93, 1978.

89d. MICHELS, R. *Political Parties*. Dover Publications, New York 1959.

90. MILIBAND, R. *The State in Capitalist Society*. Weidenfeld & Nicholson, London 1969.

90a. MILL, James. 'Liberty of the Press', in *Essays on Government, Jurisprudence, Liberty of the Press and Law of Nations*. Augustus M. Kelley reprint, New York 1967. (Each essay separately paginated.)

90b. MILL, J. S. 'Notes on Some of the More Popular Dialogues of Plato', in *Essays on Philosophy and the Classics*, Ed. by J. M. Robson. University of Toronto Press, 1978.

91. MILL, J. S. 'On Liberty', in *Utilitarianism*, Ed. by M. Warnock. Fontana, London 1962.

91a. MILL, J. S. 'Grote's *Aristotle*', in *Essays on Philosophy and the Classics*. Ed. J. M. Robson and Intro. F. E. Sparshott. University of Toronto Press and Routledge & Kegan Paul, London 1978.

91b. MILL, J. S. 'Autobiography', in M. Lerner (Ed.),

Essential Works of John Stuart Mill. Bantam Books, New York 1961.

91c. MILL, J. S. 'Grote's *Plato*', in *Essays on Philosophy and the Classics*, Ed. J. M. Robson and Intro. F. E. Sparshott. University of Toronto Press and Routledge & Kegan Paul, London 1978.

91d. MILL, J. S. 'Representative Government', in *Utilitarianism, Liberty and Representative Government.* Everyman Edition, Dent, London n.d.

91e. MORRIS, C. *Foundations of the Theory of Signs.* Chicago University Press, 1938.

91f. MUELLER, C. *The Politics of Communication: A Study in the Political Sociology of Language, Socialization and Legitimation.* Oxford University Press, New York 1973.

91g. MUELLER, C. 'Notes on the Repression of Communicative Behaviour', in H. Dreitzel (Ed.), *Recent Sociology, No. 2*, pp. 101–13. Macmillan, New York 1970.

92. MURRAY, R. & WENGRAF, T. 'The Political Economy of Communications', in *The Spokesman*, No. 5.

92a. NOVITZ, D. 'Picturing', in *Journal of Aesthetics and Art Criticism*, Vol. 34, pp. 145–55, 1975.

92b. NOVITZ, D. *Pictures and their Use in Communication.* Nijhoff, The Hague 1977.

92c. NOZICK, R. *Anarchy, State and Utopia.* Basil Blackwell, Oxford 1974.

92d. OAKESHOTT, M. 'Political Education', in P. Laslett (Ed.), *Philosophy, Politics and Society*, Vol. 1, pp. 1–21. Basil Blackwell, Oxford 1956.

92e. OLSON, M. *The Logic of Collective Action.* Second edn., Harvard University Press, 1971.

92f. *Organise against the National Front, the new Nazis.* Socialist *Worker* pamphlet, London n.d.

93. ORWELL, G. *Nineteen Eighty-four.* Penguin Books, Harmondsworth 1954.

93a. PAPPÉ, H. 'The English Utilitarians and Athenian Democracy', in R. R. Bolgar (Ed.)., *Classical Influences on Western Thought AD 1650–1870*, pp. 295–307. Cambridge University Press, 1978.

94. PASCAL, B. *Pensées.* English trans. by A. J. Krailsheimer. Penguin Books, Harmondsworth 1966.

95. PATEMAN, C. 'Political obligation and Conceptual Analysis', in *Political Studies*, Vol. XXI, 1973.

95a. PATEMAN, C. *Participation and Democratic Theory*. Cambridge University Press, 1970.

95b. PATEMAN, C. *The Problem of Political Obligation*. John Wiley, Chichester 1979.

96. PATEMAN, T. 'Sanity, Madness and the Problem of Knowledge', in *Radical Philosophy 1*, 1972.

97. PATEMAN, T. 'The Making of a Course Critic', in *Hard Cheese*, 2, 1973.

98. PATEMAN, T. Review of R. Barthes *Mythologies*, in *Human Context*, Vol. V, 1973. (Incorporated in Chapter IV, Section 3a of this book.)

99. PATEMAN, T. 'The Experience of Politics', in *Philosophy and Phenomenological Research* (USA), Vol. XXXIII, 1973. (Reprinted as Appendix 1 above.)

99a. PATEMAN, T. 'On Samuel Beckett's *Waiting for Godot*', in *The Fox*, No. 2, pp. 154–63. New York 1975.

99b. PATEMAN, T. *Television and the February 1974 General Election*. British Film Institute, London 1974.

99c. PATEMAN, T. *How is Political Knowledge Possible?* Unpublished M.Phil. thesis, University of Sussex 1978.

99d. PATEMAN, T. 'Accountability, Values and Schooling', in T. Becher and S. Maclure (Eds.), *Accountability in Education*, pp. 61–94. NFER, Windsor 1978.

99e. PATEMAN, T. 'Marxism and Linguistics: A Reply to Jacob L. Mey', in *Journal of Pragmatics*, Vol. 2, pp. 361–4, 1978.

100. PATON, K. *The Great Brain Robbery*, Keith Paton, 102 Newcastle Street, Silverdale, Newcastle-under-Lyme, Staffs.

101. POPPER, K. *The Logic of Scientific Discovery*. RKP, London 1968.

102. POPPER, K. *Conjectures and Refutations*. RKP, London 1969.

103. POSTMAN, N. & WEINGARTNER, C. *Teaching as a Subversive Activity*. Penguin Books, Harmondsworth 1971.

104. POWELL, E. *Powell and the 1970 Election*, Ed. by J. Wood. Elliott Paperfronts, Surrey 1970.

104a. PRATT, M. *Toward a Speech Act Theory of Literary Discourse*. Indiana University Press, 1977.

104b. PUTNAM, H. 'The Meaning of "Meaning" ' in *Mind, Language and Reality, Collected Papers, Vol. 2*, pp. 215–71. Cambridge University Press, 1975.

104c. PUTNAM, H. 'The Refutation of Conventionalism', in *Mind, Languague and Reality, Collected Papers, Vol. 2*, pp. 153–91. Cambridge University Press, 1975.

104d. PUTNAM, H. 'Is Semantics Possible?', in *Mind, Language and Reality, Collected Papers, Vol. 2*, pp. 139–52. Cambridge University Press, 1975.

104e. QUINE, W. *Word and Object*. MIT Press, Cambridge, Mass. 1960.

104f. QUINE, W. *Philosophy of Logic*. Prentice-Hall, New Jersey 1970.

104g. QUINTON, A. 'The Tongue Tied Masses'. (Review of *Language, Truth and Politics*), in *Times Educational Supplement*, 21 November 1975.

105a. RAWLS, J. *A Theory of Justice*. Oxford University Press, 1972.

105c. REE, J. *Descartes*. Allen Lane, London 1974.

106. REICH, W. *The Mass Psychology of Fascism*, trans. by V. R. Carfagno. Farrar, Strauss & Giroux, New York 1970.

107. REICH, W. *What is Class Consciousness?* Socialist Reproduction (1971).

107a. REICHE, R. *Sexuality and Class Struggle*. New Left Books, London 1970.

108. REIMER, E. *School is Dead*. Penguin Books, Harmondsworth 1971.

108a. ROBSON, J. *The Improvement of Mankind*. University of Toronto Press and Routledge & Kegan Paul, London 1968.

109. ROSEN, H. *Language and Class: A Critical Look at the Theories of Basil Bernstein*. Falling Wall Press, Bristol 1972.

110. ROSENHAN, D. 'On Being Sane in Insane Places', in *Science*, Vol. 179, No. 4070, 19 January 1973. For criticisms, see *Science*, Vol. 180, No. 4084, 27 April 1973.

110a. ROUSSEAU, J. *The Social Contract*, trans. by M. Cranston. Penguin Books, Harmondsworth 1968.

110b. ROUSSEAU, J.-J. *Emile ou De L'Education*. Garnier-Flammarion, Paris 1966.

111. SAUSSURE, F. de. *Course in General Linguistics*, trans. by W. Baskin, McGraw-Hill, New York 1966.

112. SCHATTSCHNEIDER, E. *The Semi-Sovereign People*. Holt, Rhinehart & Winston, New York 1960.

113. SCHATZMAN, M. *Soul Murder: Persecution in the Family*. Allen Lane, London 1973.

114. SCHREBER, D. *Memoirs of my Nervous Illness*, trans. and Ed. by I. MacALPINE and R. Hunter. Dawson, London 1955.

114a. SCHUMPETER, J. 'Two Concepts of Democracy', in A. Quinton (Ed.), *Political Philosophy*, pp. 153–88. Oxford University Press, 1967.

114b. SEARLE, J. *Speech Acts*. Cambridge University Press, 1969.

114c. SEARLE, J. 'What is a Speech Act?', in M. Black (Ed.), *Philosophy in America*, pp. 221–39. Allen & Unwin, London 1965.

114d. SEARLE, J. 'Indirect Speech Acts', in P. Cole and J. Morgan (Eds.), *Syntax and Semantics, Volume 3, Speech Acts*, pp. 59–82. Academic Press, New York 1975.

114e. SEARLE, J. 'A Taxonomy of Illocutionary Acts', in K. Gunderson (Ed.), *Language, Mind and Knowledge*. University of Minnesota Press, 1975.

115. SLATER, P. *The Pursuit of Loneliness*. Allen Lane, London 1971.

115a. SLOMAN, A. *The Computer Revolution in Philosophy*. Harvester Press, Hassocks 1978.

116. STEINER, G. *Language and Silence*. Penguin Books, Harmondsworth 1969.

117. STEINER, G. *Extra Territorial*. Faber, London 1972.

118. STEINER, G. *In Bluebeard's Castle*. Faber, London 1971.

118a. STRAWSON, P. 'Grammar and Philosophy', in D. Davidson and G. Harman (Eds.), *Semantics of Natural Language*. Second edn., pp. 455–72. Reidel, Dordrecht 1972.

119. SULLIVAN, H. Contribution in item 65.

119a. TOULMIN, S. *The Uses of Argument*. Cambridge University Press, 1958.

119b. ULLMAN-MARGALIT, E. *The Emergence of Norms*. Clarendon Press, Oxford 1977.

120. VYGOTSKY, L. *Thought and Language*. MIT Press, 1962.
120a. WALLAS, G. *Human Nature in Politics*. Constable, London 1914.
121. WASON, P. & JOHNSON-LAIRD, P. *Psychology of Reasoning: Structure and Content*. Batsford, London 1972.
122. WATZLAWICK, P., BEAVIN, J. & JACKSON, D. *The Pragmatics of Human Communication*. Norton, New York 1967.
122a. WELDON, T. 'Political Principles', in P. Laslett (Ed.), *Philosophy, Politics and Society*, Vol. 1, pp. 22–34. Basil Blackwell, Oxford 1956.
123. WERTHEIMER, M. *Productive Thinking*. Tavistock, London 1961.
124. WHORF, B. *Language, Thought and Reality*, Ed. by J. B. Carroll. MIT Press, 1956.
125. WILDEN, A. *System and Structure*. Tavistock, London 1972.
125a. WILLIAMS, R. *The Long Revolution*. Penguin Books, Harmondsworth 1961.
125b. WILSON, B. (Ed.), *Rationality*. Basil Blackwell, Oxford 1974.
126. WITTGENSTEIN, L. *Philosophical Investigations*. Second edn, Blackwell, Oxford 1958.
126a. WOLIN, S. *Politics and Vision*. Little, Brown & Co., Boston 1960.
127. WOLLHEIM, R. 'John Stuart Mill and the Limits of State Action', in *Social Research*, Vol. 40, 1973.
127a. WOOTTON, A. *Dilemmas of Discourse*. Allen & Unwin, London 1975.
127b. ZIMAN, J. *Public Knowledge*. Cambridge University Press, 1968.
127c. ZOHN, H. *Karl Kraus*. Twayne, New York 1971.